**Deschutes
Public Library**

There are few decent family-owned media c‹
story of one of the best of them, and shows in telling detail how careful
attention to the business side of a media company, coupled with a tradition
of high-minded news values over generations, can lead to remarkably good
— and sustainable — journalism.

Richard H. Meeker, co-owner of Willamette Week and author of
Newspaperman: S.I. Newhouse and the Business of News

This remarkably honest account intertwines the stories of a family, a newspaper
company and Oregon's colorful (sometimes admirable, sometimes disturbing)
history. It's a fascinating read for anyone who cares deeply about those
communities, about newspapers or about Oregon.

J. Mark Garber, President and publisher, Pamplin Media Group

Grit and Ink is small-town family business history at its best. Colorful, candid,
and fast-moving, this masterfully written and richly sourced account follows the
path of an independent Oregon family newspaper group that has expanded and
remained financially viable through more than a century of tumult, adaptation,
and fluctuating management styles.

Richard A. Baker, US Senate Historian Emeritus

Although presented as a historical reference Grit and Ink captures timeless
elements of successful stewardship of a family enterprise. This detailed account
of how a shared and compelling vision, entrepreneurial skill and the willingness
to sacrifice built trust among and between generations is a lesson to all in passing
on a stronger business to well-prepared successors.

Sherri Noxel, PhD, Director, Austin Family Business Program at OSU

Grit and Ink is the book title, but it is also a literal description of tough travel
through hard times, public controversy, and some of the most challenging and
beautiful country in the state of Oregon.

Rich Wandschneider, Director, Josephy Library of Western History and Culture

Full of fascinating insights into the inner workings of a family business and to
the critical importance of community journalism, "Grit and Ink" tells a story
that is very worthy of being told.

Kerry Tymchuk, Executive Director, Oregon Historical Society

At a time when Donald Trump relentlessly attacks independent media, and our
country needs independent media to survive more than ever, this Oregon
newspaper family is showing how to do it.

Mark Kirchmeier, Author of Packwood: The Public and Private Life,
from Acclaim to Outrage

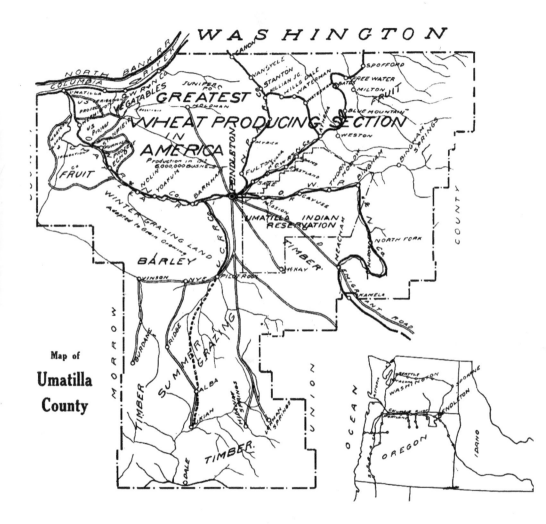

1916 Agricultural map of Umatilla County.

D0028991

GRIT
AND INK

An Oregon Family's Adventures
in Newspapering, 1908 - 2018

WILLIAM F. WILLINGHAM

Grit and Ink

An Oregon Family's Adventures in Newspapering, 1908 – 2018

© 2018 EO Media Group

All rights reserved. No part of this book may be reproduced, stored in a retrieval system, or transmitted in any form or by any means, electronic, mechanical, photocopying, recording, or otherwise, without the written permission from the publisher.

Distributed by Oregon State University Press,
121 The Valley Library, Corvallis, OR 97331, 541-737-3166
Toll-free orders: 800-426-3797

Author: William F. Willingham
Directed by: Stephen A. Forrester
Designer: John D. Bruijn

ISBN 978-0-87071-955-4

On the cover:
Photos clockwise from top left: C.S. Jackson, Edwin B. Aldrich, Amy Aldrich Bedford and J.W. Forrester.

EO Media Group
P.O. Box 2048, Salem, OR 97308
503-385-4911

CONTENTS

FOREWORD

BY R. GREGORY NOKES

B eing part of a community is the clarion call to any newspaper. And few have responded to that call better than newspapers of EO Media Group, which began life as the East Oregonian Publishing Company.

From Pendleton to Astoria, these papers have helped bring forth an array of fixtures. They include a bridge across the Columbia; a dam for cheap power, navigation and irrigation; survival of the Pendleton Woolen Mills; launch of the Pendleton Round-Up; preservation of Astoria's Liberty Theater. These newspapers' eyes have been focused on community development to create jobs, readers and civic betterment. They have also stood up to destructive forces such as the Ku Klux Klan and the Aryan Nation movement.

J.W. "Bud" Forrester, editor of the *East Oregonian* until 1970 and *The Daily Astorian* until his retirement in 1987, perhaps said it best: "A good newspaper is the voice of its community."

My late father, J. Richard Nokes, editor of *The Oregonian,* was a peer, friend and admirer of Bud Forrester. Both played a large part in the rapid growth of newspapers in Oregon at a time when newspapers were the main source of news in cities large and small.

Although I was away from Oregon for twenty-five years during my career as a foreign and diplomatic correspondent for The Associated Press in Washington, D.C., and Latin America, I had the pleasure of meeting Forrester.

The first of the properties that would become today's EO Media Group was the four-page *East Oregonian*, established by Virginia-born Mathew Bull in 1875. It went through several ownership changes before acquisition by C.S. Sam Jackson, the future owner of the *Portland Evening Journal.* Jackson was succeeded in 1908 by Edwin Aldrich, who would remain with the paper for 42 years. He was a graduate of Oregon Agricultural College (now OSU). He joined the paper as a reporter in 1904 and is described in this book as "an activist, unafraid to take up a public issue or controversy or promote a cause."

Aldrich helped engineer the major acquisition in 1919 of the *Astoria Evening Budget,* now *The Daily Astorian.* A dozen other newspapers and publications would be added during subsequent decades. The company spans the region with eleven newspapers and other publications in four states and a news bureau in Salem.

In this detailed history of the growth of the newspaper chain from its fledgling beginnings, you will read about the enterprising editors and publishers who guided the growth. Among them are Jackson, Aldrich, Merle Chessman, Bud Forrester,

Amy Aldrich Bedford, Eleanor Aldrich Forrester, Mike Forrester, Steve Forrester, Kathryn Bedford Brown, Fred Andrus, C.K. Patterson, John Perry and many more. Beyond reporting the news of their communities, these leaders kept abreast of changing technology that included photo-offset printing, computers, digital journalism, centralized design and solar power.

Editors moved among the newspapers as required. On technology, they could not afford to sit still. From four-page weeklies there would emerge color in photos and advertising, faster presses and what we used to call wire services. The demands of technology were constant. Making the right decisions on presses was critical.

The reward was an improved product that was reflected in rising circulation and advertising gains when times were good. Also, there were many awards for news coverage. The group's yearlong series "Our Climate is Changing" won a Special Merit award in the national Grantham Prize for environmental reporting in 2007. The company-wide series "The Fate of Our Forests" won the Dolly Connolly Award from the Pacific Northwest Newspaper Association. The *Blue Mountain Eagle*'s coverage of the Aryan Nation's arrival in Grant County won awards and was nominated for a Pulitzer Prize in 2011.

Sometimes, however there, was no choice for the newspapers' owners to retreat. Faced with declining circulation in a changing readership market, the *East Oregonian*, which had proudly added a Sunday edition in 2000, contracted in 2012 by combining Saturday and Sunday into a weekend edition. This change, and moving from afternoon to morning publication, led to a total sales gain for the first time in four years.

Disaster plays a role in this story. The Astoria newspaper lost its building, presses and production facilities in the Great Fire of December 8, 1922 that destroyed 32 city blocks and 240 businesses. Under the fast-thinking leadership of Chessman and Lee Drake, the newspaper didn't miss a beat. A Dec. 8 edition was printed on a multigraph machine at the Astoria YMCA. To cope with a shortage of cash during the Great Depression, the newspaper issued its own scrip, known as Budget Beaver Pelts.

Owners were ever on the lookout for expansion opportunities, to strengthen market base and add circulation. One of the most successful purchases, in 1991, was the *Capital Press*, the Salem-based agricultural weekly.

Corporate headquarters were moved to that Capital Press' Salem building.

Other purchases proved a poor fit. Acquisition of the Twin Falls *Times* in 1928 was sold at a loss two years later. The *North Coast Citizen* in Manzanita was purchased in 2007 and sold in 2011.

The final chapter of this family ownership hasn't been written. Unless everyone turns to the internet and cable news – perish the thought – these newspapers will be part of their communities for decades. Their communities will be better for them.

Growing up in the Church of Baseball and the School of Newspapering

BY STEPHEN ALDRICH FORRESTER

My father raised me in the Church of Baseball, as Susan Sarandon calls it in the movie *Bull Durham*. Few people knew that J.W. Forrester pitched for a semi-professional baseball team in Idaho. His budding career ended when he threw his arm out.

My dad also brought me up in the school of newspapering. My education in journalism consists mainly of observation – of what my father and mother went through running small town newspapers.

When I was in my teens, the *East Oregonian* was sued for libel by a county commissioner. With the redoubtable George Corey as the newspaper's attorney, we prevailed. But observing my parents' tightly controlled distress over a few days left a lasting impression.

My grandmother Elsie Aldrich, through her reminiscences, contributed to my education in how history is passed from one generation to the next. She told me how a man called their home one afternoon to say that her husband would not reach home alive. She ran to the *East Oregonian* office to join him for the walk home. "He would have to kill me, too," she told me.

My mother Eleanor told me that her father's luxury was to be shaved every workday. On the walk to work, he would stop at the barbershop. While lathering the editor's face and shaving him, the barber whispered Pendleton's latest gossip.

My grandmother surprised me with a story of how she and her husband went to the White House to meet Franklin Delano Roosevelt. My grandfather lobbied for a dam at Umatilla Rapids (McNary Dam). Of being in Roosevelt's presence, my grandmother said: "You wanted to listen to him all afternoon."

Being an editor in the first half of the 20th century included direct contact with presidents. I have two letters that Woodrow Wilson sent – from Princeton and from the White House – thanking E.B. Aldrich for his support in the presidential election.

Race is a thread in this book, as it has been in the regions we inhabit. During the civil rights era of the 1960s, my mother added a dimension to E.B. Aldrich, whom I did not know – I was four years old when he died. She said: "I don't think my father would have done well with this."

My parents had a remarkable workplace partnership, in which she ran the business side of the newspaper while he ran the news side. One evening as I drove her across the Megler Bridge from Astoria to Washington, she said: "You know, your father never fired anyone. I had to do that." In that morsel, she illuminated a significant practicality of their business relationship.

When they operated a weekly newspaper in Coos Bay, if there wasn't sufficient advertising on publishing day, she would hit the streets to sell more, before the press ran.

My father nursed a disappointment that he was not able to give new life to the empty *East Oregonian* building at Main and Emigrant streets. He thought about putting a restaurant into the building. In his concept, my dad was ahead of his time. Also, it would be another decade until the restoration ethic took hold in America and Oregon.

Well beneath the altitude of the national newspapers, there is a layer of journalism that our family has inhabited for more than 100 years. This journalism is more intimate than that of the national papers. It is no less exciting, contentious and significant. When I had the opportunity to tell Howell Raines, then-editorial page editor of the *New York Times*, about my experience in Astoria, he reminisced about his own small town beginnings. He said that often when you wrote a strong editorial and left your offices, "you could feel the ground move."

My father did that on a number of occasions. In 1954, he was one of only three Oregon daily newspaper editors to endorse the successful candidacy of Richard L. Neuberger, who became the first Democrat to represent Oregon in the U.S. Senate since 1914. Of the adverse pressure that came his way, he told me: "It was pretty bad."

In 1968 at *The Daily Astorian*, my brother Mike wrote an eloquent editorial titled "Why this newspaper will not endorse Richard Nixon." His news editor Gary Conkling has told me that the news staff was especially proud of that piece. Conkling added that Mike weathered considerable adverse comment from community leaders, who were largely Republican.

This volume is at least two things. It is the astonishing array of stories our newspapers have reported – from the Ku Klux Klan's political offensive in Astoria in the 1920s to the Aryan Nation's attempted incursion into Grant County in 2010. It is also about how our company's owners adapted to a series of calamities – a downtown's immolation, the Great Depression, World War II newsprint rationing – and adopted changing technologies, from the earliest wire services to the digital age.

What strikes me in reading Bill Willingham's telling of our story is how the right people – smart, tough and resilient – showed up at the right time. For all of our reliance on equipment, and now the cyberworld, human talent is the thread that runs through this story.

I gained my yen for history in the early Sixties in the same classroom that Bill Willingham occupied two years prior. It was the American history class of Philip G. Farley, a remarkable Pendleton High School history teacher. Farley's admonition to read critically and read widely inspired me as a journalist. For Bill, it was a ticket to become a professional historian. So in a small sense, it was Phil Farley who generated a good bit of this book's energy.

Circa 1900, Inside the East Oregonian building on Main and Emigrant streets, opened in 1887 are C.S. Jackson and family. From left – Unknown, Frank Clopton, C.S. Jackson, Maria Clopton Jackson, and Mrs. Clopton (mother of Frank and Maria).

CHAPTER I

Frontier town gets a newspaper

"Print the truth. Fight for the right. People like a fighting newspaper."
Charles Samuel Jackson

The publishing company that is the focus of this history had its origins in a feisty, nineteenth century frontier newspaper located in Pendleton, Oregon. Following its 1875 founding and gestation under several owners and editors, providence intervened in the form of a 20-year-old Virginian who would become a legend of Oregon journalism. Charles Samuel Jackson took control of the *East Oregonian*. Under Jackson's leadership, the *EO* became a respected and influential daily newspaper.

Before leaving for a larger enterprise in Portland, Jackson became a mentor to a 1900 graduate of Oregon Agricultural College, today's Oregon State University. This conjunction – between Jackson in his forties and Edwin Burton Aldrich in his twenties – began a family publishing history that would endure for more than 100 years.

When Jackson left the *EO* in 1902 to rescue the struggling *Oregon Journal* in Portland, he placed the Pendleton paper in the hands of several veteran newsmen on his staff, while keeping a controlling interest in it. Aldrich joined the paper in 1904 and quickly demonstrated his journalistic chops as a reporter. In 1908, when Jackson again reorganized the ownership of the paper, he made Aldrich the editor and a part-owner. For the next 110 years, Aldrich and his direct descendants continued Jackson's tradition of community-focused journalism. This happened in Pendleton, Astoria and nine other locations in Oregon and Washington – at papers acquired under the banner of the East Oregonian Publishing Company, subsequently renamed the EO Media Group.

Success with the *EO* led Aldrich and his partners to acquire the *Astoria Evening Budget* in 1919 and the *Morning Astorian* in 1930. Beginning in the 1970s, with the purchase of the *Blue Mountain Eagle* in John Day, Oregon—the state's oldest continuously published weekly—the EOPC bought more weekly newspapers. The weekly publications are clustered around Pendleton and Astoria, home of the company's flagship dailies. The family-run EOMG has weathered adverse economic times and the challenges of changing technology. Through it all, the company's lodestar has been a commitment to community journalism and a fierce desire to remain independent.

The *East Oregonian* gained life in a newly settled country as white pioneers flocked to northeastern Oregon – the traditional homeland of the Umatilla, Walla Walla and Cayuse tribes. Pendleton was a raw frontier town of about 275 when Mathew P. Bull launched the *EO* on October 16, 1875. The town rose from the crossroads of the Oregon Trail and the Umatilla River at the base of the Blue Mountains.

Though small and isolated in the northeastern corner of the relatively new state of Oregon, Pendleton was perceived to have excellent prospects. It was surrounded by thousands of acres of luxuriant bunchgrass. During the 1860s, the region attracted cattle and sheep men. The cattle supplied mining booms in eastern Oregon and Idaho. The surplus was driven to eastern markets and to stock other ranges. Wool was shipped to east coast markets. A component of the larger Columbia Basin rangelands, Umatilla County – according to a state census taken in 1865 – counted 5,687 cattle and 7,446 sheep. By 1875, the number of cattle had grown to 28,024, and the count of sheep stood at 80,241.

Initial settlers in Umatilla County (which included a portion that became Morrow County in 1885) also grew limited amounts of grain along well-watered, bottom lands of the region. Some farmers successfully experimented with dry land farming on elevated bench lands in the late 1860s and early 1870s, and this brought a new wave of settlers. Soon, farmers began sending large quantities of wheat down the Columbia River by steamboats to Portland, where it was then shipped to markets in the eastern United States and Europe. The production of wheat in Umatilla County rose dramatically from 16,789 bushels in 1865 to 137,575 bushels in 1875. The county's population showed similar growth over those same years, going from 1,805 to 4,426— a 145 percent increase.

The rising numbers of Umatilla valley settlers and the steady traffic of freighters and miners through the area over the Oregon Trail led to the creation of Umatilla County in 1862 and the selection of Marshall's Station on the north side of the Umatilla River opposite the mouth of McKay Creek as the temporary location of the county seat. In 1865, the county seat was moved to Umatilla City on the Columbia River. This town served as the freight forwarding point on the Columbia River for shipments of supplies headed overland for the mines in eastern Oregon and Idaho. Freight arriving upstream by steamboats was transferred at Umatilla City for shipment inland by wagon and pack trains. By 1868, new supply routes to the mines caused Umatilla City to begin a slow decline. This economic decay coupled with increased settlement in northeastern Umatilla County led to a movement to return the county seat to a location on the Umatilla River between Wild Horse and Birch creeks.

In late 1868, the voters of Umatilla County decided to relocate the county seat. Commissioners chosen to select the precise site accepted an offer of two-and-a-half acres for county buildings from Moses Goodwin, who had a claim on the south side of the Umatilla River, west of Wild Horse Creek. To strengthen this offer, Goodwin platted part of his land as a town and, on the advice of County Judge G. W. Bailey, named it Pendleton for Democratic U. S. Senator George Hunt Pendleton of Ohio.

In 1870, Oregon had 30 newspapers. By 1880, that number more than doubled to 74.

The choice of George Pendleton as the namesake for the new town was unsurprising, given the politics he represented and the background of the community's early settlers. Most had emigrated from the South or border states in the decade following the Civil War. Senator Pendleton, during the Civil War, was aligned with the peace faction of the Democratic Party and served as the vice-presidential candidate with General George McClellan when he ran against Lincoln for the presidency in 1864. In 1865, Pendleton voted in Congress against the 13th Amendment, which outlawed slavery. This dramatic event would later be immortalized in Steven Spielberg's movie, *Lincoln*. Senator Pendleton later earned fame as the father of the modern federal Civil Service Reform Act of 1883, which ended the "Spoils System" when selecting government employees.

At the time it became the county seat, Pendleton consisted of a house, small hotel, trading post, and a toll bridge across the Umatilla River. Soon, county officials erected a two-story frame courthouse. Other businesses and residences quickly followed. In October 1869, federal postal authorities established a post office in Pendleton. By 1870, the federal census recorded that Pendleton had a population of 243. The original plat of the town included 20 blocks bounded by the present SE 6th Street on the east, SW 2nd Street on the west, the Umatilla River on the north, and Dorion Avenue on the south. The southern boundary of Pendleton was also the northern edge of the Umatilla Indian Reservation as established in the Treaty of 1855. That led to illegal building on reservation land as the town expanded.

In 1880, after much pressure from the citizens of Pendleton, the Umatilla Indians agreed to sell 640 acres along the town's southern edge. Congress approved this agreement in 1882, and lots were surveyed and sold at auction in 1884. As the center of a rich agricultural area based on dry land wheat farming and livestock raising, Pendleton grew rapidly in the 1880s and 1890s. As it matured, it sought the trappings of permanency.

On the western frontier after the Civil War, having a newspaper was a way of proclaiming that a town was real and here to stay. Along with schools and churches, a newspaper provided an important measure of civilization and order. A newspaper also served as a potential unifying element and a sense of identity as it attempted to speak for the community. As one observer of the western scene noted, "just as every community in the land must . . . have a railroad of its very own, so did every hamlet and crossroad in the West pant . . . for its own newspaper." (Quote in Cloud, 6)

Oregon's enterprising newsmen avidly sought to fill this desire. In 1870, Oregon had 30 newspapers; by 1880, that number more than doubled to 74. Oregon was fertile ground for newspapers. Across the eleven western states and territories in 1880, about 73 percent of the counties had at least one newspaper, while in Oregon, 87 percent of the counties possessed papers.

The frontier publisher needed to make a careful calculation of a town's ability to support a paper. One measure of market conditions for a newspaper was the population. Evidence from a U. S. Census report on newspapers indicated that a viable weekly newspaper needed a countywide population base of at least 2,500. With a population of 2,916 in 1870, Umatilla County barely reached that threshold of newspaper viability. But by 1880, the county had 9,607 inhabitants, and by then was supporting three weekly newspapers. In addition to a sustainable population base, the anticipation of a community's future economic growth could serve as a key enticement to an enterprising newsman. A locale, for example, with a growing population and a promising agricultural economy, coupled with a lively business community seemed to offer a sufficient subscriber base and the potential advertising income necessary to sustain a newspaper. If a town, moreover, happened to be a county seat, it held the further potential for lucrative legal advertising.

An important additional source of income for newspapers in newly settled areas of the West arose from the legal requirement that all persons who had successfully proved up on their homestead or other types of claims on federal public land had to publish notice of such action in a local paper. These advertisements usually cost between $7.00 and $11.00 per ad—a sizeable sum—and thus a welcome source of income for a struggling frontier newspaper.

The *East Oregonian* occasionally ran a free column for subscribers containing cattle brands.

Pendleton, by 1875, as both service center of a thriving agricultural area and a county seat, seemed to meet the criteria necessary for founding a newspaper. Over the long term, however, a successful newspaper in Pendleton, or anywhere in the West, would need to promote the future growth and prosperity of its community.

Two newspapers had preceded Bull's *East Oregonian*. The *Pendletonian* had lasted only a short time in 1871 before fire consumed it. In 1873, Milton H. Abbott of Baker City moved to Pendleton and started the *Eastern Oregon Tribune*, but within two years he moved his newspaper to The Dalles. In the short time he published in Pendleton, Abbott strongly supported the Democratic Party, even if he thought its nominee unfit for an office. He declared, on one occasion, that should the Democratic "Convention nominate . . . any . . . man against whom we have raised objections, we shall acquiesce in such decision, and support the nominees to the best of our ability." (*Eastern Oregon Tribune*, May 29, 1875) Abbott, in common with most white settlers in Umatilla County at that time, also held racist views about Native Americans. He wrote in the *Tribune* his fervent wish "that the red pagans now on the Reservation will have been removed, and the fertile lands they occupy be owned by and cultivated by hundreds of white Americans." (ibid.)

Mathew P. Bull

Mathew Bull was a bit of a mystery. Apparently born in Virginia, he came West in the 1860s; and practiced law and edited newspapers in Portland for a time. By 1870, he had relocated to eastern Oregon, and in 1872, he took over the *Mountain Sentinel* in La Grande and edited it for two years. When voters transferred the county seat from La Grande to Union, he decided to sell the *Sentinel* back to its former owner. The following year he established the *East Oregonian* in Pendleton.

Starting a newspaper in a frontier setting required great optimism. Success depended on the growth of the new country. Such a gamble was questionable during the national economic hard times that dominated much of the 1870s. With farm prices stubbornly low and transportation costs high, most Oregon farmers could ill afford a newspaper, even if it typically—like the *EO*—only cost $4.00 or less a year. Moreover, all too often newspapers folded without warning, leaving subscribers and advertisers no refund.

To provide some sense of Bull's determination to succeed in the newspaper business in Pendleton, he secured the backing of four highly regarded local residents to guarantee subscribers against loss. J. H. Turner, a lawyer; A. Jacobson, a saloonkeeper; Lot Livermore and I. C. Disoway, merchants, provided the necessary assurance against financial harm.

The design of Bull's *EO* was typical of most western small town weekly newspapers. It consisted of four pages, with those on the outside called patent pages. This term referred to the fact that those pages were supplied by a company that aggregated national news and advertising in a standardized newsprint format. The front page typically consisted of brief telegraphic reports of national and international news, though dated, were new to the isolated rural readers. The back page usually contained short stories, social commentary, and advertising from national brands of sewing machines, farm implements, canned foodstuffs, patent medicines, and other items aimed at a rural or small-town readership. The inside pages held the local and state news written and organized by the newspaper owner/editor, local advertising, and correspondence from readers or others from communities within the subscription territory of the paper.

The inside pages conveyed the paper's editorial stance and personality, while the outside patent pages made weekly production with sufficient content financially feasible. Every ambitious weekly editor, however, wanted to produce enough local news and advertising to drop the patent outsides and print a totally fresh and homegrown newspaper. While at the beginning of publication the *EO* cost subscribers $4.00 a year in advance, Bull dropped the price in April 1877 to $3.00. Subscriptions, advertising, and occasional job printing kept the paper going.

In its early years, as a service to readers and a lure to potential patrons, the *EO* occasionally ran a free column for subscribers containing cattle brands.

Small town newspaper proprietors of that era spoke to their readers more directly, even bluntly, than a twenty-first Century publisher would. As was typical of that era, Bull operated on a financial shoestring. Bull frequently printed appeals for payment

To provide some sense of M.P. Bull's determination to succeed, he got four highly regarded residents to guarantee subscribers against loss.

of past due amounts. From time to time, Bull would remind his readers why they should support their local newspaper:

> The liberal sustaining of a newspaper by the people in whose locality it is published and in whose interests it must necessarily operate, is a much greater source of wealth, not only to patrons but to the community in general, than is ordinarily supposed. There is nothing which more correctly tells the character and grade of community, village or town than the local paper.

After listing in detail all of the things a local paper does for its community, Bull went on to make his main point:

> A newspaper, like a child, wants support and nurturing care in the beginning of its existence, so that when it can stand alone it may be able to bring credit upon the community in which it is located. Everyone should take the local, home newspaper; it gives more real information than one possibly be given by any other paper; when other papers misrepresent you, in any way, your home paper speaks in your defense. . . . Hence you should support your home paper, not grudgingly as a disagreeable duty, but willingly, in such a spirit as will satisfy the editor that you understand the investment will pay the expense intended to bring a benefit to both you and it. (*EO*, August 4, 1877)

At other times, Bull directed his ire at delinquent advertisers:

> There are several men in this town who know that they owe us. If they would come forward and pay their little bills it would relieve the proprietor of the embarrassment common to the half-paid, half-appreciated county publisher. . . . If you want a paper published in your midst, patronize it! And pay for your paper and the advertising space used by you. (*EO*, August 11, 1877)

Like most small town editors in the American West, Bull fiercely boosted his community and pushed for civic improvements. The cry for street improvements and sidewalks, better schools, and enforcement of community moral standards appeared regularly in editorials and news columns. Bull promoted local industry and businesses, sought railroad connections, and better mail service. Typical of his writing about Pendleton industry occurred in March 1877, when he took notice of the additions to a planing mill and a flour mill. After noting the arrival of several new main street businesses, Bull wrote:

> the most notable improvement lately affected in our town is that made by . . . what is called a 'planing mill.' First, the power propelling the machinery of this establishment has been increased 40 percent by cutting a new tail race 300 feet long and 7 feet deep, with a flume therein 3 feet in width. Additional machinery has been placed in the building by which the firm can now manufacture anything from a magnificent house front to a potato masher. To give an idea of the capacity of the establishment we here name some of the machinery which can be set running all at the same time: planer, buzz saw, re-saw, tenon machine, mortising machine, turning lathe, scroll saw, boring machine, wabble saw, etc. etc. (*EO*, March 3, 1877)

But Bull saved his grandest praise for the accomplishments of W. S. Byers' flour mill. After reporting that

> Mr. Byers is now turning out 100 barrels of flour every 24 hours . . . he needs more power, and additional burrs. The power will soon be procured by excavating a new tail race, and the additional burrs will be in position ready to assist in grinding the new and immense crop of wheat which will be harvested this season. Mr. Byers has expended $17,000 on this mill which to-day stands unexcelled as a master piece of machinery . . . and ere another six months rolls around he will have expended at least $1,000 more.

Bull went on to remind his readers that Byers' investment

> has gone to build up your town and added to your wealth, to the value of your lots, to your business, and everything that goes to make Pendleton a business point.

He couldn't resist, at this point, to connect his own newspaper with Byers' achievement:

> An enterprise of this description [Byers' mill], which stands parallel to a live newspaper, needs, demands and is entitled, other things being equal, to the united support of every man who is a friend of Pendleton, its success present and future, and of his own prosperity, which depends on the business enterprise which surrounds him. We hope this and every other enterprise (not excepting even your local paper) which advances our country will be heartily endorsed and sustained. (*EO*, March 10, 1877)

Above all, Bull and other small town editors in the West wanted growth—more settlers and investment equaled an improved quality of life on the frontier. The *EO* duly reported on the steady progress of Pendleton in his two years running the paper. In the March 24, 1877 issue he wrote "one year ago the population was 260; now it numbers 322, as a minimum number. This certainly is a flattering increase in our population." He also noted the continued influx of settlers taking up free homesteads under the terms of the Homestead Act or filing on pre-emption claims for as little as $1.25 an acre for unimproved lands.

Most small-town newspapers in the last half of the nineteenth century were fiercely partisan as politics served as the national pastime during that period. Bull was no exception in this regard, championing an independent Democratic Party editorial stance. This political leaning appealed to many in and around Pendleton, as most of the early settlers hailed from southern and border states, traditionally Democratic in politics. In fact, until the late 1930s when a renaming project took place, Pendleton streets bore the names of Confederate Civil War heroes as Stonewall Jackson, Robert E. Lee, P. T. Beauregard, and Jefferson Davis.

After about two years of running the *EO*, Bull's health began to fail and even though his sons helped in printing the newspaper, he decided to sell. Staunch Democrat that he was, Bull refused to sell to any potential buyer that promoted Republican Party politics. Bull eventually found a buyer who met his qualifications: J. H. Turner, a sometime school teacher and fulltime lawyer. Turner agreed to purchase the newspaper but only if he could find other investors, which he soon did. For the next four years and with a succession of partners, Turner ran the business end of the *EO* and, at times, wrote editorials. The transition in ownership took place in October 1877. After selling out, Bull moved to Milton, Oregon, evidently to take up farming. In the fall of 1878, however, he went to Portland for medical attention and died at St. Vincent Hospital on November 26, 1878. C. S. "Sam" Jackson, the editor who would do so much to establish the journalistic fame of the *EO* would not assume ownership of the paper until 1881. Before he took the helm, Turner and a few other colorful characters ran the paper.

Turner, a hot-tempered and highly opinionated man, guided the *EO* through a turbulent period in Pendleton's early days. A Confederate Army veteran from Missouri, Turner arrived in Oregon in 1865 and was admitted to the bar in Washington County. In 1870, he settled in Pendleton as one of the earliest permanent residents, opening a law office. He continued to practice law while running the newspaper. In the inaugural issue under his leadership, Turner announced that "the paper will continue as heretofore—Democratic in politics—and as a Democratic paper it will be firm and positive in support of Democratic measures. Yet we intend to do this in a manner that will not give offence to those who differ with us in politics." (*EO*, October 13, 1877) Two weeks later, Turner assured his readers that all would continue to benefit from publication of the *EO*: "We have commenced the publication of this paper under the most favorable auspices. We intend to make it a success, and we assure the people of this county that before the end of the year we intend to have them all as regular subscribers. The paper will be made so interesting that none can afford to do without it." A few months later, Turner expressed similar views, while taking a dig at Republicans. He wrote: "We are making the *East Oregonian* pay and expect to make it pay better still, and kindly ask the assistance of all, without regard to politics or previous condition, and will endeavor to give all the worth of their money. We intend, however, to reprove the world of sin (that's Republicanism) and of the judgment to come which means democratic victory." (*EO*, February 2, 1878)

> **"We intend to reprove the world of sin (that's Republicanism) and of the judgment to come, which means Democratic victory." 1878**

Turner took the helm of the *EO* at the time of the last great conflict in the Northwest between Native Americans and white settlers, known as the Bannock War. In June 1878, Bannock and Paiute Native Americans from southern Idaho swept into Oregon and headed in a northwestern direction, hoping to link up with disaffected tribes on the Umatilla Reservations. If successful in this move, the rebelling tribesman planned to cross the Columbia River to gather more support from angry tribes on the Yakama Reservation and generally lay waste all of the white settlements in their way. The hostile Bannocks and Paiutes entered Oregon in what is today northern Malheur County and rapidly pushed on through the John Day River Valley and turned north, pausing briefly in Fox and Long Creek valleys, before joining battle on July 8 with United States Army troops under General O. O. Howard just south of Pilot Rock, Oregon, at the head of Butter and Birch creeks. The army decisively defeated the Bannocks and Paiutes in the ensuing battle. In skirmishes over the next few weeks, the Army pressed its campaign to defeat and round up the scattered remnants of hostile Native Americans and return them to their respective reservations.

During the rapidly unfolding events of the Bannock War, people in Umatilla County were thrown into a panic, fearing that the Umatilla Indians would join the invading hostiles and wipe out the town and surrounding ranches. Hundreds of families crowed into Pendleton from the surrounding area and townsmen hastily threw up defenses around the courthouse. Women and children went to Byers' substantial flour mill for shelter.

Responding to federal action, Editor J.H. Turner wrote: "the Indian is a dirty, lazy, filthy vagabond."

In words that could be a screenplay for a John Ford western, in the July 6, 1878 issue of the *EO*, the editor wrote, "The Indian excitement has been at fever heat for several days. . . . Teams arrived at all hours during the night and up to a late hour Wednesday morning. Campers on every street; the school houses are filled and the rest take shelter where opportunity offers. Calico was seen on every fence corner wondering, what next. A company was organized to guard the town and another party of 10 which took their departure for the scene of war. Several more joined at Pilot Rock and started in company with several Umatilla Indians."

The volunteers skirmished with the hostile tribesmen but generally proved ineffective until the regular Army troops arrived and systematically suppressed the uprising. By the end of July life began to return to normal in Pendleton, but hereafter editor Turner turned his ire towards all Native Americans and especially those on the Umatilla Reservation. In one particularly vivid editorial, Turner stated:

> One thing is now demonstrated, viz: The whites and Indians cannot longer live together in peace. . . . Every Indian found off the Reservation will be killed, and this strife will in this way soon be ended. Indian Agents may cry peace, peace, but there can never be peace until the last one of the red demons, whose fingers are dripping with the blood of our Coggans, our Jewells, our Nelsons, our McCoys and others are numbered with the good Indians who have fallen. It will not suffice that after they have killed and plundered they return to their allegiance and join in the fight against the Snakes. They must die. Scarcely a day passes without some of them being picked off, and thus it will continue 'till they are all gone or until they are removed from our midst and every time one of them bites the dust every good citizen will say amen; so be it; bless the lord; hallelujah! (*EO*, July 27, 1878)

On another occasion, an adamant Turner bluntly asserted that "the time is approaching, as we are all well aware, where public opinion will boldly proclaim . . . the Indian must go." (*EO*, Nov. 16, 1878) In exasperation at the government's Indian policies, Turner flatly asserted that "the Indian is a dirty, lazy, filthy vagabond, wherever you find him; and as long as the present policy of the government prevails, just so long may we expect to have trouble with the Indian." (*EO*, Dec. 28, 1878) Turner was especially vocal in calling for the breakup of the Umatilla Reservation and the removal of its tribes to the Yakama Reservation in the Washington Territory.

Although the Bannock War briefly traumatized Pendleton, the town and surrounding area quickly recovered. In the final two years of the decade, crops were good and wool and cattle sold well. Settlers continued to pour into eastern Oregon and Pendleton's businesses thrived. A local census taken in February 1879, found 672 inhabitants in Pendleton. Turner boasted in an editorial that "there is perhaps no city on this coast that has made so rapid and healthy growth within the past three years as has Pendleton" and he went on to urge "the emigrant who is weary and worn, looking for a good home . . . to first take a look at our lovely country and converse yourself with the facts regarding its climate and agricultural resource, before seeking other locations." (*EO*, Sep. 1879)

By August 1879, the *EO*'s circulation had reached 1056, which was typical for frontier weeklies; the average circulation for a weekly paper in the West in 1880 was 1,156. The paper had three typographers and advertised for a fourth. Turner even added on to the *EO* building and bought a new power press. In the fall of 1879, Turner announced that he hoped to do away with the patent outsides and produce the entire paper at home. Others around the state took notice of the newspaper's quality. The Portland *Bee* wrote, "*East Oregonian*, which both for original news and wit and neat appearance, has no equal in the eastern country."

The November 30, 1878 issue of the paper announced that George Munson Bull, one of the founding editor's sons and press foreman for the paper, had become Turner's partner. Bull had bought out several of the businessmen associated in the *EO* and boasted that his part of "the business consists in manipulating the type" and he would "allow nothing to go from the office unless well printed. Seven years of experience has taught us that 'Guess it will do' will not answer." (*EO*, Nov. 1878) From time to time, Bull also wrote news briefs. Another man involved in running the paper was B. B. Bishop, Turner's law partner; he occasionally wrote editorials, especially in Turner's absence.

More change came a year later. In October 1879, Munson Bull sold his interest in the *EO* to Bishop and moved to Portland. Under the new arrangement, Turner continued to manage the business end of the paper while Bishop assumed more of the editorial duties. Over the next couple of years, Turner gradually spent more time on his law practice and less on the *EO*. In August 6, 1880, Bishop sold his interest in the paper to another lawyer newly arrived from Virginia, L. B. Cox. Bishop ruefully noted in his final editorial:

> L B. Cox, a man of ability takes the place which I have poorly filled for the last six months. I thought that my opinions were worth something to mankind, but as I proceeded along, I found that I and the opinions I entertained amounted to little to the great multitude of humanity and in the hopes that the paper would contain better articles than I could possibly write and to relieve the weight that had to be carried by my friends, I 'stepped down and out.' Jim Turner had to Father too many of my articles which appeared in the E. O. which I wrote. I found he got all the credit as well as all the cursings and it was no fair thing. (*EO*, Aug. 14, 1880)

Under Cox's editorship the *EO* continued to thrive, printing more regional news from correspondents in nearby communities and attracting more readers.

Cox, as did Turner, disliked using the patent outside pages format, so they took the financial plunge and ordered the equipment and supplies to print the entire paper in the *EO* office. In announcing this plan, Turner and Cox stated that "it shall be our aim not to make money on a worthless sheet, but to provide our fellow citizens with a respectable newspaper, having for its object the promotion of the interests of Umatilla County and the State. We only request the support of our friends in this enterprise and then if it proves a failure we will bear the censure." (*EO*, Sep. 4, 1880) Weather delays prevented shipment of the press and printing supplies during the winter months. Finally, on March 5, 1881, the weekly edition proclaimed, "Published entirely at home!"

No sooner did the *EO* start appearing in its new garb than it once again changed hands. Turner and Cox sold out to Charles Christie of Portland in April 1881. Cox said at the time that the change was necessary because he had tired of doing the editorial work at night after a full day with his law practice, and Turner was not interested in resuming the editorship. As Cox ruefully put it:

> I have been, and now am, engaged in the practice of law. This was my first choice of a profession and I was unwilling to subordinate it to anything else. I have been unable to bestow such time and attention upon the paper, therefore, as it required, and the greatest portion of the work done upon it was accomplished at night after a day's work had been finished. But I have honestly made every effort in my power to give our patrons a readable sheet in return for their subscriptions. . . . Seeing at an early date, however, that it would be impossible for me to furnish to the people of this great county such a journal as it was justly entitled to, I made it my object to endeavor to get the paper on a firm foundation and then turn it over into abler hands. This has been done.

Cox also wanted it known,

> That whatever has appeared in the editorial columns of the paper since my connection with it has been written by my own pencil, and be the same good, bad or indifferent, I claim the authorship of it. Mr. Turner has been more than once unjustly,

and without cause, criticized in an unfavorable manner for
publications in the paper. He wrote nothing during my association
with him, and it may be added had no connection with the paper
editorially for a long time previous thereto. . . . I have not
knowingly injured any man without cause, but for everything
which has appeared in the paper during my connection with it I
stand responsible, and I have no explanations or apologies to
offer therefor. (*EO*, Apr. 2, 1881)

The new ownership did not last long. Starting off with the best of intentions,
Christie noted on his assumption of editorial duties that "the *East Oregonian* has
now a fair name and fame, and is counted as one of the best papers in Eastern Oregon.
My aim shall be always to labor for the best interests of Umatilla county and her
people. The politics of the paper will be Democratic, first, last, and always." (*EO*,
Apr. 2, 1881) On May 27, 1881, however, Christie announced, "Owing to continued
ill health I am compelled to relinquish control of the *East Oregonian*." Turner and
Cox resumed ownership of the newspaper, but apparently did not intend to stay in
charge longer than necessary to find a new owner or owners.

By August, they had found their man. C. S. "Sam" Jackson. He, along with John
Hailey Jr., bought Turner's interest and became Cox's partners. The masthead listed
Jackson as the paper's business manager. Apparently, Hailey and Jackson purchased
an interest in the paper for a quick profit, for within two months, they sold out to Cox,
notifying readers that "we bought it to make money and did not buy to gain
notoriety—we sold for the same necessary article—we got it." (*EO*, Oct. 7, 1881)
Cox, after sole ownership for a short time, conveyed the *EO* to Jackson and J. A.
Guyer for $3,500 on January 13, 1882. Guyer, a lawyer, put up the money for the
EO as an investment. He took Jackson's note for his share ($1,750) and, intending
to be a silent partner, let Jackson run the paper. Time would show that his faith in
the journalistic ability of the 21-year-old Jackson was not misplaced.

Jackson, born in Virginia on September 15, 1860, had heard of Pendleton from
family friends who had settled in the town. Intrigued, he came west in 1880, and
arrived in Pendleton with five dollars to his name. He took a job with the Utah, Idaho
and Oregon Stage Company at $40 a month, a typical unskilled workers wage for the
day. The stage lines owner's son, John Hailey Jr., became a friend of Jackson, and he
lent Jackson the money when the two of them briefly bought into the *EO* in 1881.

Young Sam Jackson arrived in Pendleton around 1880 with $5 to his name.

Young Jackson quickly impressed people with his business ability, integrity, decency, and thrift—traits that would exemplify in his management of the *EO* over the next 21 years.

When Cox turned over the newspaper to Jackson and Guyer, he warned them "that their pathway will not be strewn with roses nor will their bed be without thorns." Further, he confessed that "I never liked this business and am glad to be out of it." (*EO*, Jan. 27, 1882) Despite his weariness of the newspaper business, Cox had done well in his tenure at the *EO*. He increased news coverage and circulation, while making enough money to print the entire newspaper with its own plant.

Rapid changes in newspaper ownership were not uncommon on the western frontier, so the *EO* was rather typical in this regard before Jackson took over. One study of newspaper publishers in Washington territory demonstrated that two-thirds of them stayed with a particular newspaper two years or less, and half of them stayed no more than a year.

Upon taking ownership of the *EO*, Guyer and Jackson quickly announced their editorial stance: "Our predecessors made the paper what it is—we will be responsible for what it will be. Our aim will be directed toward the right, and to work always in that direction is our desire. . . . [W]e hope to do that which will receive the generous approval of our patrons and the public. We will try to please, but will not sacrifice our principles, beliefs or rights in doing so." They also made it clear that "we are Democrats, 'staunch and true,' and the paper remains a journal interested in that party's advancement." (*EO*, Feb. 3, 1882) Under the new ownership the paper immediately became a semi-weekly.

At the time Jackson took over the *EO*, his was not the only newspaper in Pendleton. In 1878, Republicans in the community wanted a paper of their own, so several local businessmen of that political persuasion started the *Pendleton Independent*. Two years later it changed its name to the *Pendleton Tribune* and had a long run as both a weekly and a daily paper before closing in 1923. Jackson and the *Tribune* sparred with each other constantly. In expressing his feelings about the *Tribune* early in his editorship, Jackson exhibited a talent for colorful invective: "A man of any sense at all can tell, after reading one or two of your productions that you are not an advocate of truth or right. But an unconscientious, worthless, unprincipled

In the early 1880s, almost every issue told of fist fights, pistol whipping, knife fights, racing horses on the major streets of the town.

adventurer who, by accident, gained control of a patent outside. . . . You care not for the truth, of any statement, for your purpose is low, and unbecoming a thief. You are fast establishing a reputation among your friends and acquaintances as a libelous, unprincipled newspaper man." (*EO*, May 2, 1882)

When Jackson assumed control of the *EO*, he operated as a one-man show. He sold advertising, kept the books, solicited subscriptions, and wrote the news columns as well as the editorials. As newsman Fred Lockly later put it: "He had no money to hire bookkeepers, editors, circulation managers, or advertising men, so he learned every detail of the publishing business by doing the work himself." (quote in Turnbull, 318) Early on he used his bully pulpit to prod Pendletonians into shedding many of their frontier habits, including violence, gambling, and saloon patronage.

Pendleton in the early 1880s exemplified a cinematic image of the Wild West. Almost every issue of the *EO* told of fist fights, pistol whipping, knife fights, racing horses on the major streets. Soon after taking charge of the *EO*, Jackson reported that opium dens existed in Pendleton, moralizing "there are at least three dens in Pendleton where opium is the sole drug for sale, and where life is given up almost nightly, for when once indulged in, 'tis seldom that a creature ever reforms." He went on to urge the town authorities to "destroy the opium dens in our midst and place the keepers of such infamous houses where they would not see daylight anymore." (*EO*, July 20, 1882)

Saloons thrived in Pendleton, and Jackson saw them as a major nuisance and deterrent to good order. In 1882, the town had eleven saloons—five in one Main Street block—to serve a population of about 1,000, and Jackson railed against the problems they created: "Our principle street is lined with saloons in front of which hourly congregate drunkards and gamblers so thickly that it's very difficult to even pass along the sidewalk and ladies can never go the length of Main street without being compelled to hear vile and profane language from these loafers. . . . The town ordinances are stringent enough to prevent these abuses but the trouble is that the law is not enforced. Let us have a change." (*EO*, Jul. 7, 1882)

Town authorities mostly chose to look the other way, as the taxes the saloons paid constituted an important source of revenue. Jackson did not let go of the issue and soon crusaded against those violating the town's ordinance requiring closing on Sunday. Finally, a grand jury did its job and returned indictments against a saloon-keeper for Sunday violations, allowing minors to loiter, and for permitting gambling. Still, the grand jury made clear its reluctance to act, noting that it did so only "at the request of all the best citizens of our county whom we consulted in the matter and was resorted to not in a spirit of malice but for the purpose of enforcing salutary laws and bringing about an order of affairs more congenial to the business men and better class of citizens." (quote in Macnab, 61)

Shortly after Jackson and Guyer bought the *EO*, J. P. Wager bought Guyer's interest and took on the role of editor, while Jackson looked after the business side. As Jackson would later describe his position on the newspaper: "I am really the manager of it and have the financial part of it in my hands; always looked out for financially and other ways and when Wager was away I had editorial charge of the paper also." (quote in Macnab, 65)

Wager, a lawyer from New York, had been teaching school in Echo for two years when he decided that he wanted to be a newspaperman instead. Wager soon proved to be a skilled writer and an excellent orator. He won election to the Oregon state senate. Both Wager and Jackson espoused strong Democratic Party political views. Wager expressed his political philosophy in his first editorial: "Politically as heretofor the E. O. will be solidly and squarely Democratic. . . ." He added, however, that it would expose the errors or frauds caused by Democrats because the paper supported only "the success of true Democratic principles and of honest and capable Democratic candidates." (*EO*, Aug. 29, 1882)

Wager carried on Jackson's fight against saloons and gambling. Wager thought that the best way to control the excesses of saloons was to place a high license fee on them because "that eliminates a great portion of the worst features of this business and is more practical than teetotalism." (*EO*, Sep. 29, 1882) In November, the *EO* ran an editorial claiming that "the town is infested with gamblers of all sorts, sizes, sexes, ages, colors, and description . . . and should be 'cleaned out.'" (Nov. 3, 1882) Wager held the saloons and their supporters among local officials responsible for the problem and went on to urge close regulation of the ones remaining in business. He saved his special ire for public officials who failed to enforce the law:

> **In 1882, the EO declared "the town is infested with gamblers of all sorts, sizes, sexes, ages, colors and description ... and should be cleaned out."**

"Open and shameless violation of the gambling laws" could be traced "to the judges and juries and prosecuting officers who have made the courts of justice odious, who have made the house of justice a den of thieves, whose main business in such cases have been, how not to enforce the law" (*EO*, Nov. 7, 1882)

Wager's editorials bearing down on the conduct of saloonkeepers, rampant gambling, and the seeming inability of the local officials to do anything about these matters caused a good deal of controversy. Some criticized the *EO* for exposing the community's dark side. Wager, in response, sought to explain his editorial stance. In a November 7, 1882 editorial, he wrote, "It is impossible for a paper to exactly suit everybody. . . . So it is a waste of words, generally, to attempt to reply to most of the censure which is sure to fall constantly upon an editor's devoted head."

Turner ridicules Abigail Scott Duniway
Duniway fires back

J. H. Turner, as editor of the EO, reflected the all-too common racist and misogynist views of his readers during the late 19th century. Not only did he call for the extermination of the local Native Americans, he also condemned the "filthy Chinamen" who took jobs from "hard-working white laborers." (EO, Apr. 26, 1879) Turner also mocked in print the opinions of Abigail Scott Duniway, crusader for women's rights and the suffrage.

Duniway made regular lecture tours in the 1870s and 1880s through Eastern Oregon, arguing on behalf of women's suffrage. In response to one such lecture stop in Pendleton on December 13, 1880, Turner wrote a lengthy editorial attacking Duniway, asserting "that to confer the elective franchise on [a] woman is to degrade rather than to elevate her, and . . . that as an active participant in politics [a] woman would be a dangerous factor." Turner came to this conclusion, he condescendingly wrote, "after patiently and attentively listening to what Mrs. Duniway denominated reasons for the innovation [women's suffrage], we are, either through our stupidity or her unintelligibility, very much in the same situation as before the visitation was inflicted upon us. We took in what she said, but failed to see any reason, sense, or logic in her harangues." In answer to the question of how women can best exercise their influence, Turner opined: "At home in rearing sons to serve their country." (EO, Dec. 18, 1880)

Duniway, never one to back away from a good fight, responded to Turner in the columns of her own newspaper, the *New Northwest*. She wrote that the "*East Oregonian*, J. H. Turner's paper is on the rampage after us, as usual, with the classic vernacular of the Barbary Coast." She went on to assert, "The good citizens are ashamed of the thing that thinks itself an editor, and which with the sublime impudence of the puppy that barked at the moon, sent us a copy of the paper containing its scurrility—with its compliments. . . . If Mr. Turner wants any more apologies printed in the New Northwest, we'd advise him to dismiss that poor apology for an editor or take his own name from the columns of his paper." (EO, Jan. 1, 1881)

Nevertheless, he went on to lay out his editorial philosophy for his readers:

> The first duty of a paper is to give its patrons reliable news. Its second important duty is to serve as an educator of the people—advising and enlightening them upon all matters pertaining to their welfare and advancement in the world. In doing this an editor must be exceedingly careful to speak words of truth and honesty—to reason soberly and candidly—to instruct according to the very best of his ability—to himself walk in the broadest and clearest light possible of attainment. But if he does all this, he will often be mistaken, will often commit errors and blunders. He must do the best he can. Readers should not condemn him lightly, and should honor an open and honest expression of opinion, even though it may differ from theirs.

Wager, like all of his predecessors, provided editorial opinion on the great national political issues of the day. He wrote extensively on the tariff, laying out the Democratic Party's commitment to free trade. This was a courageous position in Umatilla County, because sheep men wanted high tariffs on imported wool. Among other economic issues important to agricultural interests were high railroad freight rates for wheat and wool, and Wager championed the farmer against the big rail corporations.

In 1887, the EO became the first newspaper in Oregon to advocate for the secret or Australian ballot, as it was then known.

Some readers thought Wager's criticisms of Republican officeholders were too strident or partisan. He responded editorially that "when we condemn the party we do not condemn anyone who honestly differs from us. But if we are right, the case calls for earnest speech." He went on to justify a small town newspaper's obligation to comment on the great national issues of the day: "The peace and prosperity of a great Nation is a trust of mighty responsibility, and each of us bears some small portion of that responsibility. When the very life of the Nation is at stake, it is no time for soft words and melodious phrases." (*EO*, Nov. 7, 1882).

Jackson and Wager also fought for governmental reforms such as the secret ballot for elections. The *EO* in an editorial on August 5, 1887, became the first newspaper

Horse harvesting combine, circa 1890

in Oregon to advocate for the secret or Australian ballot, as it was known at the time. From time to time, Jackson supplemented Wager's editorials with articles on his favorite subject, the single tax, which he thought was the only fair way to support government. As Jackson put it in one of his many editorials on the subject, "I believe in the 'single tax' because . . . it is plain and direct . . . [and] because it promises to reward those who labor in proportion to the productiveness of their labor, while the present system rewards the unproductive laborer more." (*EO*, Jan. 15, 1889)

Jackson and Wager's efforts at promoting civic betterment occurred at a critical moment. Over the course of the 1880s, the town and the surrounding area experienced tremendous growth and modernization. The *EO* noted in the summer of 1880 that "the emigrants from different parts of the states and territories arrive almost daily. Trains from three to eight wagons generally in one company; some of the teams consist of oxen and cows, others of horses and mules. . . . This county is comparatively unsettled and holds out inducements to the hardy workingman that few counties do today." (*EO*, July 31, 1880) While that growth rested primarily on the expanding agricultural strength of the surrounding area, the town's location also made it a commercial and transportation crossroads for all of northeastern Oregon. In addition, Pendleton as the county seat of Umatilla County served as a governmental center. A first step in gaining control of its destiny came in October 25, 1880, when Pendleton adopted a city charter and incorporated. The town's population shot up from 730 in 1880 to 2,506 in 1890—a gain of 243 percent.

Recognition of Pendleton's importance as a well-located commercial center came in September 1882 with the arrival of the Oregon Railroad and Navigation Company (ORNC), which connected with the North Pacific transcontinental line. By December 1884, the ORNC had crossed the Blue Mountains and linked up with the Union Pacific's Oregon Short Line at Huntington, Oregon, thus giving Pendleton access to another transcontinental railroad. Now farmers and livestock operators could get their wheat, wool, and cattle to market at better rates and local merchants could receive their merchandise more quickly and cheaply. Some measure of the agricultural advance of the Umatilla and Morrow (est. in 1885) counties over the course of the decade can be seen in these statistics taken from the U. S. Census records:

	Bushels of Wheat	Number of Cattle	Number of Sheep	Pounds of Wool
1880	915,571	29,231	267,782	1,738,427
1890	1,814,312	32,846	323,690	2,285,349

The *EO* avidly kept track of Pendleton's physical expansion in buildings and public infrastructure, which paced its agricultural and commercial growth. In 1880, the town got its first brick building (the two-story Milarkey Building) and its initial bank; by the end of the decade, it had a second bank and a building and loan association, and dozens of brick buildings lined Main and Court streets—the town's chief thoroughfares. In the summer of 1881, the EO—prophetically noting the large number of brick commercial establishments either under construction or planned—reported, "in short the fever for brick buildings is as catching as the California gold fever in '49 and the result is that Pendleton will soon exchange ordinary wooden houses for substantial brick edifices in all business portions of the town." (*EO*, Jul. 22, 1881) In 1886, the city financed a municipal water system with $30,000 in bonds. Two separate companies commenced in 1887 to generate and distribute electricity. The companies soon merged and began improvements. The merged companies operated out of W. S. Byers' flour mill, using the millrace to power the turbines.

As evidence of what wonders electricity brought to the town, the *EO* reported on a production of the *Mikado* at the Frazer's Opera House: "The opera house last evening was the scene of great splendor, the electric lights being put in operation for the first time. In the center of the ceiling is an arc light, while the stage and gallery are fitted with incandescent." (*EO*, Apr. 26, 1887)

Communications with the outside became easier as well during the decade of the 1880s. A telegraph connection came in 1883 and a telephone system was established as early as 1880, with a line running to Umatilla. The phone system, however, had limited utility until a network was set up within the town in 1889. The *EO* began receiving occasional news dispatches via the telegraph in 1884.

Piped water, electricity, telephone, and the railroad all demonstrated that Pendleton was leaving the frontier period behind. The growth of Umatilla County also stimulated moves to divide the county. While the effort by those in the eastern section—led by the communities of Weston and Milton—failed, the drive by those living in the western portion of the county succeeded. The state legislature set off Morrow County in 1885, which took in most of Umatilla County west of Butter Creek. The *EO* fought the eastern split but generally approved of the creation of Morrow County.

The simmering tension between the Umatilla Indian Reservation and the burgeoning town of Pendleton came to a boil in the 1880s, removing an impediment to the town's growth. The Umatilla Indian Reservation came right to the edge of the town along Dorion Street. By 1880, the town had expanded illegally over the Reservation line because a survey revealed that the patent for Moses Goodwin's claim had inadvertently included some reservation land.

The *East Oregonian* began receiving occasional news dispatches via the telegraph in 1884.

Town officials convinced tribal leaders to agree to sell 640 acres along Pendleton's southern edge, putting the new line at the top of the hills rising 200 feet high above and behind the town. Congress ratified this sale on August 5, 1882, and land office officials platted the land and sold lots at auction in the spring of 1884. Jackson took advantage of the opportunity and bought a lot at the corner of Main and Emigrant streets for $950. Three years later he built a new office building on the lot. There the *EO* would remain for over 60 years.

The desire for reservation land to allow Pendleton to expand was only one part of the drive to carve up the reservation to benefit white settlers. The pressure to diminish the reservation so that whites could take its prime agricultural land had begun in earnest in the 1870s. Over time, the *EO* had run column after column

Bird's eye view of Pendleton, 1892

pushing the idea, making the point that "Pendleton is certainly deeply interested in the matter. The sale and settlement of these [reservation] lands means a large increase in its population and volume of business." (*EO*, Aug. 15, 1888) Finally, in the mid-1880s, tribal leaders agreed to a plan allowing each Native American on the reservation to receive an individual allotment of land to replace ownership in common. In addition to the individual allotments, the reservation would include some grazing and timbered land under tribal ownership. The end result of the Allotment Act of 1885 reduced the reservation from the original 245,699 to 157,982 acres. After a lengthy survey process, federal land officials held a public auction for the surplus 87,717 acres in April 1891. The sale brought almost $80,000, which federal officials distributed to the tribal members on the reservation.

While the *EO* and others worked for the agricultural development of Umatilla County by bringing new land into production, advances in farming also took place. In July 1888, the *EO* noted, "A combined harvester left Friday for Temple's farm. . . . Six horses were all that were necessary to haul the machine to the farm although twenty horses are necessary to its complete operation in the harvest field. . . . Before leaving town the huge machine was photographed. Its trip across Main Street Bridge was a severe trial to that structure." (*EO*, July 28, 1888) A few weeks later, Jackson, writing under the name "E. O. Tramp," described the combined harvester working at Mr. J. F. Temple's ranch nine miles northwest of Pendleton. "The machine used was C. K. Myers' Improved Link and V Belt Combined Harvester. . . . Four men were operating it, and it is drawn by 26 horses. . . . The inventor of the machine was present and gave us an interesting account of the workings of this labor-saving machine which will revolutionize harvesting in this country. The machine works admirably both going up and down hill." (*EO*, August, 11, 1888) Strides in wheat farming between 1870 and 1890 are apparent from the federal census reports. Umatilla County produced 28,209 bushels of wheat in 1870; by 1890 (even without the land given to Morrow County), production reached 1,640,888 bushels.

The *EO* under Jackson and Wager steadily pushed civic betterment in its editorials, especially school improvements and the necessity of replacing the old county courthouse located on Main Street between Court and Dorion streets. The paper's efforts succeeded on both accounts in 1888. The newspaper proudly announced completion of an $18,000 brick school house on the hill south of downtown. In its crusade for a new courthouse, the *EO* used the example of the December 1887 collapse of a bridge over the Umatilla River under the weight of too many cattle attempting to cross it. The paper made an analogy between the bridge collapse and the similar danger posed by the rickety condition of the courthouse. An editorial pointed out that "during a trial in the Court House . . . probably 100 persons were in the room upstairs when someone asked if the Court House was any safer than the Main Street bridge. Several persons left. There should be no further delay in getting a new Court House." (*EO*, Jan. 31, 1888) The editorial had its effect, and the county commissioners decided to build a new one. In the process, they sited the new building four blocks east from the existing one on land that had been set aside originally for a college. Contractors completed the new courthouse in 1889.

Though both Jackson and Wager were men of strong will and deep convictions, they worked well together during the 1880s. In the summer of 1890, however, they had a falling out over the printing of letters by anonymous authors. The letter in question, signed "Nemo," attacked the conduct of saloons in Pendleton, giving several examples of alleged illegal activity and, in particular, singled out the Hotel Pendleton as an egregious example of such bad behavior. It was not unusual for letters to appear in the *EO* under a pseudonym; but these usually contained straight news or made innocuous comment on some issue of the day and the author's real name had to be known by the editor.

The day after the letter appeared, Jackson wrote a signed editorial stating, "if the gentleman wishes to rectify the abuses which he so oratorically points out, let him give the weight of his name to his complaints." Jackson went on to state his doubts about the accuracy of the complaint and noted that "assertions can easily be made over nom de plumes that a writer will hesitate to make over his real name. Citizens who desire to make specific criticism, point out abuses and make public their complaints against officials and their fellow citizens in this paper, must have the nerve and faith in the truth and justice of their cause, to sign their real names to their communications sent to this office for publication." (*EO*, August 27, 1890)

Wager did not agree and he followed with a signed editorial of his own. He stated that while the *EO* had high regard for the saloonkeepers mentioned in "Nemo's" letter, "we see nothing wrong in the communication. If it accused anyone wrongfully, let them make it known. If not, why should they wince?" Wager observed, after all, that the point of the letter was that town ordinances were not enforced, and it was fair to ask "who is the government of this little town." (*EO*, August 27, 1890) Jackson felt

Wager's position violated the long held rule of the newspaper that it know the identity of the writer before publication of a letter or other communication and that the person stood ready to defend the public value of his utterance. There may have been more to the rupture than this one issue; in any case, Wager was gone within four weeks. Jackson now resumed writing editorials as well as carrying on all the business matters of the newspaper. It is perhaps of some significance that Wager had sold his interest in the East Oregonian Publishing Company to Jackson the previous year. Wager passed his seventy shares to Jackson for $2,800 on April 1, 1889. (notarized document, EOPC Archives)

The departure of Wager marked the closure of a strong decade for the *EO*. Under Cox and then Jackson and Wager, the newspaper had established a firm financial foundation and a strong editorial stance. The business was profitable enough to move into new quarters in October 1881—a new brick building on Court Street built by William Matlock. After beginning to print all four pages at home in 1881, the *EO* had to upgrade its presses. In 1882, it bought a power press and new type; then, in 1883, it became a semi-weekly. The semi-weekly was a four-page, seven-column sheet, issued Tuesdays and Fridays. In 1887, Jackson and Wager took the bold step of building a two-story, Italianate style brick building designed by Portland architect George Marshall on the southeastern corner of Main and Emigrant streets to house the newspaper's operations. The building cost $21,000 and the owners advertised that it had steam heat, electric lights, and piped water.

In the new office, Jackson and Wager once again upgraded the printing equipment, including the purchase of a $3,400, two-revolution Campbell press capable of printing 2,000 copies an hour of a four-page paper. The editor boasted that "this is the next best press in the state, the daily *Oregonian* only, being supplied with a better press." (*EO*, March 5, 1888). With their new press and type, the publishers took a momentous step in 1888 when the *EO* began daily publication, while continuing the semi-weekly edition.

Maintaining two separate editions was a typical response by small town papers attempting to appeal both to town and country readers, for many rural mail subscribers had little need of a daily paper. The *EO*'s owners gambled that Pendleton had grown large enough at approximately 2,500 inhabitants to support such an ambitious undertaking. Indeed, Jackson and Wager doubled down on their bet by increasing the size of the daily from four to eight pages. This action brought much astonishment within the journalism profession in the Pacific Northwest.

The *EO* started its afternoon daily publication with a small staff, consisting of one editor, a manager, a secretary, a bookkeeper, a reporter, a carrier, a correspondent in Portland, and eight printers and pressmen. It published at 5 p.m. except Sunday and charged subscribers nine dollars a year by mail or 25 cents a week by carrier. In the first issue of the new daily, the *EO* stated that its success

> Will depend chiefly upon the amount of substantial, willing patronage which is accorded to it. The plan of the publishers is to make it as much of a newspaper . . . as is possible in a town of this size. The dispatches published today are a sample of what we intend to furnish daily if sufficient interest is manifested in them. They are more than has ever been attempted by a newspaper in Eastern Oregon or Washington. To obtain them, and put them in readable shape, takes labor and money. If Pendleton is to advance . . . as we hope and expect; if it is to double its population and largely increase its wealth; if it is to be alive, active, progressive, pushing; if it is to become in a short time the unrivaled metropolis and commercial center of the great inland Northwest as it can and ought—no one enterprise will be of greater service and assistance in this direction than a daily newspaper such as the *East Oregonian* hopes to be. . . . We ask a general support and a liberal, not a grudging one, intending to deserve it and believing that our enterprise will materially assist the development of the town and county. . . . The Daily *East Oregonian* is not started for campaign purposes. It is started as a NEWSPAPER and has come to stay, if possible. Very likely and quite probably it will support the Democratic nominees. It usually does. But it makes no promises beforehand. Its first business is to furnish the people with a newspaper which shall be a credit to a small inland town like this. Politics it will certainly be interested in and readers may depend on it for all political news; but politics is after all a secondary consideration. (*EO*, March 1, 1888)

The daily got off to a rocky start. While advertising support came in, subscribers were not sure if they needed this much news. In three months only 175 had signed up, while 300 were necessary for the daily to break even. Jackson held on and dropped the price from nine dollars to five dollars a year by mail and from 25 to 15 cents a week by carrier. Circulation finally increased and the daily became a success. Many rural subscribers remained content with a less frequent diet of news and features, and the *EO* continued a semi-weekly until 1911 and the weekly until 1947.

Although the 1890s began with great promise, in the summer of 1893, a financial panic on Wall Street soon turned into a national Depression. Pendleton and eastern Oregon did not escape the economic hard times that hung on until 1897. The *EO*'s newspaper competitor, the *Pendleton Tribune*, went broke; and many businesses in town failed, including the National Bank of Pendleton. Unemployment soared, and church women distributed clothing and food to the needy. Worst of all for the farming community, the price of wheat fell from 66 cents a bushel in June 1893 to 28 cents by December of that year. Members of the Oregon contingent of "Coxeys Army"— unemployed workers headed by railroad to Washington, D. C., to petition Congress for relief measures—passed through Pendleton in April 1894.

In the midst of hard times, the *EO* pushed for industrial development in Pendleton. This proposal took the form of a woolen mill. First, came the drive for a scouring mill in 1894, which cleaned the wool. Then in 1896 the town got a woolen mill, which turned the wool into cloth. The plants were designed to take advantage of the vast amount of wool produced in eastern Oregon. In both cases, the *EO* and the businessmen belonging to the Pendleton Commercial Association urged local residents to subscribe to the capital

Jackson sends a reporter to the Klondike

Every newspaper hungers for the "Big Event." When such incidents occur, they test a news organization. In the late 19th and early 20th century, four big ones came the way of the EO. Often as not, in covering the "Big Event," the EO would issue an extra edition to get out the quickly unfolding news. This was typical before the advent of instant reporting by the radio and television, because newspapers were the chief means of informing people of the events of the day.

Even after sixteen years at the helm of the EO, Sam Jackson still found novel ways to promote the newspaper. When prospectors discovered gold in the Klondike in 1897, Jackson sent—on six-hours' notice—his city editor, John E. Lathrop, to provide first hand coverage of the event. This audacious move by a small-town daily was something that only big city dailies normally could afford. To help underwrite the expense, Jackson enlisted the help of E. Y. Judd, owner of the local woolen mill. Lathrop started his assignment in July 1897, and for a year sent back to the EO detailed accounts of the thrills and hardships of his adventure. Readers eagerly awaited his published dispatches, which sometime filled as much as four columns of space. Jackson editorialized in August 10, 1897: "The East Oregonian is the only paper in Oregon having a reliable special correspondent writing from the gold fields of Alaska." Lathrop would later state that "I am proud to have been known as a writer on the East Oregonian, because never . . . has it failed of its duty to the public. Perhaps larger responsibilities have come to me in later years, ... yet the training and the principles which were developed by the East Oregonian have been my most valued assets." (Dec. 29, 1910, EOPC Archives)

Edwin Burton Aldrich, graduation photo, Oregon Agriculture College, 1900
OREGON STATE UNIVERSITY ARCHIVES

stock for these industrial operations. The mill soon established a reputation for high quality woolen blankets and clothes.

Jackson not only pushed for industrial development but also presciently recognized the great advantages that would flow from the development of the irrigation and power potential of the Columbia River. In 1891, he editorialized, "Some enterprising, vigorous, big-minded man will form a company some day and dam the Columbia at some place where nature makes it possible." (*EO*, Oct. 10, 1891). His chief successor at the helm of the *EO*, Ed Aldrich, would continue this campaign in the 20th century until the federal government completed the McNary Dam at the Umatilla Rapids in 1953.

By 1897, agricultural prices had rebounded to 72 cents a bushel for wheat, and the Klondike Gold Rush stimulated the national economy. Politics during the 1890s mirrored the economic turmoil of the period. The Populist Party and various factions of the Farmers Alliance fed on the farming and labor unrest caused by low agricultural prices and high unemployment. They were very active in eastern Oregon. In cooperation with Democrats, the Populists elected members to the state legislature and even elected one of Oregon's four presidential electors in 1892. The return of more prosperous times after 1897 led to a decline in political unrest.

During the political excitement that raged in the early 1890s, the radical farm element in eastern Oregon started a number of newspapers to spread their views.

Home of the East Oregonian from 1887 to 1956

One such paper was the *Alliance Herald* begun in Freewater, Oregon, in 1890. After a short time, it moved to Pendleton where it was printed in the *EO*'s shop. It promoted the Populist Party position on the political economic issues of the day. While Jackson kept the *EO* in the mainstream Democratic fold, he sympathized with many of the Populists' goals. These included the adoption of the initiative, referendum, recall, direct election of U. S. senators, preferential voting (primary elections), and the secret ballot. His enthusiasm for political reform made the *EO* a persistent, vocal champion of these issues.

In spite of the economic hard times in the middle of the 1890s, by the end of the decade Pendleton and Umatilla County had made measurable strides in recovery. The city's population had increased from 2,506 in 1890 to 4,406 in 1900—a gain of 76 percent. Over the same time span, Umatilla County went from 13,381 to 18,049 inhabitants—an increase of 35 percent. As the following figures show, while the number of cattle in the county declined slightly, wool and wheat production continued an upwards trend:

	Bushels of Wheat	**Number of Cattle**	**Number of Sheep**	**Pounds of Wool**
1890	1,640,888	22,100	153,719	1,006,720
1900	3,212,120	19,571	222,907	1,461,599

As the nineteenth century closed, Jackson's editorials continued to urge community improvements. He suggested in 1899 that the city pave Main and Court streets and plant street trees. He wrote, "The more that Pendleton is beautiful and made attractive, the more people that will be attracted here and the more business there will be done here." (*EO*, Nov. 16, 1899) At that time, the only Oregon city with paved streets was Portland. He continued to offer his views on events and opportunities large and small, but the new century would soon see him take his fierce blend of independent Democratic politics and civic betterment to a new platform in another city.

On July 24, 1902, the *EO* announced that "C. S. Jackson, editor of the E. O. has purchased the *Portland Evening Journal* and took formal charge yesterday." Journalist Gordon Macnab has succinctly captured the situation as Jackson took over the struggling Portland newspaper:

> The *Journal* was one of the many newspapers that for a half century had found competition with the famed *Oregonian* to be too much. Each of these, after a life of a few years at most, had failed, unable to pay its bills. The *Journal* was about to join that sorry list when Jackson stepped in. He turned it into a successful newspaper, able to compete on even terms with The *Oregonian*. He did it with the enthusiasm, imagination and sense of high purpose that had made the *East Oregonian* pre-eminent in its field. (Macnab, 119)

When Jackson went to Portland, he kept a financial interest in the *EO* and sought to establish a capable team to run his well-respected, profitable newspaper. From among his employees, he selected several to operate the business and editorial functions and sold each of them, on credit, an interest in the newspaper. For editor he chose Bert Huffman, even though he had only been at the *EO* a brief time. Apparently, Jackson saw in Huffman a man of similar political and philosophical views and a quick learner. Fred Lampkin became the business manager, and Fred Lockley moved into the position of circulation manager, while Charles Sampson handled advertising. Jackson himself kept a one-third interest in the *EO*, refusing to sell until 1913. Jackson was not about to let all the work he had put into the *EO* slip away for want of strong guidance.

Country Weekly Hand Press

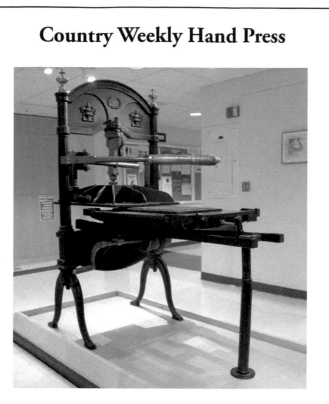

Before 1900, most small communities could not justify the expense of a powered cylinder press to put out a newspaper. Instead, newspaper owners used a hand press. Mounted on a metal frame, the Washington Hand Press took two men to operate. William Weir, editor of the *Long Creek Ranger*—located in Long Creek, Oregon—in the early 1900s, described how it worked:

> It took two men to operate the Washington hand press. One would ink the forms by running a roller over the type while the other was placing the print paper on the fly sheet. This fly sheet was brought down on the inked type and was rolled under the press by turning a hand crank. The printer would grab the handle, give it a pull, turn the crank back, [and] lift the fly sheet. There was a printed newspaper, just as good in every way as those run out on our modern presses. You could easily print 300 an hour.

> Weir recalled that the "home paper," as he called it, "was strong in personal mention, printed flowery obituaries, boosted home celebrities and attacked political issues with a force and violence." (quote in the *Oregonian*, Dec. 6, 1950)

Printing press destroyed in Astoria Fire, December 8, 1922, was rebuilt by Columbia Iron & Welding Works.

CHAPTER II

Young editors inspire
two budding western towns

"The East Oregonian is and always has been the friend of clean,
progressive government and the foe of graft."
E. B. Aldrich, Sept. 17, 1925

G reat expectations marked Pendleton as the nineteenth century waned and the twentieth loomed. C. S. Jackson and his chosen successor, Edwin B. Aldrich, chronicled the growth of Pendleton while encouraging it. In their editorial pages, they marveled at the expansion and mechanization of wheat farming and sheep husbandry. They pushed the development of new industries, especially those enterprises tied to agriculture. They advocated improvements to transportation on the Columbia River: specifically constructing canals and expanding the river's shallow-draft steamboat navigation channel in the river. The bet was that better river transportation would effectively compete with rail and bring freight rates down.

While encouraging economic growth, the *EO* also took up civic engagement. In 1910 the paper helped launch and promote the iconic Pendleton Round-Up. Over time, this volunteer community venture gained Pendleton world renown.

By the 1920s, the *EO*'s owners looked for opportunities beyond Pendleton. They had the financial resources to buy two other daily newspapers – in Astoria, Oregon and Twin Falls, Idaho. Under the strong leadership of Aldrich at the *EO* and Merle Chessman at the *Astoria Budget*, those papers thrived financially; the venture with the Twin Falls *Times* did not turn out as well. The editor/owners also took a courageous stand against the Ku Klux Klan contagion that beset Oregon during the 1920s.

In 1900, Pendleton brimmed with optimism, but events were not kind to the city. Over the course of the first decade of the twentieth century, it experienced several setbacks. A major flood in 1906 did considerable damage to the downtown, while the national financial panic of 1907 caused an important local industry—the Pendleton Woolen Mills—to close. In addition, federal authorities charged and convicted several leading citizens of land fraud, while C. B. Wade, cashier of the First National Bank, went bankrupt after using bank deposits to fund his own failed investments. Pendleton's inability to sustain continued growth was reflected in a population gain of only 54 inhabitants between 1900 and 1910. This occurred while other cities in Oregon showed greater growth during the decade:

Population of Oregon Cities

	1900	1910	Percent increase
Eugene	3,236	9,009	178.4
Klamath Falls	447	2,758	517.0
Medford	1,791	8,840	393.6
Portland	90,426	207,214	129.2
Salem	4,258	14,094	231.0
La Grande	2,991	4,843	61.9
Pendleton	4,406	4,460	1.2

Pendleton did benefit from strong agricultural output in Umatilla County between 1900 and 1910. As the following table indicates, land under production continued to increase, resulting in more wheat acreage planted. Livestock showed contradictory trends; while the number of sheep and the amount of wool increased, the quantity of cattle continued their long-term reduction. This situation can be accounted for by the changes in land utilization during the early twentieth century. As more ranchers devoted land to raising wheat, there was less open range available to graze cattle.

On the other hand, sheepmen had access to the public range available in the national forest land, so they had more flexibility than cattleman to maintain or increase their operations as the market determined.

Umatilla County Agriculture

	Wheat (bus)	Cattle	Sheep	Wool (lbs)	Improved Land (acres)
1900	3,212,120	19,571	222,907	1,461,599	382,763
1910	3,965,343	17,059	242,280	NA	544,513

Despite slow population growth, Pendleton managed to make some advances in the first decade of the twentieth century. It improved infrastructure and sought to heighten the quality of life for its citizens. St. Anthony Hospital installed the city's first elevator in 1902, while the school district built three new brick grade schools in 1904. The city also paved Main and Court streets. That made Pendleton the first Oregon city outside of Portland to pave any thoroughfares. The city council voted to update the city's water system and issued $50,000 in bonds for an improved sewer system in 1907. In 1912, the state built a branch of its mental hospital in Pendleton on a 324-acre tract of land just west of the city. As a result of the devastating flood of 1906, during which the Umatilla River broke through the embankment protecting the heart of Pendleton, the city spent $52,000 to extend and raise the levee.

Along with the community it reported on, the *EO* experienced great changes during the early years of the twentieth century. When Sam Jackson left Pendleton in 1902 to run the Portland *Journal*, he did not sever all ties with the *EO*. Over the preceding twenty years, he had built it into a strong, small-town newspaper. He was not about to let all that success go to waste. He kept a one-third interest in the paper and did not part with it for many years. Jackson left the *EO* in capable hands. He named Bert Huffman as editor; Fred Lampkin, business manager; Charles Sampson, advertising manager; and Fred Lockley, circulation manager. To ensure that these experienced newsmen—all of whom had worked on the *EO* for various periods of time—would give the paper their best effort, Jackson sold each of them an interest in it on credit. He allowed them to pay for their stock out of future dividends, if the company was profitable. To ensure the newspaper working capital, Jackson also loaned the East Oregonian Publishing Company (EOPC) $21,000 in 1909, taking a bond payable in ten years at 7.5 percent interest.

Edwin Aldrich, a young graduate of Oregon Agricultural College – one of 39 graduates in the class of 1900 – joined the *EO* staff as a reporter in 1904. Aldrich came to this profession with some genetic predisposition. In his *History of Oregon Newspapers* (1939), George Turnbull described James Harrison Aldrich, Edwin's father, as an "experienced newspaper man from Iowa." (p. 386) In Newport, Oregon, Turnbull reported that J. H. Aldrich in 1886 "launched the Newport *News*." (ibid.) It lasted three years.

Aldrich proved a good hire. When Huffman resigned as editor in 1908 to take up ranching in Canada, Jackson put Aldrich, aged 29, in that position. There were ownership changes as well. Lee Drake had rejoined the *EO* in 1904 after briefly working for other Pendleton newspapers. In the fall of 1908, Aldrich and Drake bought the stock held by Bert Huffman. The key players were now Aldrich as editor, Lampkin as business manager, and Drake in charge of advertising and mechanical operations. Jackson still held his one-third interest. The new editor assured the public that he would continue the editorial policies of the past.

1903 Heppner Flood

PENDLETON, UMATILLA COUNTY, OREGON, MONDAY, JUNE 15, 1903.

HUNDREDS OF PEOPLE DEAD AT HEPPNER

When a cloudburst swept away the town of Heppner, Oregon, on June 14, 1903 — killing about 250 inhabitants — the *EO* was quick to get the news out about this great natural disaster. On the following morning, after word reached the outside world of the scope of the calamity, a special train from Pendleton ran to Echo with relief supplies, which then were carried by wagon to Heppner. On that train rode Fred Lockley, reporter for the *EO* and the first newsman on the scene. His detailed coverage of the devastation and human suffering, carried on the front page of the paper, helped mobilize assistance from throughout Oregon and Washington for the relief of the distressed citizens of Heppner.

Oregon Agricultural College, Class of 1900. E. B. Aldrich is on far left.
OREGON STATE UNIVERSITY ARCHIVES

Aldrich wrote:

The first aim of the paper is to publish the news, as thoroughly as the conditions permit; to do so fearlessly, yet with fairness, and to comment editorially upon affairs in the same spirit. The highest creed of the *East Oregonian* is the good of the town, the county, the state and the country. With all its energy the paper will continue to work for the advancement of Pendleton and for the development of the surrounding country. It has the greatest confidence in both. As in the past the banner of the *East Oregonian* will be seen in the lead of every worthy movement for the bettering of conditions, whether the move be of a moral, political, industrial or other nature. Politically the paper will continue to be independent. This does not mean that it will be devoid of political faith. The paper has never been. But it will place citizenship above partisanship as every real newspaper does and as all good citizens should. (*EO*, Oct. 6, 1908)

In the early years of Aldrich's editorial tenure, Jackson periodically sent Aldrich advice on how to improve the newspaper. Typical of his counsel, Jackson wrote: "Never allow a paper to be personal or malicious; keep it in the front rank of enterprise and initiative and print the news, and you can't fail to succeed. The people admire a liberal, optimistic and hustling newspaper; they can't bear one that is malicious and personal, unless the personal observations are more or less friendly and favorable." (Jackson to Aldrich, Mar. 1, 1909, EOPC Archives) He also mixed his suggestions with praise: "I must say that you are making a mighty good newspaper out of the *East Oregonian*. I think it is a better newspaper now than it ever has been. You are surely 'making good' and you deserve credit for it, because it takes the hard work. Your conduct of the editorial end also, gives me quite a lot of satisfaction. It has got the right spirit to it." (ibid.)

In 1913, Aldrich pressed Jackson to sell his interest. Reluctantly, Jackson agreed to sell his stock to Aldrich for $13,000 in cash. After borrowing the money, Aldrich closed the deal with Jackson. In agreeing to sell out to Aldrich, Lampkin, and Drake, Jackson could not part without offering some words of advice to Aldrich. He wrote, "If a man is running a paper temporarily he is somewhat justified in getting out of it all the traffic will bear, but if he is in the business permanently and for the good he can do—making profit-getting a secondary matter—he should keep it as clean as a wolf's tooth and just as aggressive. It is the 'character' and 'conviction' that is behind the *East Oregonian* today, and why it is a success. If you lose this or any part of it the paper will shrink in influence and value." Jackson went on to observe that:

> I give you the credit of being a newspaperman of the right sort and I have no hesitation in saying you will continue this success—but I expect you to stay with it and not sell out at even a higher price than you pay me—as you will be able to do in a few years. And further, do not let Drake and Fred determine altogether its business policies and rates, for a newspaper must never overcharge for the service it ought to sell and never charge for the service it should not sell, any more than a true woman should sell her affection for money. Materialists cannot be good [at] newspaper making. (Jackson to Aldrich, Sept. 4, 1913, EOPC Archives)

Aldrich, Lampkin, and Drake now each held a one-third ownership in the paper; and this arrangement would continue until Lampkin's death in 1934. Out of sentiment, Jackson did keep two shares of stock, and he remained president of the corporation.

The minutes of the EOPC for 1913 also revealed a legally binding agreement that in slight variations would be included in the records of every publishing corporation that *EO* partners and their heirs would own over time. The stockholders contractually agreed that if one of them or their heirs wanted to sell their stock, they had to give the first right of purchase or refusal to the other stockholders. This ensured that the corporation would always remain closely held and protect the interests of the existing stockholders.

The annual EOPC stockholders and directors meeting in the fall of 1919 marked the closing of one era and the beginning of another one. The partners, after borrowing $25,000, paid off the corporation's debt of $9,000, using the remainder to help fund the purchase of the *Astoria Budget*. At this time, Jackson finally resigned as president of the EOPC, but sentiment caused him to retain his two shares of stock.

When Jackson chose E. B. Aldrich to replace the departed Huffman as editor, he assured the continuity of values that were so important to him. Time would demonstrate that Jackson's faith in Aldrich was not misplaced. From the moment he became the editor of the *EO*, Aldrich was an activist, unafraid to take up a public issue or controversy or promote a cause. But he did not wade into a matter without carefully considering the potential consequences. As long as he thought the matter at hand would bring community betterment, he could be counted on to back the effort wholeheartedly. For example, shortly after becoming editor in 1908, Aldrich urged that the Pendleton Woolen Mill should be reopened. The mill had closed during the national financial panic in 1907, leaving a big hole in the Pendleton economy.

> **From the moment he became editor of the EO, Aldrich was an activist, unafraid to take up a public issue or controversy or promote a cause.**

Aldrich wrote an editorial on October 10, 1908, pointing out that Pendleton was losing $75,000 a year through the mill's closure and that outside investors wanted to buy its equipment and move it to the Willamette Valley. To Aldrich, this would be a permanent loss to the city that stood at the heart of a great sheep country: "When a good thing like a woolen mill is to be taken from a town, it is the duty of the newspaper to ring the fire bell, figuratively speaking, so that the people of the city will know the danger that threatens them. The *East Oregonian* rang the bell and now hopes that the work of the rescuers will be effective." Aldrich continued his editorial by stating:

> The *EO* knows no more about the woolen mill than anyone else. But it knows that the location of the mill in this city is a splendid thing for the town and county. It believes that the mill is a money making proposition. This opinion is formed from competent evidence. . . . Furthermore, the *EO* firmly believes that the mill can be saved if the business men of this city want to save it bad enough. . . . Now is the time for the people of Pendleton to get 'upon their toes' and root for the woolen mill.

Aldrich kept up the drum beat for saving the mill and, on October 12, editorialized, "the *EO* believes the future of Pendleton depends much upon the proper handling of the woolen mill problem. . . . If this city is to advance it must have industries and payrolls. . . . If the mill cannot be retained it is doubtful if any other industry can ever be secured." On the following day, pushing his point about civic duty, Aldrich bluntly stated: "The man who allows any personal consideration, whether great or small, to block or hamper the movement for a woolen mill is a traitor to Pendleton." (*EO*, Oct. 13, 1908)

Within a year the Bishops had laid the foundations of an internationally famous brand of woolen products

By October 15, Pendleton's business and civic leaders had made enough progress on the drive to reopen the mill that Aldrich could write, "It is not yet time to rejoice, but the progress of the movement is very satisfactory to those who want to see the mills retained and Pendleton built into the better, bigger town it is entitled to be." Still, much work remained to secure the funds to buy the equipment, construct a new mill building, and find a competent operator. To reinforce the argument supporting a woolen mill, a news column in the October 17 issue of the *EO* reported that Pendleton was the largest wool shipping point west of the Mississippi River. As the mill fight dragged on into December, Aldrich reminded his readers how much was at stake for Pendleton: "If Pendleton wishes to be something more than a good country town it must have payrolls. . . . Pendleton is now on the eve of a new period. . . . The advance of the city is going to depend largely upon the efforts put forth by those who are here. The movement to retain the woolen mill marks the opening of this campaign, which is one for the industrial and commercial advancement of the town and county." (*EO*, Dec. 3, 1908)

Finally, in December 1908, the Bishop family, operators of the Thomas Kay Woolen Mill in Salem, Oregon, indicated an interest in taking over the Pendleton woolen plant if they received a subsidy. As the final negotiations got underway, the *EO* crowed, "At last something has come from it all. After many weeks of agitation and of earnest work on the part of business men it now seems certain that Pendleton will keep its woolen mill. . . . This paper has done some work on behalf of the mill—it has striven with all its power to keep the mill from leaving town. After the efforts that have been put forth the noise of the machinery in the new mill will make fine music." (Dec. 18, 1908) Indeed, Pendleton businessmen and bankers led by T. C. Taylor and G. M. Rice rose to the occasion and in a matter of weeks had pledged $30,000 to the effort, while the Bishops agreed to invest $15,000 of their own money.

When work began in late March 1909 on the new mill building, Aldrich congratulated the citizens of Pendleton on their great success: "Much, if indeed, not the greater part of the credit for the rejuvenation of the woolen mill belongs to the people of Pendleton themselves. It was largely a community affair and the success of the move shows that people of a city, when they get together under good leadership, can accomplish much towards forwarding the development of their city." (*EO*, Mar. 24, 1909) But, in the same editorial Aldrich also could not help reminding his readers of the *EO*'s role in the rebirth of the woolen mill:

> The announcement that the new mill is now to be built marks the climax of one of the best movements ever undertaken for the advancement of Pendleton. In the announcement the *East Oregonian* takes especial pride because this paper strove through thick and thin to make the move succeed. When this paper learned last fall that the old mill was in danger of being taken away it sounded the alarm and implored local people to prevent such from being done. Now that this has been accomplished and the new mill is all but here the *East Oregonian* congratulates the business men and property owners of Pendleton upon their good work. For the men who are to conduct the mill it wishes the greatest success.

Within a year, the Bishops had laid the foundations of an internationally famous brand of woolen products, including robes, blankets, shawls, and clothing.

The next big cause promoted by the *EO* under Aldrich's editorship was the Pendleton Round-Up. In the summer of 1910, a group of young business and professional men in Pendleton decided that the community ought to celebrate its western heritage and do so in a fashion that would generate great publicity. As attorney Roy Raley announced in the *EO* on July 29, "If the present plans can be successfully carried out it will do more to keep Pendleton on the map, to bring people here and to send them away satisfied than any other form of entertainment which we could give. This is not going to be any ordinary 'Wild West' show. It will be the best exhibition ever given in Pendleton or any other place also in the west for that matter. It will be worth coming many miles to see."

The show the organizers had in mind would showcase horsemanship, cowboy skills, and Native American pageantry and life ways. Participants would be actual working cowboys and Native Americans from reservations throughout the Pacific Northwest. It would have an authenticity that the typical Wild West shows of the era could not muster. As Raley would describe it during the 1911 Round-Up, the Pendleton show "gathered together all the features which comprise the West of song and story." He went on to stress that it did so in a way the spectator had "an opportunity to see the cowboys and cowgirls as they are and not as they are imitated, the Indians of the reservation and not of the circus; the untamed horse of the prairie, and best of all things which the open life of the range produces and each one at its best." (*EO*, Sept. 14, 1911)

Of course, the promoters were appealing to a popular nostalgia for the fast-disappearing American West that had already found an outlet in the frontier exhibition at Cheyenne, Wyoming, and Buffalo Bill's traveling extravaganza depicting a romanticized version of the settling of the West. Ironically, the Round-Up organizers were portraying a way of life no longer typical of Umatilla County in 1910. Bronco-busting tournaments and Native American war dances described a time in the 1870s and 1880s when cattle and cowboys dominated the rangeland of Umatilla County and the Bannock War of 1878 caused turmoil on the Umatilla Indian Reservation. Such scenes and events gradually were replaced by wheat farming and sheep raising in northeastern Oregon. On the eve of the 1911 Round-Up, Aldrich admitted as much in an editorial when he wrote, "The show is not intended to depict the life in this country at this time, for the Round-Up is not typical of Pendleton and of eastern Oregon these days." (*EO*, Sept. 14, 1911)

Ironically the Round-Up organizers were portraying a way of life no longer typical of Umatilla County in 1910

Under Raley's leadership during the summer of 1910, the Round-Up organizers, consisting of almost 250 men, moved with great speed to pull all the elements of a successful show together. Starting in late June, they incorporated the undertaking, raised funds, built a grandstand and arena, publicized the show throughout the Pacific Northwest, gathered livestock, got the cooperation of the Native American community, put together a large parade, and produced a wildly popular event in record time. Lee Drake of the *EO* handled the publicity, getting notice of the show in virtually every paper in the Pacific Northwest. He claimed credit for giving the Round-Up its name and coining the slogan, "Let 'er Buck." (Lockley, History of the Columbia River Valley, 786; *EO*, Jan. 20. 1951) Aldrich backed the idea of a frontier exhibition from the beginning, predicting in a July 30 editorial that "people like to attend broncho riding tournaments and similar events. They will come from far and near to see the

Sam and Maria Jackson's legacy

Maria Jackson
COURTESY JACKSON FOUNDATION

After leaving the *East Oregonian* in 1902 to take over the *Oregon Journal* in Portland, Jackson poured his considerable energies into building the *Journal* into a journalistic powerhouse to compete with the *Oregonian*. He was so successful that nine years later an article in the *Saturday Evening Post* declared, "Jackson is the present big man of Oregon journalism" and noted that under his leadership, the *EO* "became known as the best paper of its kind in any town the size of Pendleton on the whole map of the United States." (Nov. 11, 1911)

In addition to his successful newspaper career, Jackson engaged in singular philanthropy. He gave the city of Portland an 88-acre tract, later known as Sam Jackson Park, and a portion of land that became the site of the future Oregon Health & Science University. His charity also found its way back to Pendleton. He and his wife gave Pendleton's Episcopal Church of the Redeemer a stained-glass window, a carillon, and a chapel. In addition, the Jackson family presented the Pendleton Round-Up with a sterling silver trophy, known as the Sam Jackson Trophy, to be awarded for the all-around cowboy championship. Jackson died in 1924 after a lengthy illness. When Maria subsequently visited the annual rodeo, she was recognized in the arena as "the little mother of the Round-Up."

In her will, Maria created the Jackson Foundation. With some $15 million in assets, the foundation gives in excess of $500,000 annually.

big frontier celebration this fall and in doing so they will . . . be of benefit to the city in general."

The opening day crowd of 7,000 spectators greatly exceeded expectations and the *EO* declared it a "whirlwind success." (Sept. 27, 1910) At the close of the three-day extravaganza, the *EO* proudly asserted that "if Pendleton was ever off the map which is doubtful, she has been put back on with a vengeance and in letters so big that the whole country cannot help but see. The words 'Pendleton' and 'Round-Up' are on the lips of thousands and will continue to be for the months and years to come." (Oct. 1, 1910) The following year, the *EO* quoted Roy Raley on the element that would continue making the Round-Up so vital to the city's identity over time:

> The Round-Up is unique. Owned and controlled by the entire business population of the city. It is practically a municipal institution. It is run without profit, for the glory of Pendleton and the old West. There is scarcely a man, woman or child in the City of Pendleton who has not freely done his part in bringing the Round-Up to a wonderful success. . . . The Round-Up has made Pendleton the capital of the great horseback country of the West. (Sept. 14, 1911)

In the early decades of the twentieth century, the *EO* under Aldrich also actively supported the agricultural interests of Umatilla County. In particular, he was a big booster for irrigation projects located in the west end of the county. These were expected to bring increased population and enhance the economy of Umatilla County. In fact, while Pendleton's population had remained static between 1900 and 1910, it jumped over the next decade from 4,460 to 7,387, an increase of 66 percent. During those years, the population of Umatilla County grew from 20,309 to 25,946, an increase of 27.8 percent. This growth reflected, in part, the continued expansion of agriculture, especially irrigated farming. Between 1900 and 1910, the irrigated acreage in Umatilla County expanded from 5,168 to 31,022 acres, an increase of 500.3 percent. By 1920, irrigated land had shot to 56,000 acres, an increase of 80 percent over 1910. Another overall measure of the agriculture boom was seen in the expansion of county farm land, which jumped from 703,852 acres in 1900 to 1,075,400 acres in 1920, an enlargement of 53 percent.

Typical of Aldrich's numerous editorials on the subject of irrigated agriculture was one that appeared in August 9, 1910: "Time and time again the *East Oregonian* has called attention to the negligence displayed by the people of this city and vicinity in not taking up irrigation enterprises. Thirsty land is all about us and is producing but a biennial crop and sometimes a light crop because of drought while at the same time 500,000-acre feet of water flows annually down the Umatilla river and goes to the sea." He went on to underline the paper's advocacy of irrigation: "From appearances at this time the chidings of the *East Oregonian* have not been in vain and if it is a fact that the utterances of this paper have helped wake people up to the importance of irrigation in this vicinity then the *East Oregonian* will be glad." He closed by reminding his readers why Pendleton should care about the success of irrigation projects in Umatilla County:

> That Pendleton people should do everything in their power to encourage irrigation in this vicinity goes without question. Nothing could be of greater direct benefit to Pendleton than to have the lands in this vicinity watered. This town cannot hope to go forward except as its tributary territory is developed and settled. What Pendleton needs is a closer developed country immediately adjoining the city, improved transportation connections with its outlying territory and more industries within this city. Any work toward bringing about any of those things is work for Pendleton. Just now we seem to have more to hope from nearby irrigation than from any other one source.

The *EO* also promoted other water resources development such as improved navigation on the Columbia River. Under Jackson, the paper had backed the federal projects to build a canal and locks at the Cascades of the Columbia and establish and maintain a navigation channel for shallow-draft steamboats plying the Columbia and Snake rivers as far as Lewiston, Idaho. Before the transcontinental railroad arrived in the 1880s, steamboats were essential in transporting eastern Oregon and Washington grain to market and hauling passengers. Even after the railroads came, interior agricultural interest continued to argue that river transportation offered valuable competition to the railroads, helping to keep down freight rates. Aldrich carried on Jackson's call for federal completion of an "open river," championing the construction of The Dalles-Celilo Canal and Locks. At the completion of the The Dalles-Celilo project in 1915, Aldrich proudly pointed out that "the *East Oregonian* was credited with being the first Oregon newspaper to advocate the building of the Celilo canal. As is well known Mr. Jackson was owner and publisher of the paper in those days. He is no longer the owner but the spirit in which he served Pendleton and eastern Oregon is still the spirit of the paper and its pride." (*EO*, May 11, 1915)

During the first decade of Aldrich's editorship, Pendleton underwent a number of great physical changes. Some of the more prominent public structures constructed during those years included the city hall (1908), a new railroad station (1909), a high school (1913), state mental hospital (1913), city natatorium (1915), public library (1916), and post office/federal building (1916). During those years, the city also paved all of its major streets and built a gravity-flow water system (1911-13). Aldrich wrote editorials and served on committees backing these additions to Pendleton's betterment and when necessary personally lobbied prominent citizens to get behind these public projects. Many involved public controversies, but Aldrich never backed away from a good fight.

To handle the local, regional, and national news and meet the competition from Pendleton's other daily newspaper, the *EO* added staff and modernized equipment. In addition to an overall editor, the paper had a city editor, two reporters, a telegraph editor, and a social editor. The paper also upgraded its mechanical operations by installing a press in 1911 that could turn out 3,200 eight-page newspapers an hour. In 1917, it bought a new Duplex press that could regularly print 10 to 14 pages. Aldrich and his staff made such an impressive showing with this new equipment in printing the Round-Up special editions that the western representative of the United Press Association wrote, "From the presswork and other improvements I judge that your new Duplex must be working fine. I don't believe there's another city in the country anywhere near the size of Pendleton where a 28 page paper has been printed even for two days in succession." (T. Gerber to Aldrich, Sept. 27, 1917, EOPC Archives) By 1919, the *EO* had a staff of 25 full-time employees, 28 regional correspondents and part-timers, and a daily circulation of about 3,200. It experimented with such popular features as comics in the Saturday edition, regular automotive news, and greater sports coverage. It was the only newspaper of its size to receive news from the three major wire services: Associated Press, United Press and International News Service.

Astoria had evolved into one of the most important cities on the coast between San Francisco and Seattle

The owners of the *EO*, after profitably perfecting their operations at Pendleton, decided to branch out. While they searched the Pacific Northwest for a newspaper property, the opportunity came in Astoria. Like most medium sized towns in Oregon during the early decades of the twentieth century, Astoria had two daily newspapers—the *Morning Astorian* and the *Evening Astoria Budget*. In 1919, the owners of the *Budget*, the Gratke brothers, wanted to sell their paper. Aldrich, Drake, Lampkin, and Merle Chessman—a young newsman at the *EO* and a 1909 graduate of the University of Oregon—formed a corporation and, using their own funds plus a loan of $25,000, bought the paper for $42,000. By the terms of the corporation, the four stockholders each received 105 shares valued at $100 apiece.

Chessman, only 33 years old at the time of the purchase, had been carefully trained by Aldrich as a reporter and news editor over the preceding ten years. Aldrich wanted Chessman to edit the paper, while Drake would be the operations manager. Each received an initial salary of fifty dollars a week. At first, Drake split his time between Astoria and Pendleton; but Chessman became unhappy with this arrangement, feeling the Astoria paper needed Drake's full attention as business manager. Drake soon spent more of his time in Astoria, and Chessman concentrated on editorial and news matters.

When the owners of the *EO* decided to purchase the *Astoria Budget*, they were placing a bet on the current and continued growth of Astoria. Situated at the mouth of the Columbia River, Astoria—by the first decade of the 20th century—had evolved into one of the most important coastal cities between San Francisco and Seattle. A multi-ethnic community of Scandinavians, Anglo-Americans, and Chinese, Astoria counted 14,027 inhabitants in the 1920 census. A thriving economy based on salmon fishing and canning and timber harvesting and processing generated substantial wealth for a few and steady work for many. By 1920, Astoria was the third largest city in Oregon. In short order, Chessman and Drake doubled the paper's circulation and grew its revenues.

Early success with the *Budget* led Aldrich, Drake, Lampkin, and Chessman to expand and modernize the paper's operations. In early 1922, they bought real estate on Exchange Street between 11th and 12th streets for $7,500 and erected a 50 by 95-foot, 1-story, poured-in-place concrete building with full basement, costing $15,000 to house the paper's operations. To improve production processes, Drake also purchased new equipment. The contractor completed the building in October 1922, and business looked positive for the foreseeable future. On December 8, 1922,

Downtown Astoria smolders in the wake of the Dec. 8, 1922 fire.
CLATSOP COUNTY HISTORICAL SOCIETY

however, disaster struck when a fire destroyed most of the town's commercial district, including 32 blocks and 240 businesses. The loss to Astoria came to approximately $15 million. Drake and Chessman worked frantically to save the new *Astoria Budget* building. As Chessman's daughter later recalled, he:

> rushed to the roof of the new *Budget* building on the morning of Dec. 8. Wooden structures on three sides of the plant were aflame. Sharing a hose with the Methodist church and the telephone exchange, he was able to keep the roof wet enough to resist flying sparks, but as the fire proceeded westward and endangered large gasoline storage tanks, his water supply was cut off. He had to abandon the building and watch as flames ignited the *Budget* roof, which collapsed and gutted the interior of the building. Only the concrete walls were left standing. (*Cumtex,* Fall 1986, 5)

Aldrich was at a dinner party in Pendleton when he received a telephone call from

Chessman and Drake, telling of the disastrous fire. Aldrich immediately left the party and travelled by the night train to Astoria. A few days later, he wrote home—in an article published in the *EO*—that the *Budget*'s business records and files had been saved and that the newspaper was being printed on another paper's press in a nearby town. He assured his readers that "the building will be rebuilt at once." (*EO*, Dec. 13, 1922)

Showing great pluck under Chessman's and Drake's leadership during the emergency, the *Budget* staff shifted to the Astoria YMCA building—one of the few that escaped destruction—and used a multigraph machine to get out the December 8 issue. The next day, a page-one editorial in the rival *Morning Astorian* called upon

Astoria's many Finnish language newspapers

Small western towns commonly had more than one newspaper in the 19th and early 20th centuries. One of those newspapers would endure and prevail while others came and went.

Astoria was unique among such towns, because it spawned no less than ten Finnish-language newspapers between 1891 and 1951, according to the archive of Finlandia University in Hancock, Michigan. In the context of all Finnish language papers published in American cities and towns, Astoria stands out for the number of such papers in ratio to its population.

One of the longest-lived among these Astoria publications was *Toveri*, 1907 to 1930. It circulated on the entire West Coast. Loosely translated, toveri means comrade, which is an allusion to the newspaper's socialist editorial sentiment. Among Finns in Clatsop County as well as back in Finland, there was a passionate divide between establishment forces such as landed people and the church versus socialists. Some of *Toveri's* editors faced deportation.

Why so many Finnish language newspapers? These papers were evidence of a highly literate culture. Joanna Chopp, archivist of Finlandia University said: "There have been so many different groups in Finnish culture — church, political and temperance — that had a means of communications. Combine that with the Finnish emphasis on education and literacy and that produces this national proliferation of newspapers."

In Astoria this multitude of papers addressed certain niches: women, socialist, temperance. And on one particular occasion, *Toveri's* existence was vital to the *Morning Astorian*. Following the Fire of 1922, in which the *Astorian's* press was destroyed, it was printed on *Toveri's* press.

the citizens of Astoria to rebuild:

> Let every citizen unite with the common purpose to advance, to grow again; let none lag; let none be dismayed. Every *Astorian* should echo the cry of those, who called upon to do the impossible and dare the utmost on an embattled front in a foreign land, made their slogan of two simple words: 'Lets Go.' (Dec. 9, 1922)

Both papers met the printing challenge of the moment. Until the *Budget* reconstructed its building and replaced printing equipment, subsequent issues came off the *Seaside Signal* presses, while the *Astorian* was printed on the press of *Toveri,* a Finnish-language newspaper based in Astoria.

Using insurance proceeds and loans, Drake rebuilt the building and purchased new equipment, moving back on January 22, 1923. All told, the *Budget* partners sustained a considerable loss from the fire: the building and equipment had a book value of $49,500, salvage came to $15,000 and insurance paid out $21,500, leaving a loss of almost $13,000. As Drake later wrote Aldrich, "the fire of December 8, 1922 raised hell with us." (Drake to Aldrich, Jun. 10, 1928, EOPC Archives) Still, business was good the rest of the decade; and the *Budget* was out of debt when the Great

Astoria became fertile ground for the KKK's nativist message because it had a large immigrant population

Depression hit in 1930. Drake would boast in a 1928 interview: "When we bought the *Astoria Budget* a good many people prophesied we were biting off more than we could chew. We have not only chewed it successfully, but digested it, because we doubled the circulation of the *Budget* within a year of purchasing it, and we increased the business from a little over thirty thousand dollars to nearly one hundred thousand dollars a year." (quote in Lockley, History of the Columbia River Valley, 786)

While the *Budget* prospered financially, the editorial side had a rocky ride in the early 1920s. Chessman confronted the Ku Klux Klan (KKK), active in Astoria and around Oregon. Claiming to be "pro-American," the KKK appealed to longstanding racial and religious biases in Oregon's past. These views promoted anti-Catholic, anti-Semitic, and nativist beliefs. Boasting a statewide membership of approximately

14,000 members, the KKK held their greatest strength in Multnomah, Jackson, and Clatsop counties. The Astoria Klavern supposedly had 900 dues-paying members. In her 2003 thesis for the Pacific University History Department, Annie McLain wrote: "The (Klan's) anti-Catholic rhetoric led to the resignation of the Catholic president of the Astoria Chamber of commerce, the firing of Finnish foremen from the Union Salmon Cannery as well as the removal of Catholics from the School Board."

Prodded by the KKK and other nativist groups, Oregon's voters enacted an initiative measure in 1922 (the Compulsory School measure) that required all children to attend public schools, while the legislature passed a law in 1923 that prohibited Japanese from owning and leasing land. The federal courts struck down the former measure but upheld the latter. The Klan also tried to prevent the election of Jewish office holders. Oregon politics became badly muddled as Republicans split over the support of the Klan candidates and Democrats generally tried to avoid taking a stand on KKK activities. It was widely thought that in 1922, Walter Pierce, the Democratic candidate, won election as governor with Klan support.

The Klan called for boycotts and bans on the *Budget* and demanded that Aldrich remove Chessman or sell the paper.

In this politically contentious atmosphere, editor Chessman took a forthright, courageous stand against the Klan. Astoria became fertile ground for the KKK's nativist message because it had a large immigrant population. While Oregon's population in 1920 counted 85 percent as native born, 60 percent of Astoria's inhabitants had a least one foreign-born parent. The KKK made inroads in towns like Astoria by making a show of supporting community causes and Protestant churches. Klan members watched for perceived threats to social order, such as bootleggers, violators of Sunday closing ordinances, and radical union activities. They tried to bully opponents and used boycotts and misinformation to accomplish their mission of social and political control. The November 1922 elections became the central focus of KKK efforts to dominate Oregon. The Astoria Klavern ran candidates for local and state offices.

Amidst this highly charged environment, Chessman made his position clear. While he could accept some of the candidates that had Klan support and the general patriotic values of the organization, he editorially denounced the Klan's political agenda and its blatant falsehoods. "Carry on Knights of the Ku Klux Klan," he wrote, "Carry on until you have made it impossible for citizens of foreign birth, of Jewish blood or of Catholic faith to serve their community or their country in any capacity, save as taxpayers." (*AB*, Jan. 30, 1922)

To an old friend he wrote: "I have very well-defined views on the KKK and am not publishing anything to further their program." Chessman went on to note that the KKK "claim to have 700 or 800 members but a good many, I think, joined for reasons of political or business expediency, or were coerced into joining or became members by following the line of least resistance." He concluded by stating, "I know that there is considerable resentment against them [the KKK] and that this resentment is not confined to the ranks of those who are the particular target of the organization." (Chessman to Steven Lowell, Mar. 6, 1922, CCHS Archives)

The KKK leadership in Astoria complained about Chessman's anti-Klan editorials. In a letter to a local Klan leader, Chessman clearly and succinctly explained his news and editorial philosophy:

> In the matter of handling news, the *Budget* has a fixed and permanent policy of fairness and impartiality, and a conscious effort is always made to adhere strictly to that policy. There has been no attempt to discriminate for or against the Ku Klux Klan or any other organization or body of citizens, nor will there ever be. News value alone is the determining factor in the publishing of news matter.
>
> Editorially, its [i.e., *Astoria Budget*] opinions are its own, to be agreed with or disapproved as its readers see fit, but as long as they are honestly held and honestly expressed, no person has a right to ask that they be surrendered, and no newspaper that has any conscience or courage or any regard for its character will do so. (Chessman to E.P. Hawkins, June 28, 1922, CCHS Archives)

In response to Chessman's editorials, the Klan sought to undermine Chessman by calling for boycotts and bans on the *Budget* and by demanding that Aldrich remove Chessman or sell the paper. A Klan spokesman in Astoria, after receiving the Chessman letter quoted above, wrote to Aldrich "demand[ing] that some person other than Mr. Chessman, whose attitude is more liberal towards said organizations [the

This Ku Klux Klan meeting took place in front of the stadium at Columbia Field,
below J.J. Astor School. The stadium was constructed in 1922.
CLATSOP COUNTY HISTORICAL SOCIETY

KKK and its supporters] than his, edit the *Evening Budget* in the immediate future"
or consider selling the paper to the Klan. He added that Chessman, "in the recent
past, so freely, caustically and sarcastically expressed his views in an adverse nature
. . . that he cannot now change his views . . . and maintain self-respect." (Hawkins to
Aldrich, Jun. 30, 1922, CCHS Archives)

In response, Aldrich made it clear that he supported the editorial independence
of Chessman. He wrote: "No true newspaper wants to make any promise of editorial
action in advance of an event because it is impossible to foresee what may develop
and to make a pledge of that sort would mean to sacrifice a paper's independence.
That would not be good journalism and it should not be expected of us. . . . We wish
to remain free to praise or criticize as conditions may demand and we would not
give up that right even for the president of the United States." (Aldrich to Hawkins,
Jul. 3, 1922, CCHS Archives) Eventually, the KKK backed down, called off its
boycott, and dropped its plans to start another newspaper in Astoria.

But for much of 1922, Chessman was at war with the Klan. Throughout the
summer and early fall leading up to the November election for state and local

offices, he kept up a steady drumbeat of editorials denouncing the Klan and its candidates for office. He carried on an especially biting war of words with Lem Dever, editor of the Klan's Portland-based paper the *Western American*. Chessman resented Dever's attempts to manipulate Astoria's civic affairs by promoting the election of Klan officeholders.

Chessman's attacks on Devers reached a climax in a front-page editorial on election eve, November 6, 1922. Chessman asserted that Dever "perhaps more than any one person, is responsible for the bitterness, the strife and factional turmoil which is so apparent that even a stranger is shocked by it." He went on to assert that Dever "had injected himself so perniciously into the life of this city and has become such a baneful and baleful influence that some notice must be taken of him." What particularly galled Chessman was that Dever "is the kind of man who seeks to say to you how you shall vote" even though he has not "a dollar invested here [and] who pays not a cent in taxes here." Chessman closed his lengthy editorial by urging Astorians to reject "false prophets" and "the leadership of agitators, of blatant demagogues, of hysterical alarmists and exhorters who appeal, not to the intelligence of men, but to all that is narrow and mean and selfish in them."

Alas, on election day, the voters failed to heed Chessman's advice and instead elected the Klan slate to local offices. In time, however, the Klan in Astoria and Oregon destroyed itself through financial irregularities, personal scandal, and in-fighting within the organization. In the aftermath of their battle in Astoria, Dever admitted that Chessman had been a tough opponent, grudgingly writing, "We have been trying to hate each other, and I guess we do, but I recognize you as a fighter worthy of respect, and I hope the feeling is reciprocated." (Dever to Chessman, Mar. 23, 1923, CCHS Archives)

In the *EO*'s circulation territory, the political wars between the Klan and its opponents seemed less intense, so Aldrich tried to play down the rancorous nature of the political scene in Oregon. In a May 18, 1922 editorial he wrote: "This newspaper has been through many political campaigns but in some respects the present primary campaign is the most unusual of them all. It is supposed to be a very heated campaign with much bitterness evinced on all sides. Perhaps this is true to some extent, yet there have been many hotly contested elections in the past and everybody lived through the ordeal alright." Trying to calm the religious tensions fanned by extremists on both sides of the political divide, Aldrich went on to state,

"The *East Oregonian* does not take the so-called religious issue quite as seriously as many do. We are not willing to believe that perfectly honorable and upright men become 'marauders' and a 'menace to society' by the mere process of joining a secret society that is pledged first of all to uphold the Constitution of the United States and the laws of the land. Nor are we willing to look as many do upon the members of a certain great church [*Catholic*] as being open to question through membership therein."

Finally, Aldrich tried to restore some moderate perspective to the heated political rhetoric of the campaign:

> We may be wrong with reference to those on both sides of the supposed controversy but we don't think so. In the last few days we have had occasion to deal with many visitors at the *East Oregonian* office. Among them have been devoted Protestants and devout Catholics . . . candidates of every known description, their backers and their opponents, [and] ardent Ku Klux Klansmen and men who think they are waging war upon the Klan. But they all look a good deal alike and seem to be a good sort of people. . . . The thought we wish to express is that it will be well for people on both sides to 'keep their shirts on' and have the consideration for the rights of others.

He concluded his appeal to reason by noting that "it does not pay to get too heated about certain matters because none of us know enough about the subject to be absolutely authentic . . . and while we are privileged to have our squabbles and our scraps there are bounds we should not overstep."

The Klan, however, remained active in Umatilla County for several years after 1922, for the *EO* reported in March 18, 1924:

> Under the light shed by a fiery cross in the arena at Round-Up park a class of more than 100 candidates were initiated in to the Pendleton branch of the Ku Klux Klan last night in the first public ceremonial ever held here. The grand stand was packed with people who attended to see the ceremony. Preceding the ceremony, klansmen to the number of approximately 275 in costume, paraded from the hall on Main street to the Round-Up grounds. . . . Fiery crosses on the both the north and south hills burned during the evening for several hours. Following the parade and ceremonial a big banquet was served in the klan hall which

was enjoyed by several hundred kansmen and their families.

The *EO*'s competition, the *Pendleton Tribune*, did not fare so well in its relations with the KKK. Henry Kuck, the editor of the morning *Tribune*, took a vocal stand against the KKK. In the early 1920s, after taking over the *Tribune*, Kuck began a crusade against local officials whom he accused of graft and collusion with bootleggers. One of the accused, the popular Police Chief Jinks Taylor, brought a $10,000 libel suit against Kuck. At trial, one of Kuck's employees stated that the real reason Kuck attacked Taylor and other officials was that he believed they belonged to the Klan and "wanted to drive them out of office." (*EO*, Jan. 23, 1923) Indeed, on the eve of the November 1922 election, Kuck called out the Klan candidates for the Pendleton City Council and warned voters that in "the interests of good government founded on the law and according to the mandates of constituted authority that their anti-klan opponents be elected." (*PT*, Oct. 16, 1922)

In January 1923, after a week-long trial, a jury sided with Taylor and awarded him a judgement of $1,050. From that point, it was all downhill for Kuck. By May 1923, the *Tribune* had suspended publication, blaming poor economic conditions in the community, which it said had led to a substantial loss of advertising. In his final *Tribune* editorial, however, Kuck alluded to the negative consequences of his recent editorial fight with the KKK:

> This paper attempted to fulfill its conceived sphere in the community life and did so without fear or favor. Results of this policy could not be foreseen and would have made no difference were they clearly to be foreseen. Considerable strife arose as a result of its news policies and in a measure this strife was echoed through every agency of group organization. Such a condition was perhaps not the best thing for Pendleton. (*PT*, May 30, 1923)

While Chessman battled the Klan, Aldrich carried out a more forward-looking editorial agenda—one promoting water resources development on the Columbia River. He sought dams on the river to produce hydroelectric power and provide locks that would allow improved navigation for commercial transport via tug powered barges. He had long championed Columbia River development, first for transportation and then for power production and irrigation. As shown above,

Aldrich was merely continuing an editorial stance long held by the *EO* under Sam Jackson.

Aldrich wrote his first editorial on Columbia River improvements on January 15, 1913, in response to a report by the Oregon State Engineer, calling for development of hydropower at Celilo Falls. The resulting cheap electricity would, according to Aldrich,

> Would mean everything to Oregon. It would reduce lighting rates. It would develop manufacturing, foster irrigation, cheapen transportation and better the state in a thousand ways. Such power development would provide electricity for rural districts as well as for cities and towns. It would do much work on the farm. It would mean people could not only light their houses by electricity but they could also cook by electricity and heat their homes through use of the magic current. It would revolutionize society in the northwest. This may seem a dream but it is one that may be made to come true. The power is there and now goes to waste.

He cautioned that development of Columbia River hydropower must be a public undertaking: "To bring such results, it is necessary of course that the work be done by the state or national government or by the co-operation of both. It will not do to leave the matter in the hands of the electric trust for when the trust does the work it insists on prices that will not merely meet interest and operating charges but will also provide big dividends as an overcapitalization."

Aldrich continued to press the case for development of the Columbia River water resources. During 1922 alone, he wrote over a dozen editorials promoting dams on the Columbia, especially at the Umatilla Rapids location. Typical of his editorials was this one in February 14, 1922:

> The true solution for the problem [i.e. river navigation] lies in canalization. That is one reason why the Umatilla rapids project seems so desirable. By damming the river for power purposes the swift water is eliminated and the river becomes virtually a mill pond for many miles above the dam. It is estimated that the Umatilla rapids dam would do away with all swift waters from Umatilla rapids to Pasco. A dam at Celilo would do the same for the stretch of water between Celilo and Umatilla and power development at Bonneville would eliminate the swift water just

below Cascade Locks. When the Columbia is harnessed and made to produce the hydro electric energy it is capable of producing the transportation problem will also be solved to such an extent that it may even be possible for ocean ships of certain draft to take wheat direct from the upper river.

On April 29 of that same year, Aldrich demonstrated just how important the Umatilla project stood in his view by writing a highly unusual front-page editorial blasting the position that the *Oregonian* took on the matter:

> In an editorial this morning the *Oregonian* seems to take a position in favor of strictly private development of hydro electric power. Does that mean the Portland morning paper is averse to federal cooperation in harnessing the water power of the Columbia? If so can the *Oregonian* reconcile such views with the plain necessities of the situation?

He pointed out that when the federal government reclaimed arid land, it was creating competition with established farmland. He went on to argue his case:

> As the *East Oregonian* sees the subject the chief hope of power development on the Columbia rests upon securing federal aid. Yet government aid in such work would not work unjustly against private electrical concerns. The power developed would in all probability be distributed by private corporations, not by the government direct. The government does not farm the land it reclaims, the farmer does that. If it is good business for the United States to reclaim arid land for the framer's use, why is it not good business for the government for the government to harness water power, the power to be sold through corporations under regulation?

In a tone of mild exasperation, Aldrich concluded by stating, "Under private development we have waited 100 years and not a bit of power is being developed on the Columbia river. We are letting one of our greatest natural resources run to waste. Are we to continue this situation indefinitely or shall we get together behind a fair and logical plan to utilize our water power for the good of all concerned, including the electric companies."

Aldrich also had a keen understanding of world affairs, which he demonstrated

Before their rounds, newsboys gather in front of the Astoria *Budget's* offices during the post-fire 1920s.

in a series of astute editorials concerning the buildup to war in Europe during 1914. While the front page of the *EO* reported on the ominous diplomatic and military moves as Europe edged ever closer to war, Aldrich wrote editorials providing context to those events. He sought to untangle the historic ethnic and cultural issues between the Serbs and the Austro-Hungarian Empire. As Aldrich explained, the assassination of Archduke Franz Ferdinand represented a "savage response to the menace of arms and statecraft long exerted by Vienna against Serbs." (*EO*, Jul. 4, 1914) While Aldrich opposed United States intervention, once war broke out he made sure that the *EO* provided clear and accurate information about the progress of European news. The paper contained maps of key battles and regions almost on a daily basis.

When the United States finally entered World War I in April 6, 1917, the tone of the news coverage and editorial posture became one of patriotism and calls for wartime sacrifice. Daily news reports continued to provide progress on the war, especially concerning the American involvement and its effects on the home front. Although he was 39 years old and had two children, Aldrich tried to get a direct officer's commission in the army. Failing in that effort, he and others on the *EO* staff did their part, with Aldrich, Drake, and Chessman participating in close order drill in the streets as part of the local home defense unit. Chessman would eventually take a leave of absence in 1917 to supervise the county war bond drives.

In support of the war effort, Aldrich actively pushed Liberty Loan bond drives, writing bluntly, "If you have a chance to take some of the liberty bonds and fail to do so you are a slacker. You are just as coldfooted as the man who shuns the smoke of battle when it is his time to fight." (*EO*, Oct. 19, 1917) The Central Loyalty Committee of the Umatilla County Patriotic Service League even went so far as to have published the names of those failing to buy bonds. The *EO* noted editorially after one such listing that "the yellow dog is found here and there but thankfully there are not many of them in Umatilla County." (Oct. 7, 1918)

When the war finally ground to a halt in the fall of 1918, Aldrich presciently noted that the United States' role in world affairs had not come to an end. He wrote, "The world has been badly wounded and Uncle Sam is the rescuer and the Good Samaritan. We must care for the stricken everywhere and prove to the world even more thoroughly than we have that the American republic exists to serve and elevate humanity, not to conquer and destroy." (Nov. 12, 1918) In the following years, Aldrich actively backed President Wilson's call for the United States to join the

Pendleton to Astoria and back in one day

Overseeing three newspapers—the *EO*, *AB*, and Twin Falls *Times*—in locations several hundred miles apart during the 1920s and 1930s could have been a communications challenge for part-owner/editor E. B. Aldrich. In Pendleton, however, he was linked to Astoria and Twin Falls by a railroad network that solved that potential problem. Three mainline Union Pacific trains passed each day through Pendleton, east and west bound. Each train carried the mail, but one in particular was labelled a mail and express train; and it reached Pendleton from either direction in the early afternoon. Once a westbound UP train reached Portland, it connected with Astoria, via three trains a day, going each direction six days a week. The mail to Twin Falls, Idaho, left the mainline at Minadoka, Idaho, reaching its destination each day by a local, connecting train. Of course, long-distance telephone and the telegraph could be used in an emergency, but they were expensive. Cheap, speedy, and dependable United States mail delivered by trains served the business needs of the day.

League of Nations and condemned the Senate for refusing to approve the treaty. Soon, however, he turned his attention to more pressing local matters. These included editorials on matters such as the murder of the popular sheriff Til Taylor, the troubled enforcement of prohibition by local law enforcement, and pushing the federal government to provide price supports for agricultural produce. The owners of the EOPC also had new business concerns to focus on.

After purchasing and successfully operating the Astoria *Budget* for almost ten years, the owners of the *EO* decided to extend their newspaper empire to Idaho. After looking over the field of newspapers for sale, Aldrich, Lampkin, and Drake cast their eyes on the bankrupt daily *Times* of Twin Falls. Poorly run but in a rich agricultural region, they thought they had the right touch to make a success of the afternoon *Times*. Twin Falls already had another strong daily newspaper in operation, so buying the barely functioning *Times* was a gamble. After due diligence with the business community of Twin Falls, the *EO* owners bought the Idaho paper on September 1, 1928 out of bankruptcy for $25,000 and committed to paying the outstanding debt owed for equipment and newsprint, amounting to several thousand dollars. Their business plan called for borrowing from a Pendleton banker the money necessary for the purchase and creating a separate corporation to operate the Idaho paper.

> **"We simply underestimated the size of the job of converting a bankrupt paper into a profitable one."**
>
> *John Harvey*

The stockholders of the new company consisted of Aldrich, Lampkin, Drake, and John Harvey, who was to edit the paper. Drake would assume the business management of the *Times*. Harvey owned a weekly newspaper in Hermiston, which he sold to take on his new position with the *Times*. Their plan called for Drake to split his time between his duties with the *Budget* in Astoria and the *Times* in Twin Falls, spending half of each month in each location. Drake and Harvey enthusiastically and optimistically dove into the daunting task of turning the bankrupt paper around. Unfortunately, the job of making a success of the *Times* proved more of a challenge than any of the partners bargained for.

Throughout the fall of 1928, the paper, published in the afternoon, continued to

Sheriff Taylor killed in jailbreak

THE EAST OREGONIAN IS THE ONLY INLAND EMPIRE NEWSPAPER GIVING ITS READERS THE BENEFIT OF DAILY TELEGRAPHIC NEWS REPORTS FROM BOTH THE ASSOCIATED PRESS AND THE UNITED PRESS

DAILY EDITION

East Oregonian

DAILY SEMI-WEEKLY INDEPENDENT

DAILY EDITION

COUNTY OFFICIAL PAPER

CITY OFFICIAL PAPER

DAILY EAST OREGONIAN, PENDLETON, OREGON, MONDAY EVENING, JULY 26, 1920.

SHERIFF TIL TAYLOR SLAIN; FIVE PRISONERS STILL AT LARGE; LINDGREN IS TAKEN

BELOVED OFFICER DIES FROM SHOT FIRED BY HART

Discovering Escaping Prisoners in Sheriff's Office Yesterday Taylor Gave Battle Suffering Mortal Wound.

GUY WYRICK HELPED IN DESPERATE FIGHT

Prisoners in County Jail Overpowered Deputy Jake Marin When He took Them Lunch; Took Gun and Keys.

FIVE MEN WERE STILL AT LARGE THIS AFTERNOON

Two Major Posses at Work on Clues West of Town and in Vicinity of Cayuse; But No Prisoners Found.

JINKS TAYLOR NAMED SUCCESSOR IN OFFICE

Hart and Others Reported Seen on Cayuse Bridge by Friends, Think They Sought Money Cached Near Rieth.

MANY OUTSIDE OFFICERS ARRIVE TO HELP IN CHASE FOR ESCAPES

RESOLUTE LEADING RACE IS CALLED OFF BY TIME LIMIT

$6000 REWARD

FUNERAL WILL BE HELD AT 3 O'CLOCK TUESDAY; BODY TO LIE IN STATE

Weather

THE WEATHER FORECAST

Crime received headline attention – especially when it involved well-known, local leaders. For example, bold *EO* headlines announced the fatal shooting of popular Umatilla County sheriff, Til Taylor, during a jail break on July 25, 1920. Taylor had been sheriff for 18 years before his tragic death and a key leader in the early success of the Pendleton Round-Up. A massive manhunt quickly swept up the three escaped prisoners involved in Taylor's shooting death. The killers were subsequently tried, convicted, and hanged. A statue of Taylor by famed sculptor A. Phimister Proctor was dedicated in a Pendleton park during the 1929 Round-Up.

lose money. Aldrich and Lampkin had to drain money from their successful papers in Astoria and Pendleton and borrow additional funds to keep the Twin Falls enterprise afloat. The *Times* ran a deficit of about $1,000, on average, each month, and expenses, to the new owners' surprise, proved difficult to reduce. For example, distribution costs for the daily were high because so much of the circulation was rural or in distant towns. In addition, the competing morning daily put up stiff competition, and local and national advertisers were reluctant to make major advertising buys or commit to long-term contracts, since they remained skeptical of the *Times*' claimed circulation numbers and of the paper's ability to survive over time.

On top of the difficult business conditions, the *Times*' team suffered an unexpected blow on the editorial/news side of the business when Harvey suffered medical problems, requiring major surgery. His medical condition kept him away from his duties for extended periods during the winter of 1928-29. By January 1929, Drake was becoming increasingly discouraged with the situation at the *Times* and his constant travel. In addition he felt that Aldrich and Lampkin were micromanaging the *Times*' operations without fully understanding the unique conditions prevailing in Twin Falls. For their part, Aldrich and Lampkin had become increasingly nervous about the situation after it became necessary to borrow another $2,000 at the end of December to keep the newspaper afloat. They had already provided at least $3,500 previously during the fall. As Harvey succinctly noted in one of his reports, "We simply underestimated the size of the job of converting a bankrupt paper into a profitable one." (EOPC Archives, Dec. 25, 1928) It did not help that the agricultural economy of the *Times*' circulation area took a downturn, while at the same time a flu epidemic led to a total quarantine in Idaho Falls and a cessation of normal business in the community.

After much discussion among the partners, they came up with a revised business plan in mid-January 1929. They increased the capital of the *Times* Corporation to $50,000 and issued 500 shares of stock, mostly held by Aldrich, Lampkin, and Drake. They gave their notes to the EOPC for the money advanced for purchase of the stock and their stock, in turn, would be held by the EOPC as security for the money loaned. Harvey and Leland Miller, who joined the *Times* as the advertising and business manager, would each receive 75 shares to be paid for from dividends on the stock once the company became profitable. Harvey and Miller each received a salary of fifty dollars a week. The partners expected that further staff layoffs and other expense reductions would save at least another $500 a month. Aldrich, Lampkin, and Drake would continue to offer advice and counsel but draw no salaries from the *Times*. Their plan provided the *Times* with an onsite, two-man, employee-owner management, just as existed at Pendleton and Astoria for their other papers. As the plan went into effect, Harvey needed more surgery, keeping him away from the office for an extended period; and their best advertising salesman died in a car crash. In February, the partners had to borrow another $2,000 to meet expenses at the *Times*.

It became clear that the *Times* needed to gross at least $6,000 a month to break even and about $8,000 a month on a sustained basis to assure a profit. To accomplish that profit goal, Drake estimated that the paper would need a paid circulation of at least 4,500, in combination with increased advertising sales and further cost reductions. From his vantage point, Aldrich thought the *Times* spent too much on distribution; but Drake assured him that the paper's extensive rural circulation area required extra carrier expense that was worth serving because it offered a large population base for future circulation growth. Above all, Drake, writing from Astoria, pointedly told Aldrich and Lampkin, "think there is too much long distance advice being given the business end there (Twin Falls) by those not familiar with conditions there and that it is going to wreck us there absolutely if carried out." Drake went on, "You are getting out of your field, Ed, when you start to run the business end of a newspaper without being on the ground and knowing the details." (EOPC Archives, Feb. 18, 1929)

Aldrich remained undeterred by Drake's advice and throughout the spring and summer of 1929, sent regular, detailed instructions to Harvey and Miller on how to run the paper. As he put it, "Am writing freely to you fellows because you have quite a task and I feel you are entitled to all the ideas we can give based upon our experience." (EOPC Archives, Feb. 23, 1929) Aldrich's advice covered every aspect of putting out a newspaper. He told them how to improve the news and editorial aspects of the paper and how to enhance its overall physical appearance. This work, in turn, he argued would support the drive to increase circulation and sell more advertising. With an audited base of only 2,550 paid subscribers, it was difficult to win over new advertisers; and, as Aldrich noted, "the success or failure of the paper will depend on circulation getting." (EOPC Archives, Apr. 25, 1929) Aldrich also made suggestions for increased feature stories and sports coverage, and, as a big believer in the superiority of an afternoon paper, how best to promote the advantage of having a newspaper reach its audience in the evening when the subscriber has time to read. Since late press runs had been a constant problem with the *Times*, he emphasized the necessity of getting the paper out on time. Above all, Aldrich reminded Harvey, "the paper must have "It" [i. e. interesting content] to hold its readers and that the responsibility for holding reader interest and circulation rests with the editor and his staff." (EOPC Archives, Jul. 29, 1929)

Through the process of passing on advice, Aldrich revealed much of his own personal editorial philosophy. In advising Harvey about how to handle a story of a local scandal in Twin Falls, he wrote:

> I have always taken the position that a newspaper has respon-
> sibilities and going into the homes of its people should always
> uphold law enforcement and clean conditions. That is not only
> good morally but it is good business in the end and creates respect.
> We follow a stiff policy here [at the *EO*] . . . yet we always try to
> administer it as kindly as possible, having in mind, as our rules
> state, that we are all friends and neighbors and desire to help
> people, not hurt them. Likewise that we should be very careful
> wherever the good name of a man is involved. . . . Where good
> people are involved I have tried to protect them as much as
> possible, consistent with our rules, but we never hold out names
> where criminal offenses are charged. We try to show a stiff
> backbone but also a kind heart and usually we convince people we
> are glad to do anything for them that we would do for anyone else.
> . . . A vigorous editorial policy is a good thing but an editor must
> use discretion, particularly in dealing with local subjects and local
> people. All of that of course develops with experience." (EOPC
> Archives, Apr. 25, 1929)

To prove to the *Times* staff that the owners would stay the course in Twin Falls, they sent an additional $4,000 in July to clean up the paper's most pressing debts. In the year since Aldrich, Lampkin, and Drake had bought the *Times*, they had put about $12,000 into it. By late September, however, the partners felt that drastic measures were necessary to save the paper. They sent Drake back to Twin Falls to take over complete management of the *Times*. Harvey and Miller just were not able to get the operation to run profitably. As Drake reported to Aldrich and Lampkin after his return to Twin Falls, "The whole thing is too loosely managed here and needs a real head to hold it in place when we once get it there." (EOPC Archives, Oct. 4, 1929) The biggest immediate problem still stemmed from the inability to consistently get the paper out on time. Old equipment, short staff, and organizational difficulties meant that the shop could not deliver a timely paper and simultaneously meet the demands for potentially profitable job work.

Drake struggled through the fall and winter to get all aspects of the paper running well and earning a consistent profit, but it proved to be an uphill battle. Aldrich and Lampkin wanted him "to make strong progress and make it pretty quick and it will have to be in tangible form if we make the grade." Drake, for his part, grew tired of what he considered micro-management from his partners. In apparent exasperation, Drake reminded Aldrich and Lampkin;

> We all agreed to go into this proposition and we are now into it. There is more business to be had and money to be made here than in either Pendleton or Astoria. The trouble here in the past has been lack of organization and management. I have agreed to sacrifice my home and years of work in Astoria and take charge of this paper. I have put as much money into this as either of you and am doing your work here as well, at quite an extra expense to me personally. Yet I am not complaining. This paper is about on its feet now and I think I can put it over. . . . Don't blame you both for being a bit skeptical because of the past history here, but it is different now. This thing is being ironed out. You fellows would ok my actions and do the same thing if you were here.

Drake, ever the optimist, concluded his report by assuring them "this old fight is getting into my veins and I am out to win." He could not, however, resist a final dig: "Don't forget, you fellows money is tied up here and is at stake. Also remember that I am fighting for my own money here and if I win you win. If you can't help, At least be patient and give me a chance. You have got to trust me here and believe me I am on the job. I know of no alternative by which we can all three get our money back." (EOPC Archives, Nov. 23, 1929) Still, for all of Drake's efforts, the *Times* continued to struggle and need further cash infusions from Aldrich and Lampkin to pay its bills. By the spring of 1930, the partners had put another $4,000 into the effort to make the *Times* a profitable paper.

Harvey and Miller grew impatient to learn about their employment status, especially if the paper were sold. Aldrich responded somewhat reassuringly "about all I can say is that the situation seems to be the same it was a month or two ago when I wrote you in answer to a similar inquiry. . . . We have not tried to sell the *Times*. . . .

We are interested in operating it." Aldrich went on to lecture Harvey about making sure that "the news department is clicking effectively" so that it was not the cause of the paper coming out late. He reminded Harvey that "by proper work with his desk man an editor can get the paper out on time even when the mechanical situation is adverse. Even if the composing room situation is excellent a slight, almost unobservable failure of the desk man will make the paper late. A man can be a good desk man in many ways and still not have the knack of getting his stuff up and the paper to press on time." Aldrich then gave detailed instructions on how to get copy out in a timely fashion and emphasized how crucial the desk man's role was in not only meeting press time but also in getting and using late-breaking news: "The desk man's game however is not merely to go to press on time but to do so and yet use vital news. It is quite a game and he must be really interested in getting results both ways or he won't protect the paper. He concluded by advising Harvey "to handle the desk some and get familiar with it so you can instruct a man or take over the desk in an emergency if you need to do so. I get quite a kick out of handling the desk here at times. It gives one a chance to check on the wire news and also an insight on paper making you don't get from reportorial work." (EOPC Archives, Nov. 30, 1929)

> **"I have been awake nights more than once and at least twice was told on good authority men proposed to shoot me."**
>
> *E.B. Aldrich*

At the end of the year, Drake retained his stubborn optimism that he could make the *Times* a success. To insure that he could devote full time to that effort, he sold his interest in the *Astoria Budget* to Merle Chessman, its editor, who was eager to manage that paper by himself. For his part, Drake wanted his own operation in Twin Falls. As he put it, in apparent frustration with having to work with Chessman, "No more Astoria situations for me." As he noted, "We all grew up together under the C. S. Jackson principles of honesty, good government, law enforcement and common sense. . . . I may have my shortcoming but when it comes to a showdown I think I know something about the newspaper business." (EOPC Archives, Dec. 10, 1929)

Aldrich responded by cautioning Drake about wanting to have control of the editorial functions as well as overall management of a newspaper:

There is this about local editorial control Lee. If you had it you would find it more grief and worry to you than you know. The local angle is the ticklish part and I know from experience. I have been awake nights more than once and at least twice was told on good authority men proposed to shoot me. We have also had phone calls to the house, during heated fights trying to scare my folks about my safety. Those things are all in the game but they are none too pleasant at times.

He went on to warn:

If you had an editor who was subject to your orders on local subjects he would be in the clear if trouble arose and would pass the buck to you and you would be the fall guy. You would be vastly happier with a strong editor who would work neither above you nor under you but with you. He should be good enough to take responsibility and stand or fall by his own work. . . . Another point is that local issues require a lot of time, thought, investigation and talking to people. . . . If you should take on that load and handle it intelligently you would have scant time for business getting and management which makes quite a job itself if carried on right.

Finally, he summed up:

As a rule where one man is IT a small daily is not well balanced. If a business man he devotes first attention to that end but neglects the editorial end. If a news man the business end is neglected. The scheme we work here [EO] is the best and we have no trouble with it. It is chiefly a matter of horse sense and mutual courtesy. (EOPC Archives, Dec. 14, 1929)

In January 1930, Aldrich, Lampkin, and Drake made yet another change in the operations of the *Times*. They reorganized the *Times* corporation with themselves as sole stockholders and reduced Harvey and Miller to the role of salaried employees. Although Drake felt that Aldrich and Lampkin did not sufficiently appreciate his hard work and talents, he continued to soldier on at Twin Falls. The paid circulation had reached almost 4,500; and he further reduced staff and continued improving the business and management aspects of the paper, but a hard winter cut advertising and slowed collections. For all Drake's newspaper skills and the potential of the *Times'* territory to support the paper's ultimate success, it appeared that the partners lacked the financial resources to stay the course.

Suddenly, in mid-March, Aldrich received a telegram from a newspaper broker that a publisher in Iowa wanted to buy the *Times* in an all cash deal. At first, Drake was reluctant to sell, having invested so much effort into making the *Times* successful; but Aldrich and Lampkin were only too happy to get out from under the financially draining newspaper adventure in Twin Falls. By April, the partners had sold their stock in the *Times* corporation to the Iowa newspaperman for $25,000, with the new owner assuming all unpaid debts. The parties to the deal split the accounts receivable due as of March 31, 1930. While the partners got out of the *Times* for what they originally paid for it, they still lost about $15,000 in the gamble to make it a success. Given the darkening economic clouds rapidly building as the Depression took hold in the early 1930s, the partners were probably fortunate to sell when they did.

Given the darkening economic clouds, the partners were fortunate to sell the Idaho paper when they did.

During the first thirty years of the twentieth century under Aldrich's editorship, the *EO* continued to focus on community betterment. The paper steadfastly functioned of and for the people of Pendleton and Umatilla County. Whether through promoting industrial development by reviving the shuttered Pendleton Woolen Mills, encouraging agricultural expansion by championing irrigation and improvement projects on the Columbia River, or stimulating general economic prosperity by campaigning for better farm-to-market roads, Aldrich pushed a positive, growth-based agenda. Editorial and business success with the *EO* led the owners of the EOPC to expand their newspaper operations by purchasing and personally running the *Astoria Budget* and the Twin Falls *Times*. The former proved to be a success, with Chessman operating the Budget in much the same fashion as Aldrich and the other partners ran the *EO* in Pendleton, while the latter turned out to be a mistake. With the Great Depression appearing over the horizon, Aldrich and his fellow partners in the *EO* and *Astoria Budget* now would face new and challenging situations in the newspaper business.

CHAPTER III

Hard times hit Pendleton and Astoria

"Towns are built; they do not grow."
E. B. Aldrich

Editors in Pendleton and Astoria showed pluck and business acumen in handling the challenges they encountered during the 1920s. Success in Pendleton and Astoria had emboldened them to take on the newspaper opportunity in Twin Falls. Only good fortune prevented financial disaster in that gamble on expansion. Aldrich at the *EO* and Chessman at the *AB*, moreover, would need every bit of luck, business smarts, and journalistic skill that they could muster to survive the twin tempests of the Depression and World War II, while making sense of the continuous economic and political turmoil of the era for their readers.

At the beginning of the 1930s, before the full effects of the Depression had been felt, the owners had managed to escape the ill-fated adventure operating a newspaper in Twin Falls. At the same time, they shrewdly took advantage of the opportunity to buy the evening *Budget's* morning competition—the *Morning Astorian*. Chessman then integrated that paper into the *AB*. The two editors worked feverishly to keep their newspapers financially solvent during the depths of the Depression, while expressing the hope that President Roosevelt's policies would save the nation. Even though generally supportive of the New Deal, each editor worried about the consequences of a growing national debt.

After surviving the difficulties of the Depression, World War II presented its own unique problems in the form of wage and price controls and material shortages. Still, each newspaper managed to make improvements to plant and equipment during the two decades and ended the period stronger than ever. This strength would enable the *AB* and *EO* to weather changes in leadership as both Chessman and Aldrich passed from the scene in 1947 and 1950, respectively.

Like the nation, Oregon felt hard times during the 1930s. Banks failed, businesses went broke, and high unemployment added to the misery caused by the struggling agricultural and timber sectors of Oregon's economy. The Oregon economy had suffered in the 1920s from glutted agricultural markets and weak demand for lumber as the construction industry languished in California. When the Depression set in in earnest in 1931, lumber mills on the West Coast operated at only 38 percent of capacity. Soon 90 percent of the Oregon's timber companies were on the edge of bankruptcy and one-half of all state timber land became tax delinquent. The state's farm income plummeted from $136 million in 1929 to $49 million in 1933. Delinquencies on the county and local tax rolls reflected financial suffering and curtailed support for schools and various community services. Private relief efforts quickly became overwhelmed throughout Oregon. By the time of Franklin Roosevelt's inauguration as president in March 1933, 40,000 in Portland were on relief. In 1933, the number of production workers in Oregon was only 62.8 percent of those in 1929. Statewide between 1929 and 1933, wages declined 77 percent and total income dropped by 29 percent. Pendleton and Astoria did not escape the tough times.

The collapse in farm prices weighed especially heavily on the Pendleton community. Wheat fell from just over a $1.00 a bushel in June 1930 to 43½ cents in July 1931. By the end of 1932, $500,000 in Umatilla County property tax remained unpaid and more than $700,000 was outstanding from previous years. The city of Pendleton cut its employees' pay by 15 percent in August 1931, and the school district had to issue warrants instead of paychecks. Even Pendleton's population of 6,621 in 1930 reflected a decline of 10 per cent from 1920. The city's two banks merged in the fall of 1931 but could not stave off closure in 1932. The bank stayed closed until June 1933, when New Deal legislation allowed banks nationwide to reopen. In July, U. S. National Bank of Portland opened a branch in Pendleton; and later that year the First National Bank of Portland bought the assets of the defunct Pendleton bank and re-opened it as a branch. Astoria experienced similar difficulties from delinquent taxes, bank failures, high unemployment in the timber and salmon canning industries, and business bankruptcies.

The owners responded to the economic tough times by taking a number of cost-saving measures without resorting to overly drastic changes. During much of the 1920s the *EO* had a staff of about 25 full-time employees, 28 correspondents and part-timers, and a daily circulation of about 3,200. The paper had added comics to the Saturday edition and extensive coverage of sports—even on page one. It claimed to be the only newspaper of its size in the country to receive news from the Associated Press, United Press, and International News Service. The *AB* also showed great strength during the 1920s; and it had engaged in a spirited circulation war with its competitor, the *Morning Astorian*. By 1922, the *AB* had an audited circulation of 3,500 copies daily. It also boasted of carrying news from both the Associated Press and United Press services.

Eleanor Aldrich Forrester recalled seeing farmers pay for subscriptions with eggs during the lean years of the Depression.

Merchants in both towns either dropped or cut back advertising with the onset of the Depression, so the two papers responded by reducing their size from the usual eight to twelve pages to a meager six pages. For a while, the *AB* printed only five days a week. The owners of the Pendleton and Astoria papers steadily cut their own salaries and reduced workers' pay. At the *EO* stockholders and directors' meetings in 1933, both Aldrich and Drake decided to borrow against their life insurance policies to get operating cash. Aldrich even quietly accepted produce in payment for subscriptions. Aldrich's daughter Eleanor – who had dropped out of the University of Oregon for financial reasons – worked at the newspaper and remembered seeing farm families bring eggs to pay for a subscription. In line with the press generally, neither the *EO* nor *AB* reduced advertising rates during the 1930s.

The winter months between the election of President Franklin D. Roosevelt in November 1932 and his inauguration in March 1933 were perhaps the bleakest, especially as most of the nation's banks failed or were closed during so-called bank holidays. In December 1932, Chessman noted, "Business has certainly taken to the storm cellar here" and then went on to list the firms that had either closed or gone

The *Astorian-Budget* offered its own scrip, Budget Beaver Pelts, during the Depression.

bankrupt. Still, in comparing his results in November 1932 with those in November 1928—"when we had real competition"—he could show "that expenses [in 1932] were less and revenue more, so we have been getting by up to date." Not one to take his current situation for granted, Chessman planned—"with three lean months a certainty just ahead'—to cut wages and other expenses further. (Dec. 8, 1932, EOPC Archives)

Lampkin replied in January 1933, with a letter explaining all the actions taken at the *EO* to offset the loss of business, stating "we have eliminated every item of expense possible." In particular, he listed wage cuts, reduction in payments to suburban carriers and country correspondents, dropping professional memberships, cutting newsprint consumption to the minimum ("but never less than six pages [for the paper]"). (Jan. 14, 1933, EOPC Archives) To get around the lack of cash when the banks closed, Chessman adopted a novel approach. The *AB* issued its own scrip, known as the "Budget Beaver Pelts." As Chessman explained,

> It was just a temporary expedient but it worked out very well. We're getting some bills paid thereby which would be unpaid as yet. We issued 50 per cent of the payroll a week ago in scrip and 25 per cent today and also paid the carriers 50 per cent. In all we have issued about $650 in scrip and it is returning to us at a lively pace. Practically all of the business houses accepted it at face and numbers of them gave back cash change. We do not expect to continue it. (Mar. 18, 1933, EOPC Archives)

At least four other Depression-era Oregon newspapers resorted to issuing scrip redeemable only at firms that traded it for advertising space.

With such measures, the papers held on until the economy started to improve in the late 1930s. While the owners of the *EO* decided in December 1935 to set the salaries of Aldrich and Drake at $75 per week until economic conditions improved, they were able to start paying dividends by December of the following year. Although they did not raise their salaries until December 1943, as directors of the EOPC, they did receive a monthly fee of $100 starting in 1937. While often delayed, the *AB* managed to cover its directors' salaries each year during the 1930s. In the depths of the Depression, the *AB* had a debt of $60,000, which Chessman remarkably managed to pay off by 1936. In fact, in 1936, *AB* partners remodeled their building, bought a new job press and linotype machine, and managed to pay a dividend as well. The next year, they secured a lot adjacent to their building at a tax sale; and in 1938, they bought another lot. These purchases were to prepare for future expansion, as the business was outgrowing the existing building.

In all, the *Astorian-Budget* seems to have weathered the Depression years better than her sister paper in Pendleton.

In the midst of dealing with the financial struggles of the early 1930s, the owners of the *EO* faced a new challenge when Fred Lampkin, stockholder and business manager of the paper, was killed in a hunting accident. Dorothy Engle, Lampkin's sister, inherited his 166 shares and became a director. At that time, the other directors found it advisable to restate the option contract in the bylaws of the EOPC to include Engle. This agreement held that if one of the owners wanted to sell, transfer, or by other means dispose of their shares, they had to initially offer the other shareholders of record the right of first refusal. The agreement also stipulated that as long as Aldrich held at least 125 shares of EOPC stock "he shall remain and be retained as editor . . . and shall be president of said corporation, and shall control the editorial policies of, . . . [and] the general business policy and direction of the said newspaper." The agreement further stated that as long as Drake held at least 125 shares of company stock, he would "be retained as business manager, but his duties and actions shall be fixed by and subject to the approval of the president." (corporate minutes, EOPC Archives)

The financial condition of the two papers became further complicated by an opportunity that presented itself in Astoria. The owners of the *EO* and *AB* had barely escaped financial disaster with the Twin Falls *Times* by selling it in the spring of 1930, when another newspaper opportunity appeared. In December 1929, the owner of the *Morning Astorian*, John Dellinger, proposed a 50-50 merger of his paper with the *AB*. Aldrich, Lampkin, and Chessman refused, arguing that their afternoon paper was doing more business than the *Morning Astorian*, which was struggling and in debt. Still, Aldrich thought the property too good to pass up. As he wrote Chessman, "The merger is a logical thing if we can work it out. We will be happy with the business if it makes good money." (undated letter, EOPC archives)   Before negotiations had proceeded very far, Dellinger died suddenly in late February 1930. His estate decided to sell but wanted $90,000 for the paper and its building. The *AB* partners rejected that price, believing, that, at best, the *Morning Astorian* was worth no more than $50,000, excluding the building. Since the partners already owned a building, they had no need for the other papers' plant.

No sooner had the *EO* and *Budget* escaped the debilitating effects of the Depression, then they descended into the unknown perils of operating under wartime conditions.

In a cautious frame of mind, both Aldrich and Lampkin remained skeptical that the *AB*, with the field to itself, would make as much extra as Chessman estimated. They based this opinion on their experience in Pendleton when the *Tribune* quit. While the *EO* charged more for advertisements, neither the lineage nor subscriptions increased as much as had been expected. Aldrich and Lampkin also worried, wisely as it turned out, that if they raised advertising rates too aggressively, someone else could sweep in and establish a new paper in Astoria on the basis of offering lowball ad rates. As Aldrich speculated to Chessman, "Someone might start another paper and if he had a small plant, say in connection with a job shop and kept his expenses down he could make us a lot of competition for a while at least. I would hate to pay $50,000 for the field and find we had secured nothing but the *Astorian* name and the machinery which would sell for but little if junked." (Aug. 4, 1930, EOPC Archives)

To make the deal work for them, the *AB* partners had to get the price down while

Dorothy Engle, whose company stock was critical to Aldrich family control.

getting advertisers to sign long-term, exclusive ad contracts at higher than current rates. They succeeded in doing both. No doubt the uncertainty stemming from the steadily deteriorating economic conditions caused by the national Depression helped bring the *Morning Astorian*'s price down; and advertisers seemed happy to have only one local paper as long as it was in solid, competent hands. Chessman reported to Lampkin that "most of the leading advertisers signed to an agreement that they will not advertise in any other paper for five years and will get the few others I want before the week ends." (Aug. 13, 1930, EOPC Archives)

After lengthy negotiations, Dellinger's wife agreed in August to sell the paper to the owners of the *AB* for $50,000. The terms of the deal called for the assumption of an existing bank loan of $26,000, 25 shares of A-BPC stock valued at $5,000, and the balance in cash on September 1, 1930. At first, the partners considered bringing in another investor but decided against it. Instead, they borrowed the money necessary to complete the purchase. This transaction gave Aldrich, Lampkin, and Chessman complete control of the Astoria newspaper market. Chessman, since Drake had sold his interest in the *Budget* to him, alone held the positions of editor and manager of the combined Astoria newspapers. Initially, the stockholders of the renamed newspaper corporation—the Astorian-Budget Publishing Company (A-BPC)—consisted of Chessman (189 shares), Lampkin (148 shares), Aldrich (123 shares), and three minority shareholders (80 shares total). Lampkin's survivor—his sister—Dorothy Engle, inherited his shares and became a director of the A-BPC.

Carrying out the consolidation proved to be a complicated, exhausting task, taking several months to complete. Chessman tackled the job with gusto. His first problem involved a small group of investors trying to start a rival daily paper, "on a shoestring," as Chessman put it. Although the new paper managed to begin in February 1931 and operated for almost three years, it never thrived. As noted above, Chessman moved quickly to sign up the community's major advertisers to five-year contracts. While dealing with the new competition, he had to combine the staffs of the two merging papers, letting go unneeded or weak performers and retaining the strong employees. Early in the process, Chessman expressed satisfaction with the merger from the personnel side. He reported to Aldrich and Lampkin that "our crew here has certainly gone to bat, most of them working every night without overtime in order to get organized. I certainly did not overestimate the amount of work involved in making the consolidation and there have not been hours

> **"This newsprint rationing is hitting us as we have several hundred more subscribers than we had in 1941."**
>
> *Merle Chessman*

enough in the day to get all of the work accomplished." (Sept. 7, 1930, EOPC Archives) He also had to decide what printing equipment from the two plants to keep and what to try and sell. He purchased a used duplex printing press from Texas for $7,300 and over time successfully sold the worn out or duplicate equipment. After a quick review of the first month's results, Chessman pronounced himself "very well satisfied with . . . business in view of the disorganization incident to the merger." (Oct. 2, 1930, EOPC Archives) By January 1931, he reported his expenses related to consolidation—all paid—at $6,940.

Despite the steadily worsening economic conditions and the inability to pay directors' salaries on time, Chessman showed the *Astorian-Budget* earning a profit for all of 1931. He also continued to battle the rival daily known as the *Messenger*.

Crucially, he managed to secure the city and county legal business for both 1931 and 1932. Still, though insolvent, the *Messenger* hung on because none of its creditors wanted to pay the court costs and attorneys' fees necessary to push it into bankruptcy, fearing that there was nothing to attach since there was an outstanding mortgage on the plant. As Chessman described the situation, "The *Messenger* is getting to be quite a thorn in our flesh and I am disposed to think that we are justified in using any legitimate means to bring about its demise." Chessman was particularly frustrated that the *Messenger* took job business away from the *AB* by bidding below their costs. He noted that the pressmen and typographical unions had declared the *Messenger* unfair in its treatment of their workers, especially since it was not able to pay its workers on time or in full. (Aug. 11, 1932, EOPC Archives)

What bothered Chessman the most was that the newsprint supplier, Blake, Moffitt, and Towne, had invested in the *Messenger* and was continuing to keep the paper afloat while trying to find a buyer for it. At one point, the *Messenger* sold subscriptions for as low as 25 cents a month and advertising for 12.5 cents an inch—about a quarter of the pre-Depression open rate. By September 1933, Chessman reported a rumor that the *Messenger* would be sold and converted to a weekly. In October 1933, however, the bankrupt paper was shut down through foreclosure action and a sheriff's sale of its equipment.

Neither the *East Oregonian* nor the *Astoria Budget* panicked or engaged in journalistic sensationalism merely to survive.

In all, the *AB* seems to have weathered the Depression years better than her sister paper in eastern Oregon. Directors' salaries, while often deferred, were ultimately paid. In addition, the owners were able to invest in new printing equipment and make other physical improvements to the Astoria plant, buy out minority shareholders, pay off the mortgage, and even pay dividends. In the summer of 1936, moreover, the A-BPC bought and successfully operated a radio station in Astoria: KAST. The partners initially took on two other men experienced in radio as part owners and operators of the station. The A-BPC partners decided to enter the radio business because, as Chessman put it, they "believe[d] that the newspaper of the future without a radio station is going to be handicapped and that we can never acquire a station cheaper."

(May 25, 1936, EOPC Archives) The venture proved financially successful, and in 1937 the A-BPC partners bought out the other investors. The *AB* continued to thrive, and by 1940 it had a circulation of 4,950 copies daily, which exceeded the low mark of the previous ten years by 1,250 copies, and a staff of about 40. Also, for the first time in a decade, the *AB* increased its advertising rates about three cents per column inch.

The survival of the *EO* and *AB* during the worst of the Depression was typical of the newspaper business in Oregon as a whole. Between 1930 and 1937, the number of daily and weekly newspapers in the state only declined from 205 to 203. What neither the *East Oregonian* nor the *Astoria Budget* did was to panic and engage in journalistic sensationalism merely to survive. They both maintained their reputation for editorial quality and accurate news coverage, while preserving such staples as sports and women and society sections.

No sooner had the *EO* and *AB* escaped the debilitating effects of the Depression, than they descended into the unknown perils of operating under wartime conditions. The nation's entry into World War II presented a whole new set of challenges to the business of running a small-town, daily newspaper. With war came manpower shortages and then the rationing of newsprint. By November 1942, Chessman reported that he had "lost over 45 per cent of our personnel and have four women in back shop. Getting along very well under the circumstances." At the same time, he worried that "with gas rationing into effect we'll have to cut out our rural routes and go to mail. We shall probably lose several hundred subscribers as the mail service is bad." (Nov. 12, 1942, EOPC Archives) Worst of all, he feared the effects of paper shortages. Indeed, in January 7, 1943, he wrote Aldrich, "This newsprint rationing is hitting us as we have several hundred more subscribers than we had in 1941. We are cutting to two six-page papers a week, eliminating some exchanges and service copies and cutting 550 off our free weekly list." Staffing at the two papers proved especially difficult, both at the news desk and in the mechanical department. Those who were not called up for military duty could usually make better wages in wartime industries such as the local shipyards. With wage freezes in effect, Aldrich and Chessmen resorted to bonuses to

The Astoria partners entered the radio business because they "believed the newspaper of the future without a radio station is going to be handicapped."

try and stem the hemorrhaging of their work forces. During the war years, both papers continued to earn a profit and to pay dividends to the owners and bonuses to the employees.

Throughout the hard times of the 1930s and the drama of wartime in the 1940s, Aldrich and Chessman, in their respective papers, editorially continued to promote those actions they thought would better their communities. Aldrich kept up his fight for the Umatilla Dam on the Columbia River. He argued forcefully that the dam construction would provide needed jobs while improving navigation and producing cheap electric power. He even went to Washington to lobby Congress for the Umatilla Dam. He was disappointed but undaunted when President Roosevelt selected Bonneville Dam in 1933 as the first federal dam to be built on the Columbia. Eventually his efforts for the Umatilla Dam bore fruit following World War II.

Throughout the 1930s, Aldrich strongly backed President Roosevelt's New Deal program, especially its work relief and agriculture price support components. Aldrich wrote that "in complex modern life all responsible governments must enlarge their field of supervision to protect the weak from the rapacious. That is New Deal Doctrine and it is sound." (Quote in Macnab, 224) In 1935, he editorialized, "The country wants neither radicalism nor reaction. It wants recovery

When Republicans nominated Oregon Sen. Charles McNary as Wendell Wilkie's running mate, Aldrich jumped to the GOP ticket.

and economic security. This is the president's goal and he is entitled to support." (*EO*, Jan. 4, 1935) During the run up to the 1936 election, Aldrich reminded voters, "By a wise and workable program he [Roosevelt] got us out of the black tunnel of depression in which we were baffled, helpless, disheartened and dying. He gave us rescue and recovery by means of policies that were honorable and fair. He saved the United States from chaos and possible revolution." (*EO*, Oct. 26, 1936) Still, by the late 1930s, Aldrich began to worry that the massive deficit spending was creating problems of its own. He wrote, "Emergency spending for relief is justifiable but as a promoter of prosperity the policy is questionable. It is too much like relying upon a larger faucet in the kitchen to make up for a water shortage. It is necessary to look to the watershed, not to the household hydrants for a permanent solution." (*EO*, Mar. 16, 1940)

Aldrich's continued support of President Roosevelt and adherence to the Democratic Party came into question when Roosevelt ran for a third term in 1940. His concern over the third term issue led Aldrich to question what he saw as an excessive growth in government, especially continued deficit spending. As he worried in an editorial, "Excessive peace time spending with terrific federal debt increases can only lead to some form of repudiation or inflation. . . . If you think that people or nations can ignore mathematics observe those that try it. At the end of the trail you will find misfortune and sorrow." (*EO*, Oct. 28, 1940) Then, when the Republicans nominated Oregon Senator NcNary as Wendell Willkie's running mate, Aldrich made the jump to the Republican ticket. In an editorial on October 30, 1940, Aldrich wrote, "If Willkie and McNary are elected the third term rule will not be broken and if that rule is broken the American people may have occasion to deeply regret this action. . . . Sen. McNary is entitled to Oregon's support on November 5 and we cannot give him that support unless our five electoral votes are cast for Willkie and McNary."

Aldrich's only other break with the Democratic Party came in his endorsement of the Salem newspaper editor Charles Sprague for governor in 1938. He justified that switch by stating "He [Sprague] has a better grasp of Democratic principles than some of the Democratic extremists." (*EO*, Oct. 29, 1938) Even the *Oregonian* took notice of that bold step by running a cartoon showing Aldrich on horseback riding into Sprague's camp. When Roosevelt ran for a fourth term, Aldrich did not depart the Democratic Party, as the United States was still at war and deficit spending could not be avoided.

Local issues dominated much of Aldrich's editorial attention in the 1930s. He championed, for example, the rise of the pea industry in Umatilla County as a valuable diversification of agriculture. The first important experiments with peas occurred in1931, when L. L. Rogers planted 400 acres on summer fallow. Soon mechanization led to extensive planting of peas as a rotation crop with wheat. In 1934, the Rogers and Barney Foster built a pea cannery and in three years, Umatilla County supported three more. Aldrich chronicled this progress for his readers, noting in an April 13, 1937 editorial, "The county's newest industry, pea growing and canning is flourishing. . . . Pea raising not only aids farmers in crop diversification but pea harvesting and canning take care of the common labor problem." Again, on June 7, 1939, he observed, "The pea industry has meant a great deal to Umatilla county—and other counties—in the way of new prosperity." By the 1940s, peas became second only to

I1 \ND SEPTEMBER 11 1938

A Good Outfit Always Welcomes a Top Hand

When the *East Oregonian* supported Charles A. Sprague for governor in 1938,
The *Oregonian* in Portland ran this editorial cartoon. It was the first time Aldrich
had given editorial support to a Republican.

wheat as Umatilla County's most important crop.

Aldrich also worked to bring the Harris Pine Mill operations to Pendleton. After three years the campaign bore fruit in the construction of a sawmill and box factory in 1939. Aldrich was also pleased that company would be building new houses for some of its employees, noting in an editorial, "Pendleton needs such a program because this is a growing town and there has long been a problem in connection with housing." He went on to state that the Harris "lumber operation is to be on a permanent basis. Harris

J.W. "Bud" Forrester

brothers will cut government timber on a sustained yield plan and those informed say the operation can be made to last indefinitely. Naturally the forest officials want the program to succeed and like Harris brothers, they desire that the workers live in attractive homes that they can afford to rent or own." (*EO*, April 15, 1939)

Aldrich avidly promoted attracting new industries to Pendleton – even if they needed subsidies in the beginning because, as he put it, "Towns are built; they do not grow. They are built by people who know how to work together eagerly and unselfishly for the common good." (*EO*, Sept. 28, 1938)

The *EO* had long championed good roads, especially through southern Umatilla County and northern Grant County to John Day. Editorial after editorial complained that western Oregon got most of the state's highway appropriations. Finally, with the help of federal money U. S. Highway 395 was completed through eastern Oregon in 1935. Aldrich played a key role in improving highways statewide when Governor Julius Meier appointed him to the Oregon Highway Commission in 1932. For example, he actively promoted building the five major bridges along the Oregon Coast Highway—a goal that Chessman also would actively push from his editorial chair on the *AB*. Aldrich continued to serve on the highway commission until 1940.

The last half of the 1930s demonstrated gradual improvement in Pendleton's economic condition, as reflected in the town's growth in population. In 1940, the census recorded 8,847 inhabitants, a 33 percent increase over the 1930 numbers. As business picked up, so did the fortunes of the *EO*. Between 1935 and 1939, net paid circulation averaged 3,200 copies a quarter, and six-page editions were a thing of the past. Eight pages became the norm. To handle the growth, the directors of the EOPC voted in May 1940 to borrow $3,500 to purchase and install a new press and other equipment from the Duplex Printing Press Company. Important new staff additions during the 1930s included Nolan Skiff, who arrived in 1938 to handle sports reporting but soon became an associate editor. In July 1935, J. W. "Bud" Forrester Jr. became city editor. Forrester, however, did not stay long, as he married Eleanor, the daughter of Ed Aldrich, on June 20, 1936, and left the *EO* soon after to become athletic news director at Oregon State University. Following service in the Merchant Marine during World War II, he and Eleanor ran a weekly newspaper in North Bend, Oregon. In 1950, they would take over the *EO* upon Aldrich's death.

The famous "Doolittle Raiders" who bombed Tokyo early in the war had trained at the Pendleton Air Base.

The preparations for the United States' entry into World War II brought profound changes to Umatilla County and Pendleton. In 1940, the federal government constructed a massive ammunition depot west of Hermiston and an Army air base on a hilltop overlooking Pendleton. Soon, over 1,000 employees worked at the depot under guard by 245 soldiers, while the air field had 2,200 enlisted men and 300 officers. The town underwent a building boom to house the airmen. Much of the *EO*'s news space during the war years would be taken up with coverage of the military struggle in Europe and the Pacific. The famous "Doolittle Raiders" who bombed Tokyo early in the war had trained at the Pendleton Air Base, so the *EO* was proud to announce that event on the front page: "Pendleton Fliers Decorated." Because of a wartime paper shortage and rationing that affected advertisers, the newspaper had to drop to six pages daily. In another cutback resulting

Merle Chessman

from the war effort on the home front, the directors of the Round-Up cancelled the shows for 1942 and 1943. The *EO* headlined the end of war with Germany in big, bold type with the simple words "Germany Quits" and when Japan surrendered, "War is Over."

In Astoria, Chessman had his own community issues to focus on. While the effects of the great Astoria fire and the poisonous activities of the KKK consumed Chessman during the 1920s, other challenges and new enemies engaged him during the economic struggles of the 1930s. Unemployed fishermen and loggers were attracted to the blandishments of the Communist Party and other radical labor organizations. When a petition to create the Communist Party circulated in Astoria in 1934, 220 signed the document. Chessman editorialized against the evils of communism and printed the names of those on the Astoria petition.

One of the identified signatories alleged that he lost his job as a consequence of Chessman's publishing his name in the *AB*, and then sued Chessman and his newspaper for libel. A circuit judge upheld the right of the paper to criticize a political organization and affirmed that an individual member of a group cannot be libeled in such an opinion piece. The legal profession in the community strongly backed Chessman's position on communism and offered to defend him free of charge.

Chessman also took on the issue of union violence. When a jurisdictional dispute between two sawmill unions erupted in Astoria and nearby towns, Chessman wrote editorials condemning the resulting violence and intimidation. In response, the union organizers threatened violence and boycotts against Chessman and the *AB*. Chessman responded to the attempts to intimidate him in a memorable editorial:

> This newspaper is not interested in which union is right in its claim for jurisdiction or whether either is. The quarrel between them is penalizing an industry, a whole community and hundreds of men who need employment and whose families are suffering from the long controversy. We are only interested in maintaining law and order and insuring peace and security for the law-abiding citizens, whether union member or not, whether laborer or employer, and regardless of race, religion, color or political belief. (quote in *Cumtux*, Fall 1986, 10)

Chessman and the *AB* worked hard to save the city and local school system from bankruptcy in the early 1930s. Heavy unemployment led to tax delinquencies, which reached 75 percent. Chessman served on a committee that produced a plan to pay Astoria's bonded debt, and he went east to negotiate with the bondholders. By 1935, the plan had been accepted by Astoria's creditors and slowly the city met its obligations. Similarly, in 1933, Chessman as a director of the new Bank of Astoria pushed to have the bank accept warrants issued in lieu of cash by the school district until tax collections began to improve in 1935.

While working to stem Astoria's downward economic slide, Chessman also took a more proactive role in community improvement by writing editorials and serving on various local and statewide committees pushing various economic development efforts. During the early 1930s, for example, the *AB* promoted formation of the Oregon Coast Highway Association, which sought to build a scenic highway along Oregon's 400-mile coastline. Eventually, Chessman's editorials and lobbying by his association won the support of the Oregon Highway Commission and the state legislature. Using state and federal Public Works Administration money, contractors completed the hard-surfaced roadway in 1932, linking all of U. S. Highway 101 segments at the Arch Cape tunnel south of Cannon Beach. The workers completed the necessary bridges over the coastal rivers in 1936. He later served on the State Highway Commission during World War II.

Chessman also was an early and long-term promoter of a bridge across the Columbia River at Astoria. First pushed in 1935, early efforts failed to win the necessary state and federal funding. Even though he kept supporting the dream of a Columbia River bridge over the years, Chessman did not live to see it completed in 1966. He supported the bridge because of its potential to promote tourism and economic development in Astoria and lower Columbia River communities.

Chessman also served on several statewide commissions. He accepted appointment to the Oregon Fish Commission in 1936 because he felt that the lower Columbia River fishing industry needed representation on the commission. He served on the Oregon Wildlife Conservation Commission, the Oregon State Geographic Board, as well as president of the Oregon State Editorial Association. He sat on numerous local boards and societies, such as the Rotary Club, Clatsop County Historical Society, and the Clatsop County library board.

Chessman was appointed to the Oregon State Senate in 1942 to fill out the term of deceased Sen. Frank Franciscovich.

Recognizing that federal funds were necessary for carrying out projects beneficial to Astoria, Chessman sought appropriations for Fort Stevens prior to World War II and then wrote over 100 editorials in support of the effort to establish a naval installation at Tongue Point. He even made five trips to Washington, D. C. to lobby for the project. At last, in 1939, Congress appropriated funds to build a naval air station at Tongue Point. During World War II, it became a base for repair and maintenance of aircraft. After the war, the navy closed the facility; and it eventually became a Jobs Corps Center.

Perhaps the strongest recognition of Chessman's contributions to his community came in his appointment to the Oregon State Senate in 1942 to fill out the term of the deceased senator Frank Franciscovich. He spent much of his time in the legislature working on behalf of Astoria's fishing interests. His political appointment was not entirely welcome to Chessman. As he told Aldrich, "it is something I have shied away from all my life and I have no appetite for it but, under the circumstance, I could not very well turn it down." (ltr, no date, EOPC Archives) In 1946, voters reelected Chessman to the Senate, but his second term was cut short by his sudden death at the age of 60.

Speaking at Chessman's funeral at the Astoria Presbyterian Church, Rev. Philip B. Lewis said, "He denounced selfish partisanship and we united in community endeavour. He pressed for the generous spirit of fairmindedness, and we became more forebearing. He struck hard at the roots of intolerance and we were knit together as neighbors. He fought against corruption; we committed ourselves to integrity."

Before his unexpected death from a brain tumor in September 1947, Chessman initiated major operational changes at the *AB*. At the close of the war, pent-up consumer demand unleashed a period of economic prosperity. To take advantage of the potential increases in advertising and circulation growing out of the new business opportunities afforded by the post-war boom, Chessman pushed the idea of constructing a new building for the paper and replacing the old printing press. In October 1945, the stockholders of the A-BPC agreed to have an architectural firm draw up plans for a new building. Chessman, however, had second thoughts and recommended purchasing and remodeling an existing building instead of new construction. He had in mind the Troy Laundry building. It had been built in 1922 after the great Astoria fire, and according to Chessman, was "a solidly built concrete structure, 145' x 80' and in addition there is a smaller building about 30' x 50' and an adjacent lot." He did admit that "it is a factory type of building and would require considerable alterations and remodeling to make it fit our bill of needs." But, he felt, "there would be an abundance of floor space and all on one level." (Feb. 15, 1946, EOPC Archives)

In early June 1947, Chessman experienced a series of multiple blood clots in the small arteries of his brain, impairing speech and physical functions.

Chessman, reported that the owners wanted $40,000 for the building and land but the price included the laundry machinery that could be sold for $10,000 and remodeling could be done for about $32,000. In all, he thought it "a splendid property and better located than our own property." (Feb. 15, 1946, EOPC Archives) Aldrich wrote back, exhibiting less enthusiasm. He feared that the converted building would not be large enough, especially for future expansion. As he noted, "with business expanding the A-B will need considerable room as you will need a good vault, conference room, space for an eventual engraving plant and studio." (Feb 19, 1946, EOPC Archives) Undaunted, Chessman pressed ahead with the Troy Laundry building project, arguing that it would cost at least $100,000 for a new building.

By March, Chessman had arranged for the purchase of the Troy Laundry building and set the Portland architect George Jones to work on plans and specifications. Terms of the purchase required $15,000 down and $200 per month at 4 percent interest. Chessman hoped to reroof the building and make outside repairs before the rainy season arrived in the fall and then finish the inside work. With the building project initiated, he then investigated the purchase of new printing equipment, noting "it would be very advantageous to have a new press installed when we move into the building rather than take down our old one and re-erect it." (Mar. 13, 1946, EOPC Archives)

Post-war inflation and material shortages had a major impact on both the ultimate cost of the remodel and the price of a new press, as well as on construction time. When finally finished in the summer of 1947, the remodel came in at about $42,000; and the new, 16-page tubular press from the Duplex Printing Company also increased in price. The Duplex Company, however, failed to

Chessman worked to save the city and local schools from bankruptcy in the early 1930s, when tax delinquencies reached 75 percent.

deliver on the contract; and Chessman ultimately bought a press from the Goss Company instead, which cost slightly over $55,000. The A-BPC stockholders paid the cost of the building and new equipment project through savings; bank loans; and money from the sale of the old building, two lots, and the old printing equipment. Just as much of the work on the building reached completion, personal disaster struck.

In early June 1947, Chessman experienced a series of multiple blood clots in the small arteries of his brain. It slightly impaired his speech and some physical functions. While agreeing to reduce his work load and turn most of his daily business activities over to his staff, Chessman assured Aldrich that "I am fully capable of keeping an eye and hand on things, as the need arises. . . . Please do not feel alarmed over my condition. If it were critical, I would tell you." (undated ltr, EOPC Archives) He went on to report that the building would be ready by the end of July, but the press would not arrive until sometime in the "third quarter" of the year. Best of all, Chessman believed that the sale of the old building and press would cover much of the cost of the undertaking, leaving them only about $30,000 in debt at the completion of the project. Over the course of the summer, however, Chessman's condition worsened. The key question was who would replace him at the *AB*. At one time, there appeared to be two possible contenders for the position.

In 1936, Chessman's daughter had married Robert Lucas, whom she had met while a student at the University of Oregon. After a short stint as a reporter for the *Oregon Journal,* Chessman hired him to work at the *AB*. For the next eight years, Lucas learned the details of the newspaper business from Chessman. In 1945, however, Lucas left to become editor of the *Yakima Herald* and later assumed editorship of the *Denver Post* and then took over the *Hartford (Conn.) Times.* The other candidate for Chessman's place was his son, Robert. After a year at the University of Oregon, Robert Chessman served in the Army during World War II, returning home in 1945 to join his father at the *AB*. Upon the elder Chessman's death, the directors of the A-BPC would choose his son to take over the paper. At the age of 26, Bob Chessman was one of the youngest publishers of a daily newspaper in America. He would lead the paper until 1960.

When Bob Chessman succeeded Merle in 1947, at the age of 26, he became one of the youngest daily newspaper publishers in America.

During the summer of 1947, Robert Chessman took on increasing responsibility at the paper as his father ailed. Aldrich assured Merle that he was "glad Bob Chessman is on the job for he should be able to lighten your load quite a bit and the more he learns about the business the better." (undated ltr, EOPC Archives) Aldrich began offering advice to the younger Chessman, and at one point he suggested instituting a profit sharing plan to incentivize key people on the paper's staff "to take responsibility and hit the ball, so as to improve the business." He also advised that the paper should invest in new typeface: "When the A-B is in the new building and has the new press it would be nice to make the paper look as well as possible, so that the boys can go to town with reference to business getting. People like to see a paper make progress and provide improvements. There is better status and it helps advertising." (Jun. 21, 1947, EOPC Archives)

To improve the job department, Merle Chessman, in one of his last decisions regarding the paper, convinced Aldrich and the other A-BPC stockholders to invest $10,000 in a new, automatic feed press and to hire a new superintendent to go after more business. Aldrich thought that a new man to run the job department should have a salary and a percentage of the net profits rather than gross sales: "By giving him a percentage of net profits we provide an incentive for him to work for the interest of the shareholders." On the other hand, if his salary, Aldrich argued, were based on gross sales, such remuneration "would offer him an incentive to increase the business volume regardless of whether we made any money on the work." (Jul. 10, 1947, EOPC Archives)

In August, as the elder Chessman's health continued to fail, the stockholders and directors of A-BPC held an emergency meeting and elected Robert Chessman a director and executive vice president of the company. Then, in early September, Merle Chessman died and another special meeting of the director's convened to elect Robert Chessman as publisher and president to succeed his father. At the same time, the directors named Fred Andrus editor of the *AB*. The stockholders also elected Merle's wife, Daphne, to the Board of Directors and put her in charge of public relations for the paper. Since the price of the new press had increased to $55,000 and the sale of the old building brought only $32,000, the directors, in September 1947, took out a bank loan and arranged financing from the press manufacturer to cover the difference and to pay for the new job press.

In another wartime cutback, directors of the Pendleton Round-Up cancelled the shows for 1942 and 1943.

Clearly, higher operating costs incidental to the move to larger quarters and the purchase of new presses for both the newspaper and job printing department put pressure on the business and the new management under Robert Chessman. He also had to deal with inflationary wage pressure from his staff of 45, and the continuing shortage of newsprint the plagued that publishing business in general at the time. In spite of the difficulties, in the final years of the decade, the *AB* ran profitably and

This ferry that sailed between Astoria and Megler, Wash.,
was named the M.R. Chessman following Merle Chessman's death.
CLATSOP COUNTY HISTORICAL SOCIETY

made steady progress in retiring its indebtedness, while continuing to pay dividends.

The career of Merle Chessman at the *AB* had been remarkable. Fred Andrus, the managing editor of the paper at the time of Chessman's death, succinctly summed up Chessman's approach: "As publisher of the *Astoria Budget*, Chessman spoke his mind boldly and clearly on problems whether of controversial nature or not and without regard to whether the side he took was the popular one or not." Andrus went on to state, "His editorials were widely read and much quoted and reprinted by other newspapers, not only in Oregon but in other states, and he was widely known and recognized in the publishing industry as one of Oregon's ablest editors." (*AB*, Sept. 1, 1947) Some years later, Andrus recalled Chessman's approach to community leadership:

> Chessman saw no dichotomy between his roles as a newspaper editor-publisher and as a community leader, for he firmly believed that a newspaper's primary duty is to serve its community to the utmost of its ability. He used the newspaper as an instrument for that purpose, and even further by devoting his great personal talents and energies to the salvation and betterment of Astoria. *(Daily Astorian, Nov 20, 1970)*

111

Within three years, the *EO* also would experience its leadership change. In the early postwar period, Aldrich returned to his main themes of promoting Pendleton and Umatilla County, while maintaining his support of international peace and defending freedom from tyranny. The former led him to support the United Nations—just as he had championed the League of Nations—while the latter caused him to back the Korean War. The close of World War II, he editorialized, "insured peace is our No. 1 project for the future"; but later, as the Cold War set in, he observed that "appeasement leads only to other aggression and ultimately to war. . . . If criminals are permitted to operate fully they will do so." (quote in Macnab, 278-79)

For 42 years, Aldrich wrote editorials consistently grounded on the firm principles of truth-telling and fairness to the weak and underdog, while promoting the community good. Then, after a Saturday at the office, he went home and died quietly that same evening. It was November 19, 1950. While there was no memorial service, Aldrich's death was noticed well beyond Pendleton. President Truman sent Elsie Aldrich a telegram of condolence.

Aldrich's death was noticed well beyond Pendleton. President Truman sent Elsie Aldrich a telegram of condolence.

As in the case of the *AB*, the *EO* stockholders effected a smooth transition to new leadership. J. W. "Bud" Forrester Jr., the husband of Aldrich's daughter Eleanor, was ready to step in as editor and other members of the family assumed new responsibilities with the paper. As noted above, after returning from World War II, he and Eleanor had operated a weekly newspaper in North Bend, Oregon. Aldrich, before his death, had already encouraged his other daughter, Amy Bedford, to return home to Pendleton after the death of her husband and assume management of the *EO*'s commercial printing department. During the 1950s, further realignments of the newspaper's operations would soon take place, but it would remain a family-run business.

E.B. Aldrich and President Truman

In May 1950, Editor Ed Aldrich of the *East Oregonian*, introduced
President Harry Truman to a crowd at the Pendleton Railway Station.
Aldrich is at the right with First Lady Bess Truman.

Six months prior to the death of E.B. Aldrich, one of the editor's heroes visited Pendleton.
At 6pm on May 10, 1950, a 15-car presidential train rolled into the Pendleton railway station
with President Harry Truman standing on the balcony of the Observation Car.

Aldrich sat behind Truman as the president addressed a crowd estimated at 20,000. Truman
exhorted the crowd with, "I don't believe the country is going to hell." Reporter Nolan Skiff
wrote there was "round after round of applause." Atop a panoramic front-page photo, the
headline proclaimed: "President Truman's Welcome Largest Given Anyone in Pendleton."

In the wake of Aldrich's death in November, a White House telegram to Mrs. Aldrich
expressed condolences.

CHAPTER IV

New beginning, new commitments

Mrs. Aldrich drives a hard bargain

The mid-twentieth century marked a major turning point in the ownership and management of the *EO* and *AB*. Prior to their deaths, E.B. Aldrich had run the *East Oregonian* for 42 years. Merle Chessman had operated the *Evening Budget* and its successor the *Astorian-Budget* for 29. Each man held strong editorial views and promoted their communities' well-being and growth. They knew how to run small-town daily newspapers at a profit.

Would those traditions continue under new ownership and management? Two separate families held the major stake in each newspaper. The heirs of Merle Chessman controlled the *AB*, while the inheritors of Edwin Aldrich held the *EO*. The *EO* owners, however, continued to retain a minority interest in the *AB*. The transition at both papers is a pivotal chapter in this family business history.

Robert Chessman

Robert Chessman, taking over from his father at the age of 26, struggled with the management of the *AB* during the late 1940s. Astoria's economy was sluggish, especially its leading industry, commercial fishing.

Chessman also had to devote much of his attention to the problems at the radio station—KAST—owned by the *AB* stockholders. To stay ahead of the competition, the owners of KAST decided to increase the station's broadcast power from 250 to 1,000 watts. Chessman found this effort more expensive and time-consuming than anticipated. In the process of modernizing the radio station, he decided to oust the station manager (also a minority stockholder). The management change did not go smoothly and was not completed until the spring of 1950.

In the meantime, Chessman scrambled to earn a profit at the *AB*. He did manage to pay off the new press bought by his father, but the paper still carried a heavy load of debt. On the plus side, circulation in 1950 stood at an all-time high of 7,129 subscribers; in 1946, it had been 6,631.

As Chessman explained in a long letter to Aldrich, he found it necessary to raise advertising rates, cut staff, and bargain with the union to prevent an increase in the

COURTESY OF GAYLE CHESSMAN LAIRD

Daphne Chessman

wage scale—all against a backdrop of a weak local economy. Aldrich, in one of his last letters before his death, sought to reassure Chessman, who was 40 years his junior. Aldrich approved the new advertising rates because, as he noted, the old ones "were too low." Then, he went on to "advise that you not be discouraged or pessimistic. The A-B is a fine business, well established in a good town and Astoria will always be a good town. There are no problems that cannot be handled by good management and proper work. All towns have up and down periods that must be expected." Aldrich also advised Chessman to build up the job printing side of the business. He noted that since his daughter, Amy, had taken over the job work at the *EO*, the business had almost doubled. After offering further advice on managing his staff, Aldrich closed by encouraging him to write "editorials of a constructive nature", and offered a bit of prospective: "What you are facing, Bob, is nothing like as tough as the job your Dad had after we bought the *Astorian*. He had a big debt to work out of and did it during the depression years. I still do not know just how he did it but he did a grand job under very adverse conditions. I am confident you will work out your problems just as well." (Aldrich to Chessman, Oct. 25, 1950, EOPC Archives)

Elsie Aldrich

In spite of Aldrich's optimism, Robert Chessman continued to struggle with the management of both the paper and the radio station throughout the next decade. Some years the business did not earn a profit; and the Forrester family, Aldrich's heirs and minority stockholders in the *AB*, became increasingly concerned about their investment. The ownership and management of the two family newspapers had become more complex. The major stockholders of the two newspaper corporations during the 1950s were Daphne Chessman, the widow of Merle, at the *AB* and Elsie Aldrich, the widow of Ed, at the *EO*. The children of the two deceased editors, as active minority stockholders, played the major management roles at the two papers.

The *EO* had run on a profitable basis during the 1940s under Aldrich and Drake. In 1949, the EOPC bought the two shares of stock still held by the C. S. Jackson estate and purchased a new Kelly press for $10,285, which it paid for in a year. The paper was able to pay regular dividends, annual employee bonuses, and increase the corporate officers' monthly pay, while maintaining the regular salaries for the editor and business manager. In 1950, the paper needed more space, so the stockholders added a one-story addition and basement at the east end of the old building.

They also leased basement space in an adjacent building. Between 1946 and 1950, circulation had grown from 5,291 to 6,586 subscribers—a 25 percent increase.

The death of Aldrich brought new family members into stock ownership at the EOPC. When Aldrich died, he held 166 shares, while Lee Drake and Dorothy Engle (heir to Fred Lampkin's estate) each held an equal amount. Elsie Aldrich inherited all of her husband's shares, but daughters Amy Aldrich Bedford and her sister, Eleanor and her husband J. W. Forrester, needed to purchase shares from Drake and/or Engle to become part owners of the *EO*. In 1950, at the age of 68, Drake expressed an interest in retiring but drove a hard bargain in the extensive negotiations that led to the sale of his shares. In 1935, the EOPC had promised him $75 a week with cost of living adjustments so long as he held 125 shares. For agreeing to give up his contractual rights, he insisted on receiving $60,000 over ten years at the rate of $500 a month. In addition, he wanted $100,000 for his stock in the EOPC, while agreeing not to compete against the *EO* in the future by engaging in the newspaper business.

Aldrich's heirs and minority stockholders in the *Astorian-Budget* became increasingly concerned about their investment.

The Forresters and Amy Bedford accepted the terms and acquired Drake's 166 shares. J. W. Forrester received 41.5 shares, his wife Eleanor, 41.5; and Amy Bedford, 83 shares. They paid $25,000 immediately and the remainder was to be paid over ten years at the rate of $7,500 yearly. The purchase price of the stock came to $602.41 per share.

In January 1951, the new owners, as stockholders and directors of the EOPC, reorganized management of the company. The directors chose J. W. Forrester as vice president and editor, Amy Bedford as secretary and manager of the commercial printing department, and Eleanor Forrester as business manager of the EOPC. In addition, the directors selected Elsie Aldrich as President and Dorothy Engle – who resided in San Francisco's St. Francis Hotel – remained treasurer. The Forresters and Amy Bedford sold a portion of their shares to the EOPC to be held as treasury stock. Lee Drake died in 1957, and the payments continued to his heir until the purchase was paid off in 1961. When Dorothy Engle died in the mid-1960s, she left her one-third interest in both the *EO* and *AB* to Eleanor and Amy, thus confirming ownership in the hands of the Aldrich heirs.

While the *EO* moved ahead under the Forresters and Bedford, the situation in Astoria was not so positive. By mid-1952, Elsie Aldrich had become alarmed at the declining financial condition of the *AB* and KAST. Between 1949 and the end of 1951, the profits at the paper dropped about $5,000 each year, going from 7.2 percent to 2.2 percent of operating income. At KAST, the last year of profit was 1949 and by April 1952, liabilities exceeded assets by $21,875. Mrs. Aldrich wrote to the other two major shareholders—Dorothy Engle and Daphne Chessman—that in light of the declining financial condition of the two properties, "I think we should be aware from this that immediate action must be taken to correct the situation." She recommended:

> That we immediately agree to employ a qualified expert in newspaper management to go to Astoria and take charge of the entire newspaper operation and our company. I think we should get the best qualified man available and one who will have the knowledge and experience to make any changes necessary there. I do not mean that he would replace Bob as Publisher. What I have in mind is for the new man to be our general manager, and with the authority to put into practice the best ideas available. I am sure that it is feasible for Bob to work with him, and Bob could offer his advice and assistance. In the event that we decide to do this I wish the new general manger to be someone of whom I approve.

Mrs. Aldrich then stated that "if the . . . proposal doesn't meet with your approval, I wish to know as soon as possible, for I have definitely decided that unless we attempt to put our company on a firm basis by the above proposal, I no longer wish to retain my stock." However, she clearly was anguished over the thought of selling her interest in the *AB*:

> It would be with the utmost reluctance that I would do this. I remember only too well the many years our family was paying its share of the purchase of the Astoria newspaper. But I feel that I have more than a financial interest in the welfare of our company, and it is for this reason that I cannot bear to sit idly by and see it lose its stature as one of the leading newspapers in the state. I feel that the paper must not only be a leader in the community, but that it also must be financially successful. A newspaper that is weak financially can't be a strong voice in the community. (Aldrich to Engle and Daphne Chessman, May 24, 1952, EOPC Archives)

The Chessman family did not respond favorably to the proposal, so in a proactive move to protect her interest in the *AB* and KAST, Mrs. Aldrich had her accountant study the finances of the two companies and place a valuation on the stock. After her due diligence, she offered to sell her stock in both companies for $150,000. Negotiations dragged into the next year with the Chessman family only willing to pay $40,000 for the Aldrich stock. Then in the summer of 1953, Daphne Chessman suffered a severe stroke, which brought further negotiations to a standstill. Mrs. Aldrich did transfer 11 shares of A-BPC stock to each of her daughters in August 1953.

Throughout the remainder of the 1950s, Bob Chessman struggled to make a profit at either the *AB* or KAST. The paper was debt-free, however, after May 1955 when Chessman managed to make the last payment on the building and press purchased in the 1940s. In March 1956, the stockholders agreed to purchase a new Linotype and keyboard for $18,000 in installments over 60 months to replace a 30-year-old machine. The lumber and fishing industries in northwestern Oregon, however, continued a steady decline throughout the 1950s, putting pressure on both circulation and advertising. Circulation, for example, declined from 7,296 in 1951 to 6,350 at the end of 1959.

> **"A newspaper that is weak financially can't be a strong voice in the community."**
>
> *E.B. Aldrich*

Growing increasingly alarmed about the condition of the *AB* and losing confidence in Bob Chessman's ability to improve the situation, the Aldrich heirs acted to protect their investment. They also had the support of Dorothy Engle, the other substantial stockholder outside of the Chessman family. In 1959, they forced the sale of KAST and indicated that they wished to sell their interest in the paper.

Chessman remained reluctant to sell. He wrote Mrs. Aldrich that "as far as I am personally concerned, however, I have no desire to abandon the *Budget* or Astoria merely because of pressing economic conditions. Therefore, any personal decision to sell would be by necessity; not choice." (Chessman to Aldrich, Dec. 8, 1959, *EO* Archives) Chessman, however, could not raise the money to buy out the other stockholders outside of his family.

The Aldrich/Engle/Forrester/Bedford interest applied further pressure for change.

Morgan Coe, publisher of *The Daily Astorian*, looking at the last paper printed
on the Goss press September 25, 1970 before converting to a new Goss offset press.
Printing moved from the newspaper's Duane Street building (now US Bank)
to its current location on Exchange Street.

They hired outside consultants to appraise the market value of the plant, equipment, and company stock. They also employed a consultant to suggest changes in the advertising rate structure and installed Amy Bedford as a company director. By the summer of 1960, they had decided to buy out the Chessmans rather than sell their interests. As Amy Bedford put it, "we had been reluctant to do this before, mainly for sentimental reasons involving the families owning the stock, but have now decided that our common sense, rather than sentiment, should prevail." (Jul. 15, 1960, EOPC Archives) Finally, in December 1960 the Chessman family stockholders agreed to sell their interest (199 shares) to the A-BPC for $89,550.

Upon taking control of the A-BPC, the Aldrich/Forrester/ Engle/Bedford interest soon made major changes in the management and operations of the newspaper. They brought in an experienced newsman as publisher, enlarged the board of directors, and purchased new equipment. Still, the *AB* basically had a sound infrastructure. One consultant sent to evaluate the paper reported, "There is a great undeveloped potential here. Some equipment and repairs are needed . . . but on the whole the newspaper plant is OK, and can carry a lot more advertising and news with no more equipment and with little added expense." (Report to Amy Bedford, Dec. 9, 1960, EOPC Archives)

The new owners now controlling the A-BPC chose an experienced newsman, Morgan Coe, to take the helm of the *AB* and restore its former luster. Coe had almost 40 years experience in the newspaper business before coming in 1960 to Astoria from the *Juneau Daily Alaska Empire*, where he had been publisher for the previous six years. Before remaking the *AB*, he decided to keep one current, longtime member of the staff—Fred Andrus. Andrus started at the *Morning Astorian* in 1928 and then moved to the *Budget* the next year and stayed with that paper and its successors. Andrus became editor of the *AB* in 1947 after the death of Merle Chessman. He remained editor until his retirement in December 1968.

The first few years of Coe's tenure proved very difficult. As it turned out, the *AB* was in worse shape than he initially had been led to believe and Astoria's economy continued to struggle. Between 1950 and 1970, Astoria's main industries, fishing and timber, remained depressed and the Pillsbury flour mill, with a payroll of 350, closed during 1962. One of the few bright spots during the decade of the sixties was completion of the Astoria-Megler Bridge across the Columbia River. Overall, Astoria's declining population reflected the city's troubles. The numbers went from 12,331 in 1950 to 10,244 in 1970—a drop of 16.9 percent.

Contrary to the earlier report, Coe found that the equipment had not been well maintained for many years and required expensive repairs. The addition of four-color printing, to keep up with modern reader expectations, cost $2,000. Still, at the end of 1961, Coe – through stringent cost-saving measure – had increased the cash position of the corporation, cut the accounts receivable by 60 percent, and increased advertising by over $25,000. In addition, the newspaper had a net gain of 400 subscribers during the year. On the other hand, Coe reported that job printing volume was under-performing. The new owners, at the behest of Coe, also decided at their annual meeting in 1961 to change the name of the newspaper to *The Daily Astorian*. Coe was quoted later as saying, "I have never felt the word *Budget* was a descriptive, appropriate or proper name for a newspaper." (*DA*, Nov. 20, 1970)

Michael Forrester, after he became editor, discovered that Coe may have gone a bit overboard in his economy drive at the *DA*. Mike later observed, "The main thing that stood out to me was his [Coe's] frugality to the point of miserliness. I found that what he paid his news staff in the 1960s was astonishingly low. He got by in part by having a workhorse editor, Fred Andrus, who generated huge amounts of newspaper copy and photos and was willing to take a modest salary." (interview, Nov. 9, 2015)

To provide Coe with an incentive to pour his considerable talents into rebuilding the newspaper, the new owners of the A-BPC arranged for him to buy 25 shares of stock held by the heirs of Hattie Brown, long-time bookkeeper for the *AB* and one of the original investors in the purchase of the *Morning Astorian* in 1930. Also, John Dellinger, another minority shareholder, sold his 25 shares, inherited from his father, to Coe. The stockholders of the reorganized A-BPC then elected Coe and J. W. Forrester as directors to enlarge the board to six members. The directors next chose Coe as president; Elsie Aldrich, vice president; Amy Bedford, secretary; Eleanor Forrester, director; J. W. Forrester, treasurer; and Dorothy Engle, chairman of the board. The board also authorized the purchase of a new Ludlow machine and typefaces and approved modernizing the main press to print three-color as well as black and white. They also recorded the need to collect on past due accounts.

Coe struggled for the next two years, replacing worn out equipment and cutting costs. Still, business volume kept declining and the paper continued to lose money. In fact, the last time the paper had shown a profit was in 1956. Finally, in 1964, Coe's efforts began to pay off. Business in Astoria improved and so did the *DA*'s. The corporation made a profit that year and, best of all, was able to pay off all of its outstanding debt except for the amount still owing to the Chessmans for the stock purchase. The latter debt was being retired at the rate of $750 a month. Circulation stabilized at about 6,400 subscribers.

For the rest of the 1960s, Astoria's economy improved and so did the fortunes of the *DA*. Crown-Zellerbach built a pulp mill at Wauna, and the Port of Astoria attracted new business. In Astoria, the city library and Clatsop Community College constructed new buildings. Despite the need to purchase new printing equipment and make repairs to the *DA*'s building, the paper continued to make a profit and circulation rose above 7,000 subscribers. At the annual stockholders and directors meeting in October 1965, the corporation decided to discontinue the *Weekly Astorian*. In 1966, the corporation paid off the Chessman debt—four years early—and the other stockholders allowed Coe to purchase another 22 shares. That year also marked the first time in many years that the corporation paid a dividend to the shareholders. The directors also decided to switch the wire service to the Associated Press from United Press International, which had served the *DA* and its predecessors since 1912.

> **"Your editor is a registered Independent. Political candidates will be judged by their educational backgrounds and intellectual integrities."**
> *J. W. Forrester*

Over in Pendleton, J. W. Forrester began his term as editor of the *EO* in January 1951 by continuing the community-focused editorial stance of Aldrich, his father-in-law, but with a slightly different emphasis. For the first time, the editor of the *EO* was not a Democrat. Forrester declared himself an Independent with a liberal, internationalist slant. As Forrester put it in his first editorial, "Your editor is a registered Independent. His editorial viewpoint is independent. Political candidates will be judged by their educational backgrounds, intellectual integrities and beliefs on the important issues of the day. Their political parties are a minor consideration. But, we must confess, a liberal has an edge over a conservative and an isolationist is not popular around this typewriter." (*EO*, Jan. 16, 1951) He went on to state: "A good newspaper is the voice of its community. This newspaper always will be that. In its news columns both sides of controversial, local issues will be presented. Editorial judgement will be exercised in the light of what is thought to be best for all." (ibid) Like his predecessors he held government officials to account but never with malice.

In another early editorial, Forrester made a point of offering strong support to the local schools. In commenting, for example, on a move in the state legislature to reduce the state's basic school support money, he wrote, in timeless words,

> They [i.e. the legislature] are confusing the problem of education with state budget problems. Each must be treated within its own scope. The state must aid the school districts in every way possible to shoulder their heavy financial loads resulting from the increased costs of education. The load is big now and will be heavier in the future. Certainly, the answer is not to take away from the districts any help the state is giving now. The legislature had best be thinking about providing even more help in the not too distant future. . . . All the citizens of Oregon have an obligation to maintain the best possible schools. . . . The legislature must see to it that state funds take care of at least part of that job. (*EO*, Feb. 6, 1951)

Above all, Forrester believed the *EO* had a duty to report the news so that the public could be well-informed. To him, this principle represented the bedrock of democracy. Forrester wrote, in commenting on a controversial city council meeting, "The newspaper does not make the news; it only reports it. . . . Citizens of this community must know about the deliberations of their elected officials. They cannot attend the meetings of those officials. It therefore is the responsibility of the newspaper to report those deliberations accurately and completely. This, the *East Oregonian* always will do to the best of its ability." (*EO*, Feb. 24, 1951)

In taking over the *EO*, the Forresters brought a wealth of newspaper experience. For five years before returning to the *EO*, he and Eleanor had run the weekly *Coos Bay Harbor*. Before that undertaking, Forrester had done journalism work at Oregon State College and wrote for the *Oregon Journal, The Oregonian, EO*, and the Associated Press prior to World War II. Based on their years in Coos Bay/North Bend, the Forresters thought they were well-prepared to take the helm of the *EO*. As Bud Forrester later explained,

> The experience Eleanor and I had with that weekly newspaper established a pattern that made everything possible thereafter. We learned all the facets of newspapering together and in that process found that we had a superb working relationship. We respected

each other's judgment and learned what to expect of each other under all kinds of circumstances. When we went to Pendleton in 1951 we were completely confident that, together, we could do the job. . . . Together we can do anything involving the production of a newspaper. (memo, Oct. 30, 1974, EOPC Archives)

The advent of the new management at the *EO* came at a time of high anxiety in the nation. The insecurities many felt during the Cold War era—fanned by the Korean War and the anti-Communist demagogy of Senator Joseph McCarthy—led to attacks on civil liberties. Forrester was disturbed by McCarthy's antics and pointed out in editorials that McCarthy was "guilty of insidious attack upon human rights and dignity and decency" and that "McCarthyism is one of the gravest dangers this nation faces today." (*EO*, Jan. 24, 1951) Forrester became especially concerned when some attempted to prevent college students from reading about or discussing communism. The *EO* said, "Our conviction is that a university student is completely capable of weighing all sides of a subject; and that he cannot become a well-rounded product of a university if he doesn't know every side of every subject the university can possibly present to him." (*EO*, Feb. 17, 1951)

Pendleton undertook many civil improvements in the 1950s, reflecting the general prosperity in agriculture and timber processing in the county. Wheat and pea harvests were strong, although price supports for wheat fluctuated unpredictably. The cattle business changed substantially, as feedlot fattening of cattle replaced range feeding. New sawmills sprang up on the fringes of the Blue Mountains and Harris Pine Mills of Pendleton expanded. As a service, transportation, and government center for eastern Oregon, Pendleton benefitted from the region's economic growth. The city's population increased from 11,774 in 1950 to 14,434 in 1960—a 22.6 percent increase.

During the 1950s, Pendleton added civic assets: a new courthouse, high school, National Guard armory, enhanced flood control through levee and river channelization improvements, and even cable television. The Happy Canyon night pageant moved to a new covered grandstand adjacent to the Round-Up grounds, and the Round-Up stadium itself was roofed in 1954. The *EO* supported these civic improvements editorially.

The Forresters, after assuming management of the *EO*, began to put their own stamp on the paper's operations. Recognizing the steady growth in Umatilla County's

Fred Andrus

west end, they opened a news office in Hermiston in 1951. They expanded the women's section in the newspaper. To the Saturday edition, they added a magazine with family and farm news as well as radio and television listings.

In 1957, they installed an Associated Press Wirephoto receiver, which give the *EO* the ability to illustrate world news with pictures taken the same day. Perhaps the biggest change at the paper came when the owners built a new building to house its expanded operations.

The old, two-story, Italianate brick structure built by C. S. Jackson in 1887 at the southeast corner of Main and Emigrant streets had served the *EO* for 68 years. By the mid-1950s, that was no longer the case. To meet its current and future needs, EOPC had a new, one-story building erected on a lot at the northeast corner of Southeast Byers Avenue and Second Street. It was actually built to the *EO*'s specifications by the Raymond family—previous owners of the land on which the new building sat— and leased to the EOPC. Once the new plant was in operation, Forrester could carry out his next goal. As the number of newspapers and the size of editions increased, he sought efficiency through a larger and faster press. He decided on an offset press because of the fine quality of print and photographs it could produce. He told the Goss Company, which had supplied the press the *EO* had been using since 1940, that if they could make such a press, he would buy one. By 1960, the Goss Company had perfected a photo-offset press; and the *EO* became the first daily newspaper west of the Mississippi River to own one. The offset press operated like lithography to chemically transfer (through exposure of photosensitive layers on the plate material) the inked image to paper. The press printing the paper was web fed, employing a continuous roll of paper, and could print 14,000 complete newspapers an hour. It began operation on July 25, 1960.

The new press made the use of color, both in advertising and headlines, more effective. An *EO* color advertisement for the Olympia Brewing Company won a prize as the best multicolor advertisement in the Pacific Northwest in 1960. News photographs continued to be a strong feature of the *EO*, and the next advance after the AP Wirephoto receiver in 1957 was the laser picture receiver installed in 1974. The *EO* was the first newspaper in Oregon to receive one.

The Defense Department in 1969 announced plans to ship nerve gas to the Umatilla Army Depot for long-term storage.

After installing the new press, the *EO* switched to a computer-based printing process called "cold type." This required phasing out the paper's Linotypes, which it had used since the 1890s to produce lines of type in hot lead. As old-style typography gave way to cold type, operators had to learn a new system. The International Typographical Union had represented printers at the *EO* since 1898 and kept their jurisdiction in the short term. During the 1960s, however, retirements and turnover brought new printers who lost interest in the union. Eventually, the union no longer represented a majority of the printers and the union withdrew the charter. Over its long history, the *EO* had transitioned through every major change in the production process of newspapers. Through all these changes, the *EO* and its sister paper, the *DA*, also stood out among the state's daily newspapers in maintaining a job printing department.

While operating the *EO*, the Forresters and Amy Bedford continued the family tradition of involvement in community affairs. As a result, Bud Forrester was named

Mike Forrester

Pendleton's citizen of the year in 1957 and Amy received the honor in 1963. The Forresters had focused on editorial and community development issues, while Bedford had been involved in various cultural activities. Bud Forrester also served many years on the state Board of Higher Education, appointed by Gov. Mark Hatfield.

Pendleton, along with the rest of the nation, experienced the turmoil of the 1960s. Over the course of the decade, while observing the civil rights and racial upheaval and anti-war protests over the Vietnam War on the national level, local folks struggled with issues of city governance, division over the building of a second hospital, and a sex education curriculum in the junior high school. Other communities in the *EO* circulation area had their own controversies, causing civic disturbances. In most cases, the *EO* observed, the troubles resulted from uninvolved citizens: "Sloppy, incompetent city government is something to be ashamed of because it is almost always the result of citizens' apathy." (quote in Macnab, 321)

Perhaps the controversy that brought national issues to the local level in Umatilla County and Oregon involved the plan announced by the Department of Defense in December 1969 to ship nerve gas to the Umatilla Army Depot for long-term storage.

Antiwar sentiment focused on stopping this plan, while residents of the west end of the county feared the loss of jobs if the nerve gas was not accepted. The *EO* editorially asked for tolerance and understanding of those on each side of the argument. In the end, the nerve gas went elsewhere.

The late 1960s and early 1970s marked a major shift in the economic expansion of northern Morrow and western Umatilla counties. The new era represented fulfillment of the earlier vision of river improvements and agricultural development championed for so long by editors Sam Jackson and Ed Aldrich in the pages of the *EO*. They had promoted damming the Columbia River to provide improved navigation and to make economically feasible irrigated agriculture. With the completion of the John Day Dam by the Army Corps of Engineers, both goals were within reach. The dam raised the level of the river and provided cheap power to operate the pumps necessary to lift the water to farmland. Soon, large-scale investment by corporate farmers, using center-pivot irrigation, revolutionized farming on the sandy but rich soil lying along the Columbia in Morrow and Umatilla counties.

> **"The state must aid the school districts in every way possible to shoulder their heavy financial loads."**
>
> *East Oregonian*, **1951**

Potatoes quickly became the first crop to benefit from irrigated agriculture. For example, in 1969, the potato farms in Umatilla County had sales of $2.1 million from 2,800 acres; by 1974, the potato acreage had reached 7,350 worth $11 million in sales. The story was much the same in Morrow County: the potato acreage had climbed from 1,200 in 1970 to 11,720 in 1974. The value increased from $1 million to $17.6 million over the same timeframe. Soon, investors constructed processing plants in the Boardman area to handle the output. By 1975, an estimated $100 million had been invested in growing and processing potatoes. Along with the potato production came the planting of row crops and alfalfa and more processing plants. The downside of all the agricultural development was a drastic decline in the regional water table, limiting future growth unless irrigators used appropriate water conservation methods.

In the late 1960s and early 1970s, surprising changes came to the leadership of the *EO* and *DA*. In 1968, Mike Forrester, son of J. W. Forrester, went to Astoria to edit the *DA*, after longtime editor Fred Andrus retired. The younger Forrester followed the pattern of his father in learning the details of the newspaper business. After growing up in Pendleton, graduating from the University of Oregon in 1960, and serving in the military, he spent several years working on newspapers in Coos Bay and Eugene and for the Associated Press in Los Angeles before taking over the editorial role at the *DA* on January 1, 1969, at the age of 30.

Mike Forrester assumed his editorial responsibilities at an auspicious time at the *DA*. The paper had experienced two solid years of profits, the purchase price of the Chessman ownership had been paid off, and circulation had climbed above 7,600 subscribers. The potential for further growth led the A-BPC stockholders to plan a new building and the purchase of a new printing press. As part of the planning process, the corporation in October 1968 established a separate entity (Astorian Building Company) with a fund of $41,000 taken out of internal savings. Coe then purchased properties in October 1969 on the 900 block of Exchange Street. The Astorian Building Company also borrowed another $19,500 locally. Then, in May 1969 the corporation sold its existing building and land for $31,000 to U.S. Bank and began construction on the new plant with plans drawn up by the Astoria architectural firm of Brown, Brown, and Grider.

To prepare himself, J.W. Forrester enrolled in the American Press Institute seminars at Columbia University.

To complete the financing of the new building and purchase of an offset press, the A-BPC authorized borrowing up to $370,000 from the U. S. Bank with a payback period of 25 years. The A-BPC also considered selling its job printing department to some of its employees but decided instead to operate it as a separate business, called the Astoria Printing Company. In September 1970, the *DA* moved into its new building on the southwest corner of 10th and Exchange streets. At that time, the *DA* began printing with the new offset press, rather than the old hot-metal, letterpress method that it had used since 1892. The new press could produce a 20-page paper with color in one run. After completing the new building, the A-BPC dissolved the Astoria Building Company in October 1970.

In the summer 1973, the owners of the *EO* and *DA* took steps to simplify the management of the two papers and better reflect the value of each business. The first transaction entailed increasing the number of EOPC shares outstanding in order to facilitate a second transaction. The first step made no change in the percentage of ownership; each stockholder received 22 additional shares for each currently owned. The number of shares increased from 376 to 8,648, valued at $125 per share (total value: $1,081,000). The owners of the papers increased the number of shares to make it possible to merge the A-BPC into the EOPC by exchanging the A-BPC stock for shares of the EOPC. The exchange was made on the basis of two shares of EOPC stock for each share of the A-BPC stock. The A-BPC, with 1,372 shares outstanding, had a value of $250 per share (total value: $343,000).

The difference in value of the two corporations reflected the stronger financial condition of the *EO* at the time. The *DA* carried debt of $350,000 against its new plant and building, while the *EO* had a modern plant fully paid for. The *EO*, however, did not own the building where it operated. The A-BPC, moreover, was unprofitable, whereas the *EO* had always made a profit. Consequently, the *EO* could pay dividends, while the *DA* had a restriction on dividends because of its heavy debt load. Finally, the economic outlook appeared more favorable in Pendleton than in Astoria at the time of the merger. Based on these assumptions, the stockholders

In July 1973, both papers announced that the senior Forrester and his son would exchange jobs on August 1. Mike Forrester would move to Pendleton and J. W. Forrester would go to Astoria.

approved the two transactions and the merger was completed on August 1, 1973.

The summer of 1973 also brought other big changes in the management of the Forrester family newspapers. In July 1973, both papers announced that the senior Forrester and his son would exchange jobs on August 1. Mike Forrester would move to Pendleton and J. W. Forrester would go to Astoria. The elder Forrester said at the time, "Each of us is looking forward to the challenge of new interests and responsibilities. Having grown up here, Mike knows this region of the state very well. I have some knowledge of Oregon coastal conditions, having operated a weekly newspaper at North Bend from 1945 to 1950." There was, however, a backstory to this move. Personal family issues played a key role in the decision: Mike's young son had contracted a severe respiratory ailment, and doctors recommended a move to a drier climate. After a family conference on the matter, the job switch seemed the right solution.

When the exchange occurred, both papers appeared to be in a stable condition and in communities with reasonable prospects for future growth. The *EO* had a circulation of 11,500 and the *DA*, about 8,000. The Astoria paper celebrated its 100th anniversary that year, while the Pendleton paper had two more years to go until it reached the same milestone. But on a personal level, the transition for each editor had its own challenges. For J. W. Forrester, when he arrived in Pendleton 22 years before this switch, had found Ed Aldrich a tough act to follow. Over his 42 years at the helm of the *EO*, Aldrich had been a major force in promoting Pendleton and championing the interest of eastern Oregon. J.W. Forrester struggled at first. As he later commented, "I had a helluva time. There were news people and businessmen in Pendleton who'd been there forever—and then in comes this young guy as their paper's editor—and he's a son-in-law to boot!" (*Northwest Magazine*, Dec. 1, 1985: 13, 16, 20)

Forrester persevered, establishing his own editorial persona, and won the respect of the community. When he arrived in Astoria, J. W. Forrester brought a track record of accomplishment, but he still needed to show he understood the unique challenges the North Coast faced.

Mike Forrester, on the other hand, landed in Pendleton with a less established reputation as an editor and community figure. He knew he had a lot to prove in following in the path of his father. The next two decades would pose many trials for both Forresters as they navigated the turbulent newspaper environment for small town dailies during the last third of the twentieth century.

CHAPTER V

Postwar era demands
a different type of grit

"The key to our success is hiring good employees
and taking good care of them"
Amy Bedford, Dec. 1998

The kind of grit that was essential to survival in the early twentieth century – the era of Jackson, Aldrich and Chessman – gave way to a new grit that was needed to survive in the postwar era. The dominant names of this period included J.W. Forrester, Eleanor Forrester and Amy Aldrich Bedford. As the century ended, their children – the third generation of family ownership – would rise, and the fourth generation would make its initial appearance.

The company's fortunes in this period would also be defined by the leadership of top managers who were not members of the family – C.K. Patterson and John S. Perry. As the owning family's most trusted counsels, these men would guide day-to-day corporate affairs. They would also define and analyze the large choices the board faced.

During a time of economic turmoil – the thirty years between 1970 and 2000 – the EOPC went through wrenching economic times and unexpected changes in technology. In the 1970s, an energy crisis and galloping inflation gripped the nation, and in the 1980s recurrent recessions caused havoc. While economic currents buffeted the company, the internet's emergence in the 1990s marked the dawn of the Digital Age for the newspaper business—creating a new kind of challenge.

Innovative technology appeared at the same time difficult traditional business conditions still had to be dealt with. The economy of the communities served by the EOPC's daily papers relied on agriculture and natural resources extraction. These means of livelihood suffered from the vagaries of international markets and rising environmental concerns. Umatilla County—the *East Oregonian*'s home territory—rested its well-being primarily on wheat, cattle, potatoes, and food processing, while Clatsop County—the base of *The Daily Astorian*—depended upon commercial fishing, timber processing, tourism, and transient maritime fabrication and maintenance work at the Port of Astoria. The cycles of inflation and recession that coursed through the era, coupled with emerging environmental concerns, severely tested these natural resource-based activities.

While reporting the challenging economic conditions and promoting potential solutions through numerous editorials, the Forrester and Aldrich family members also provided leadership and financial contributions to important community projects in each of the towns in which they published daily papers.

The *Blue Mountain Eagle* had a storied place in Oregon journalism as the oldest continuously published weekly.

In Astoria, Bud Forrester championed the Columbia River Maritime Museum, serving as its president in 1982 as the museum moved its collection into the new building. Steve Forrester later played a leading role in the revitalization of the Liberty Theater. In Pendleton, Amy Aldrich Bedford was the prime mover in creating the Pendleton River Parkway and the Pendleton Center for the Arts.

The *EO* and *DA* also sponsored journalism scholarships at the University of Oregon and Oregon State University. The most remarkable young person to benefit was Joann Green, who applied for work at the *East Oregonian* while a junior high school student. Green would become executive editor of *The Herald* of Everett, Washington, as well as ombudsman of *The Washington Post*. At Eleanor's memorial service, Green spoke fondly of "the Bud and Eleanor newspaper academy." Celia Currin of Pendleton, another intern, benefitted from a similar apprenticeship and enjoyed a career with Dow Jones.

The Forrester family philosophy that their newspapers should provide both

editorial leadership and personal contribution to community projects is best given by
Bud Forrester in describing the impact of the *EO*:

> In countless ways, The *East Oregonian* and its editors and
> publishers have exerted great influence upon the development of
> so much that is here today. Perhaps the newspaper's proudest
> achievement is the guidance that it leaders provided both editorially
> and as workers on countless projects. . . . A newspaper is an
> institution of great importance to a community. Over more than 40
> years of newspapering I have been impressed with the evidence
> that good newspapers and communities that are good to live in go
> together. A community is fortunate that has a good newspaper
> whose managers are guided by the principle that they are
> custodians of an institution that belongs to its readers and therefore
> must at all times and in all ways act in the best interests of those
> readers. (*EO*, Apr. 17, 1975)

Population trends in Clatsop and Umatilla counties
reflected the struggling economies of the EOPC territory:

	CLATSOP	ASTORIA	UMATILLA	PENDLETON
1970	28,743	10,244	44,923	13,197
1980	32,489	9,996	58,861	14,521
1990	33,301	10,069	59,249	15,142
2000	35,630	9,813	70,548	16,354

For the most part, Pendleton and Astoria showed little growth; and in Astoria's
case, an actual decline in population over the course of the twenty-year period. The
unusual 31 percent uptick in Umatilla County's numbers resulted from the effects of
the explosion of irrigated agriculture and food processing plants in the west end of the
county. The *DA* operated in a much more difficult economic setting than the *EO*, as the
accounting firm of Green and Green noted in a report to the stockholders of the EOPC:

> The economic conditions in Astoria appear to be flat and
> indicative of the operations there. Pendleton on the other hand has
> a good farm economy which would appear may continue into the
> foreseeable future. It is of concern to the writer that it may be
> sometime before there is any turn around in the economic situation
> at Astoria. (EOPC Archives, Sep. 15, 1975)

Amy Aldrich Bedford

Against this challenging economic backdrop, the EOPC newspapers coped as best they could over the next few years. The Forrester family looked for ways to boost advertising sales and circulation, while holding down costs. The goal for corporate net profit was 15 percent, but the highest return during the period reached only 11 percent. In the 1970s, the *EO* consistently turned a small profit, but the *DA* only intermittently accomplished that feat. Overall, though, the EOPC remained profitable. This surplus allowed the corporation to pay dividends, build reserves, and to consider acquisitions.

At a minimum, the corporation had to invest in the maintenance of its facilities and equipment and look critically at purchasing a new press and a larger plant for the *DA*. Most importantly, to modernize the gathering and publishing of the news and advertising copy, the owners of the EOPC had to investigate and ultimately purchase advanced computer systems. By 1979, the EOPC had decided on a plan to add 1,992 square feet to the Astoria building at a cost of about $120,000. In a major, cost-saving decision, the *DA* transitioned to a six-column format in January 1979, and the *EO* made the same move in January 1981.

In Pendleton, the commercial printing shop moved from the *EO* building on S.E. Byers Avenue to another EOPC-owned building on Main Street to make room for a new $280,000 computer system and create more storage space for newsprint. During 1979, the *DA* also bought more land on its block to provide increased parking space, while that same year the EOPC began the process of buying the Pendleton building that it had been leasing since 1956. The company completed the building purchase in March 1980, paying $300,000 over ten years. At the end of the 1970s, the owners of the EOPC also looked at another potential change in operations. At the time, many afternoon daily newspapers began a transition to morning publication, and the *EO* considered such a move in 1979. Mike Forrester, editor of the *EO*, surveyed the paper's readers and found that they overwhelmingly wanted it to stay an afternoon paper, and so it remained.

Throughout the 1970s, the EOPC looked for opportunities to acquire other newspapers. In considering other papers to purchase, the Forresters were guided by several principles. The stockholders and directors placed the highest value on publications that, if they fell into other hands, could endanger the future of one of the dailies they owned. The next criterion concerned whether the publication could enhance one of their existing papers, either because of geographical proximity or the possession of some other feature that would complement an existing paper.

> **"We paid too much and constructed an unrewarding contract with the former owners."**
> *Pat Patterson on the Valley Herald purchase*

The lowest priority would be given to a publication that had no effect on the *DA* or *EO*, either because it lacked proximity or for other reasons. They decided not to buy any weekly that competed with one of their papers, unless a competitor's purchase of such a property would materially endanger one of their own. The stockholders and directors also thought it wise to buy existing newspapers rather than starting new ones. Finally, they had no desire to purchase non-news publications.

During the 1970s, the main properties they eyed included the *Chinook Observer* in Long Beach, Washington, the *Capital Press* in Salem, Oregon, and the *Hermiston Herald* in Hermiston, Oregon. The first acquisition opportunity, though, came in 1978 when the Moreau family, owners of the *Blue Mountain Eagle* in John Day, Oregon,

Eleanor Forrester

indicated a desire to sell. The EOPC moved quickly on this opening, as the paper fit all its key criteria for acquisition. It would nicely compliment the *EO*, was a weekly in a neighboring county (Grant), and consistently earned a profit. The EOPC started the merger process in 1978 and completed the purchase in July 1979, paying $148,000 in cash and stock for the paper. This proved a sound decision, as the *Blue Mountain Eagle* continued earning profits from the start.

With deep roots in Grant County, the *Blue Mountain Eagle* had a storied place in Oregon journalism. It is the oldest continuously published weekly in Oregon, beginning as the *Long Creek Eagle* in Long Creek, Oregon, in 1886, but tracing its origins farther back through a consolidation with another newspaper. In 1898, its editor changed the paper's name to the *Blue Mountain Eagle* and in 1900 moved it to Canyon City. In 1908, the owners of the *Blue Mountain Eagle* sold to the publishers of the *Grant County News*, which could run its ancestry—through several predecessor weeklies—back to 1869. The consolidation took place under the name *Blue Mountain Eagle*. Unfortunately, complete files of the early *Blue Mountain Eagle* and its predecessors are missing as a result of the great fire in Canyon City in 1939.

The early 1980s began a particularly busy and challenging time for the EOPC. While purchasing and integrating the *Blue Mountain Eagle* into the company, the Forresters had to complete raising the funds to pay for the *EO* building, cope with the local effects of a national economic recession, pay for computer systems upgrades, and finish a building expansion at the *DA*. The company also had large financial commitments in Hermiston to expand coverage and discourage competition from entering the west end (of Umatilla County) market, which was growing.

While FY 1979 and 1980 remained profitable for the EOPC, expenses were growing at an unsustainable rate. At a directors' meeting held in December 1981, the minutes recorded that expenses had increased 14 percent instead of the budgeted 8 percent. At their February 1982 meeting, directors registered concern that revenues were down. At the *EO*, in particular, the percent of news to advertising had worsened. In response, the directors discussed freezing salaries and cutting the workweek. The situation had not improved by May, with revenues dropping further and reserves being tapped for regular expenses. For the FY 1981-82, the EOPC eked out a small profit overall, while the *DA* actually lost 6 percent. The directors decided, based on the steadily slowing economy, to cut the yearly dividend in half. Fortunately, the Goss press outside printing (which included such items as catalogs,

In 1987, Pendleton's largest employer, Harris Pine Mills, went bankrupt and the Bon Marche announced its closure in the following year.

advertising inserts, and company newsletters) continued to carry the EOPC; without this work the company would have been in serious financial trouble. Still, the directors optimistically discussed potential acquisitions, completed purchase of a new building to house its operations in Hermiston, and went ahead with buying computer equipment. They could do this because the EOPC had no debt outside of the building purchases and already had set aside money for the new computer system upgrade and the plant addition in Astoria.

In 1983, management of the EOPC underwent a major change. Forrest "Bill" Johnson, general manager of both the corporation and the *EO* since 1970, left to run his own business. In August 1982, Johnson had asked to be named publisher of the *EO*. The major stockholders of the corporation were unwilling to grant his request.

However, they did agree to sell him the commercial printing portion of the *EO* known as EO Master Printers. This operation had been a subsidiary of the *EO* since 1979 and before that a department of the newspaper from its earliest days. Johnson had wanted to buy a newspaper in northern California, but finding none he could afford, negotiated to buy Master Printers instead. Speaking for the other EOPC stockholders, J. W. Forrester commented, "We wish Bill Johnson well. Our association has been mutually, beneficial. The company has enjoyed growth during his time in a top management position." (*EO*, Aug. 1983)

At the time of Johnson's departure from the EOPC, the stockholders decided on a further expansion. The *Valley Herald*, a weekly newspaper in the neighboring town of Milton-Freewater, came on the market. After some hesitation, the stockholders decided to purchase the paper in May 1983 for $201,000. The stockholders—as they noted in the company annual report "decided to take a calculated risk while others were retrenching"—reasoning that this purchase represented a strategic move even though it occurred during a period of flat growth and profits for the EOPC (*EO* Archives, Aug. 27, 1983). They thought it a move that would save in news and advertising costs for the *EO* in the short term and generate a good profit in the long run for the company. In summing up the performance of the EOPC for FY 1982-83, the annual report noted

> The *East Oregonian* remains the strongest of the newspaper operations. The economy of Pendleton and the five counties it serves doesn't feel the sharp ups and downs of many other areas. The effect of the slowed economy has been a flattening trend. We have experienced two years of no growth. As mentioned earlier, we purposely took an aggressive approach during this time to improve our position in what we consider to be our growth-potential areas—Hermiston and Milton-Freewater. While it has cut into our profit picture, we have benefited and will continue to benefit from these moves. (EOPC Archives, Aug. 27, 1983)

While undertaking this major corporate expansion, the directors of the EOPC also decided to pay, in part, for the *DA*'s new front-end computer system (costing $175,000) by borrowing from stockholders Eleanor and Bud Forrester. The loan ran for two years at 10 percent interest—a bargain at that time of high interest rates.

To replace Bill Johnson, who resigned in August 1983, the directors of the EOPC hired Stephen Van Cleve, a newspaperman from California. With 27 years of varied reporting, editorial, and managerial experience, the directors hoped Van Cleve could place the *EO* and EOPC on a firmer financial footing. His immediate examination confirmed that EOPC needed to increase advertising revenue and become less reliant on Goss printing to carry the newspapers. In the spring of 1984, Van Cleve instituted strict budgeting controls for each department at all the company papers and set an ambitious profit goal of 15 percent for all of EOPC's operations. He also looked at reorganizing the production process at the *EO* to break down barriers between the composing room and other departments to gain greater efficiencies. There were hints that perhaps the *EO* was overstaffed. A recent study of 24 papers with circulations similar to that of the *EO*'s showed that the *EO* had the highest annual payroll.

The EOPC annual report for FY 1983, ending on June 30, 1984, brought the sobering news that the *EO* and *Valley Herald* both lost money, while the *DA* and *Blue Mountain Eagle* showed a small profit. Van Cleve's FY report to the stockholders succinctly stated EOPC's situation in the mid-1980s:

> The continued soft economy of the Pacific Northwest—and particularly of the markets we serve—is causing us to take a careful, in-depth look at our operating procedures with a goal of cutting expenses so that we can become more profitable within the financial limitations of our markets. We have been particularly concerned about the diminishing profits from the newspapers themselves. While the company has remained profitable overall because of non-newspaper areas, we have placed the highest priority on returning the newspaper operations to industry-accepted profit levels since they are the base of our operations. As a primary means of gaining more control over our profitability, we instituted budgeting procedures for the new fiscal year which began July 1. . . . The need to tightly control expenses is illustrated by our performance in the fiscal year ended June 30, 1984—while total sales for the four newspapers showed an acceptable gain, our operating profit dipped into the red. We were able to overcome that in other areas so that the overall operation showed a slight increase in profit when compared with last year.

Van Cleve went on to explain:

> As an example of why we must switch more profit emphasis
> to the four newspapers, one need look only at the area of Goss
> printing, which is our most profitable area and is carrying the
> company at this time. At the *East Oregonian*, for instance, almost
> half of our Goss revenue comes from a single customer. If that
> business should fail or move to another printer, we would lose
> overnight a major source of revenue and profit. (General
> Manager's Report, Aug. 25, 1984, EOPC Archives)

As a beginning for the EOPC's turnaround, Van Cleve noted the sale of Master Printers at the *EO* and the elimination of two unprofitable divisions at the *DA*. He also pointed to an increase in circulation at the two dailies and two weeklies at a time when circulation had declined at newspapers across the nation.

Before Van Cleve could see any concrete results from his management initiatives, he abruptly resigned in the fall of 1984. In October, the EOPC hired a man whose managerial leadership would guide the company for over two decades. C. K. "Pat" Patterson came to the EOPC from the *Springfield News*, where he had competed against the powerhouse Eugene *Register-Guard*. In addition to his corporate position, Patterson was general manager of the *EO*. Over time, he would mentor Steve Forrester; and he would structure Kathryn Bedford Brown's orientation to the company.

Patterson's first task involved carrying out the decisions made in 1983 to close out the Employee Stock Ownership Trust (ESOT) and institute a new profit-sharing plan and 401K program. The EOPC had to take out a sizeable bank loan ($1.12 million) to cover the ESOT payouts. At the end of 1984, Patterson could report that while expenses were within budget, income still was not meeting budget across the board.

After a difficult passage during 1984, Patterson noted some room for optimism by the summer of 1985. In his annual report reviewing FY 1984, he observed that the cost containment actions, aggressive sales work, and a pay freeze had resulted in improved results, even though the changes had led to heavy staff turnover. Despite apparent employee instability, he also reported that introduction and implementation of new profit sharing and retirement plans had been well received. As Patterson put

C.K. "Pat" Patterson

it, "there is no reason to be optimistic about Oregon's immediate economic future. . . . There is every reason to believe that your company has now weathered the worst of the economic storms and is prepared to ride out the remaining months or years of slow times. We may even find ways to prosper despite our surrounding economy."

While he believed that the "decisions of 1983/84 and the subsequent changes in your company have begun the process of internal recovery," there remained a major problem in Milton-Freewater. According to Patterson, "the challenge is intense. Our staff there is maintaining operations on a status-quo basis while we search for a new, vigorous, effective leader." He went on to state that the *Valley Herald* "operates . . . under constant threat of losing its largest local ad if prices are increased. Competitors offer the service for less."

Patterson went so far as to advise that if the *Valley Herald* cannot meet operating expenses by the close of FY 1986-87, it might be wise to sell the paper. Finally, he observed generally that constraints on profits were not unique to EOPC, but rather reflected current newspaper industry realities: "We no longer operate alone in our markets. We no longer control supermarket and super drug store ad delivery. Other options exist and limit our flexibility. Those factors then combine with the stable or slumping economy to restrain growth of profits." (Annual Report, Aug. 10, 1985, *EO* Archives)

The last half of the 1980s proved as challenging as the first part of the decade. Even though the EOPC's general manager forecast flat revenue for FY 1986-87, he felt that careful expense control, modest advertising rate increases, and a strong sales push would achieve the corporate profit goal of 9.9 percent. His annual report stated that good management had held down newspaper expenses, while a strong sales effort had improved circulation at all the EOPC papers. The most perplexing situation facing the stockholders and directors involved their ownership of the *Valley Herald*. Patterson frankly summarized the problem: "As you know, we bought a troubled newspaper stumbling under the burden of a split community and poor management. We paid too much and constructed an unrewarding contract with the former owners. . . . Our own efforts at finding capable management were unsuccessful until last year." (*EO* Archives, Aug. 9, 1986) After reviewing the options of selling or folding the *Valley Herald* at a substantial loss, the EOPC stockholders decided to follow Patterson's advice to soldier on with the paper—holding down costs while pushing advertising sales to increase revenue amidst a weak economy.

The 1986 annual meeting of the EOPC also demonstrated the directors' willingness to take calculated risks, even though they seemingly had their hands full with their existing publications. Steve Forrester, the younger son of Bud and Eleanor Forrester and a company stockholder and director, recommended a new publishing venture for the EOPC. This undertaking involved creating a Washington, D. C.-based newsletter, primarily directed at California. While startup funds from the EOPC would be substantial, the potential for profit, based on Steve's analysis of the market, was thought to be strong. In fact, he projected the publication would be self-financing in the third month of operation. Steve would serve as publisher, while the editor would be an experienced newsman he had selected. The directors voted to proceed with newsletter—called "the *California Report*"—with the caveat that the board would review progress in January 1987 and decide by March whether to continue the publication.

The EOPC encountered yet more difficulties during 1987. In Pendleton, two large businesses closed. In the spring, Harris Pine Mills, the town's largest employer, went bankrupt and ceased operations, while later in the year, The Bon Marche department store announced that it would close its Main Street store in January 1988. Even before this dismal news came out, the EOPC had to deal with the fact that its newspapers earned little or no profit and that the company stayed in the black only from its Goss printing. On a more positive note, the EOPC paid off—on January 1, 1987—the debt taken on to pay for the *EO* building, and the *Valley Herald* had begun to make steady progress in improving its financial situation. The *EO* also purchased a mechanical inserter ($55,000) for placing preprints in the newspaper and expanded the production area to accommodate it. The general manager projected that the inserter would save enough in labor costs to pay for itself in three years.

Perhaps the major management change occurred at the end of 1987 when Bud Forrester retired and his son, Steve, took over as the editor of the *DA*. For ten years, Steve had been a Washington correspondent with newspaper clients in Oregon, Washington and Idaho. He also published ˆ*NorthwestLetter*" and hosted a weekly radio show that was heard on Northwest public radio stations.

The Bon's closure had the potential to put a big hole in the *EO*'s advertising revenue. Patterson, the EOPC's general manager, anticipated the loss of 18,000 column inches of camera-ready advertising a year, which would translate into a yearly loss of 425 pages of paper, or an average 5.5 pages a week. He estimated the dollar loss at $100,000. To deal with the situation, Patterson recommended a combination of staff cuts or retirements, a circulation rate increase, newsprint savings from the elimination of the 425 pages previously supported by The Bon, and an

Pat Patterson completed negotiations with the *Chinook Observer* and acquisition took place in the spring of 1988.

aggressive advertising sales campaign. In all, his plan, if successful, would cut expenses and increase revenues amounting to $154,000—covering The Bon loss and any collateral decline caused by it.

Patterson even offered to resign, if the EOPC's directors felt it necessary to further improve the company's bottom line. The directors, after a thorough discussion of the alternatives, chose to follow most of Patterson's advice. They cut personnel, mainly by offering early retirements, increased the *EO*'s circulation rate, and aggressively pushed advertising sales, but did not ask Patterson to resign. In a major move, the directors voted to solicit advertising accounts outside the *EO*'s immediate trading area. Longer than other community newspaper groups, EOPC papers had protected businesses within their market. The long reach of broadcast media had made that

Steve Forrester succeeds his father, J.W. "Bud" Forrester
as editor of *The Daily Astorian* in December 1987

practice anachronistic.

Despite the focus on the *EO*'s troubles, the EOPC directors still looked at new acquisitions. Two prospects appeared ripe for purchase during 1987: the weekly *Chinook Observer* in Long Beach, Washington, and the regional agricultural weekly *Capital Press* in Salem, Oregon. Patterson completed negotiations with the *CO* and acquisition took place in the spring of 1988.

Over time, the *Capital Press* purchase would prove to be enormously significant. The transaction grew from a relationship between J.W. Forrester Jr., and Dewey Rand Jr. Closing the *CP* deal, however, required more time, as the Rand family indicated a reluctance to sell until they completed additional estate planning. While the directors pursued new acquisitions, they decided to divest themselves of the *California Report*. It had finally turned a profit in December 1987, but Steve Forrester's attention was now fully focused on the *DA*; and the newsletter was difficult to manage from a distance. Unable to sell the publication, the directors decided to close it in the summer of 1989.

Another change in the Forrester family's management team occurred when

Jacqueline Brown, Amy Aldrich Bedford's daughter, indicated a desire to return to Pendleton and become involved in the operation of the *EO*. Brown was Mike Forrester's classmate in the Pendleton High School Class of 1956. She was a graduate of Occidental College and raised two daughters in Los Angeles, where she worked as a preschool teacher.

In the summer of 1988, Jacqueline took on the role of corporate personnel and training manager and set about learning the details of the newspaper business, beginning with the circulation and classified departments. She was also a director of the EOPC. In August 1989, the other directors elected her deputy secretary of the EOPC. At the end of the 1980s, the EOPC had survived tumultuous times caused by the rollercoaster economy of the decade. The *DA* now seemed in a stronger financial position, the *VH* had greatly improved its performance, and the *BME* continued its usual strong contribution to the company's profits. Even more remarkably, the *EO* had weathered the flattened advertising market caused by the closure of The Bon Marche department store. In the spring of 1989, the *EO* even reported that it had achieved an average daily circulation of 13,026—one of its best results to date. EOPC General Manager Patterson predicted the positive result that would flow from the purchase of the *CO*:

> **The acquisition of the *Chinook Observer* was a good buy, but certainly not a bargain.**
>
> ***Pat Patterson***

> The acquisition of *Chinook Observer* completes a purchase we had sought for many years. It was a good buy, but certainly not a bargain. . . . Consequently, acquisition costs have a temporary depressing effect on our earnings. After the first three years, that will disappear for the most part. After five years, we'll no doubt be quite pleased with the results. Meanwhile, the purchase secures a printing job which will pay for the acquisition over a fair period of time, roughly 10 years. (Aug. 11, 1988, EOPC Archives)

Management of the EOPC during the 1980s had been equally as tumultuous as the economic situation. The company went through three general managers before stabilizing under Patterson. By the end of the decade, Bud and Eleanor Forrester had

Jacqueline Brown

retired from day-to-day involvement, while sons Mike and Steve became key figures in the company's progress. Each oversaw one of the all-important dailies. Their cousin Jacqueline Brown's involvement in the EOPC and *EO* represented yet another third-generation member willing to play a role in maintaining the family ownership. The first fourth generation member made her appearance during this period. In the summer of 1986, Patterson created an internship for Kathryn Bedford Brown in several departments of the *East Oregonian.*

The early 1990s were a repeat of what the EOPC faced in the previous decade. A national economic recession coupled with sluggish local economies hurt advertising lineage, especially from large retailers, even while circulation held up reasonably well. The national trend of big box advertisers moving away from preprint newspaper inserts to direct mail distribution took its toll on the Goss printing. In short, while the EOPC's newspapers hit revenue targets, expense pressures, a heavy debt load from expansion, and the cost of equipment upgrades raised alarms for managers.

Individually, each newspaper in the EOPC had its own special market environment. Both Astoria and Pendleton experienced challenges from cutbacks in the timber industry and slack retail business. In response, both communities aggressively sought economic development. In Astoria, for example, the best prospects for growth centered on tourism and an increased Coast Guard presence. Pendleton, drawing on its wheat production, attracted a major new employer – Continental Mills, makers of Krusteaz mixes.

For much of the 1990s, the *EO* achieved an all-time high circulation of over 13,000. Population trends in the areas served by the two dailies reflected the prevailing economic situation each faced. Over the course of the decade, Astoria lost 2.5 percent of its population, while Pendleton gained 8 percent. While both counties grew, Umatilla outpaced Clatsop 19 percent to 7 percent.

For the weekly portion of the newspaper operation, the *Blue Mountain Eagle* and *Chinook Observer* achieved solid results. In spite of the decline in timber sales, the economy of Grant County held its own, buoying the *Eagle*, while tourism continued to support the *Observer's* market. Both newspapers remained profitable in the early 1990s.

The company went through three general managers before stabilizing under Pat Patterson.

After gaining ownership of the *Observer*, the EOPC went through two unsuccessful editors. In the next advertisement for the position, Steve Forrester evoked the spirit of John McPhee and said the Pacific County market was worthy of the "kind of newspaper E.B. White would give it." A young Wyoming lawyer turned journalist named Matt Winters convincingly responded to that summons. He would become one of the company's longest tenured non-family publishers.

By 1991, however, the *Valley Herald*, according to general manager Patterson, continued "to be an unsatisfactory property for the company." After almost ten years of ownership, the *VH* finally managed to make a profit; but it faced an uphill struggle in "a stagnant suburban market." The paper faced fierce competition from the *Walla Walla Union-Bulletin* and another advertising publication called the *Buyline*. The *VH's* stable circulation base of 2,000 paid subscribers seemed unlikely to grow. The question Patterson raised was whether to sell the paper. After a careful analysis, Patterson believed that "on balance, at this time, we are probably better off owning than selling the *VH*." (Oct. 31, 1991, EOPC Archives) The directors of the EOPC followed his advice.

Through 1993, however, the *VH* had shown no financial improvement, so the company finally decided to put it up for sale. No buyers could be found and in August 1994, Patterson reported: "We must face facts and close the *Valley Herald*. No buyer has appeared through brokers offering the paper for sale, and no plan we've been able to devise results in a profit. Keeping it as a separate, free-standing newspaper is no longer an option." (Aug. 24, 1994, EOPC Archives) The Board of EOPC voted at its annual meeting in 1994 to accept Patterson's recommendation.

Despite the bad experience with the *VH*, growth at the EOPC occurred with the January 1991 acquisition of Press Publishing Inc., of Salem, Oregon, publishers of the *Capital Press*. Over a 63-year period under the Rand family, the *CP* had established itself as the leading Pacific Northwest agricultural publication. The Rands finally agreed to sell to the EOPC in 1990 after a lengthy negotiation. At the beginning of the new ownership, Dewey Rand Jr. retained the position of publisher at the *CP* and joined the board of the EOPC. At the same time, Michael Forrester became president of Capital Press Publishing Co. —a wholly owned subsidiary of the EOPC. Steve Forrester was named vice president and Jacqueline Brown, secretary/treasurer. Mike also took the title of associate publisher and editor of the *CP*. In assuming his new position with the *CP*, Mike gave up his editorship of the *EO* and moved to Salem, noting, "I and other members of my family are happy to be assuming ownership of the *Capital Press.* . . . When you travel around for the *Capital Press*, you hear quite a chorus of praise for this Northwest paper. . . . We hope to make a good product even better." (CP, Dec. 28, 1990)

At time of the acquisition, Bud Forrester stated: "We feel fortunate to be associated with the *Capital Press*. It is one of the outstanding publications of its kind in the United States. I long have known and admired the Rands. We hope to pursue the course that has made their newspaper so successful." (*CP*, Nov. 16, 1990) Indeed, research on the national farm press market revealed that the *CP* had a unique position in the agri-publishing world: It exhibited both a large paid circulation base and a sizeable classified advertising lineage. Reporting to the EOPC Board, Patterson wrote, "Nowhere else could I discover a farm publication in which classified was even considered important. When combined with the size of its paid circulation, the regional content and longstanding market position, there are simply no comparable publications I could locate." (Patterson to J. W. Forrester and *EO* Board members, May 17, 1987, EOPC Archives).

The *CP* originated in 1928 as the *Hollywood Press*, a community newspaper in north Salem run by A. M. Church, a writer and political gadfly. By 1932, the successful publication had moved to downtown Salem and changed its name to the *Capital Press*. At first, farm news made up a small part of the paper's news content, but agricultural advertising soon became a prominent element. Between 1934 and 1941, the agricultural classified section increased from one to three full pages. By 1958, the *CP* was running an eight-page section of line classified ads. In 1946, insurance agent Dewey Rand and attorney Henry Hazen bought the paper and its commercial printing facility. By 1948, the *CP* focused almost exclusively on Willamette Valley farm and forest news, billing itself as "the farmer's paper." Dewey Rand Jr. joined the paper in 1955 and served as publisher and editor at the time of the sale to the EOPC.

Over 63 years, the Rand family established the Capital Press as the leading agricultural newspaper in the Pacific Northwest.

The acquisition performed well under EOPC ownership, adding solid sales and operating profits from the start. In the short term, though, the purchase depressed EOPC's net profits by increasing expenses and reducing interest earnings from cash taken from savings and invested in the new business. Over the course of the 1990s, the *CP* moved into new territory in northern California and Idaho. Previously, its circulation had been confined to Oregon and Washington. The new owners invested in new presses and production facilities at Salem and expanded the job printing side of the business. By August 1995, Patterson could report that the Capital Press Publishing Company subsidiary was performing above the projections that had guided the acquisition. Sales volume and profits had exceeded expectations over the first five years of ownership. As to the future, he stated, "the potential for growth in both categories remains large, but it is likely to cost more than in the recent past as we stretch the paper's boundaries and strive for increased market penetration." (Aug. 16, 1995, EOPC Archives)

While integrating and growing the business of the new acquisition, EOPC owners responded to the management challenges in its existing newspaper

Dewey Rand Jr.

properties. Replacing Mike Forrester as editor of the *East Oregonian* was Bill Crampton, who came from the newsroom of the *Walla Walla Union-Bulletin*. During Crampton's tenure (1990-1995), he, as well as Steve Forrester in Astoria, would confront the deeply divisive anti-homosexual ballot measures of Lon Mabon and the Oregon Citizens Alliance. Both newspapers' editorial pages strongly opposed measures 9 and 13.

The company continued to invest in new printing and office equipment, front-end production systems, and building remodels. Jacqueline Brown, after training, became its human resources manager and the assistant secretary of the EOPC Board.

After several false starts, management began a corporate newsletter to open better communications among the company's far-flung properties and personnel. Recognizing the need to strengthen the family ownership of the business as a new generation gradually assumed more control, Mike, Steve, and Jacqueline sought advice in 1992 from a consultant, specializing in family-run businesses. The next year, they and Patterson took the Myers-Briggs personality assessment to help better understand each other and improve their personal communications styles. The company directors also amended the by-laws to establish an executive committee to handle pressing matters between quarterly Board meetings.

In another move reflecting the transfer of power from one generation of Forresters to another, Mike became president of the EOPC in August 1994, and J. W. Forrester moved up to the position of chairman of the board. Both Steve and Jacqueline continued as vice presidents, while Eleanor Forrester remained treasurer and Amy Bedford continued serving as secretary.

The addition of the *CP* greatly expanded the work of Patterson. He found a move to Salem essential to oversee both corporate and *CP* operations. This in turn led to a new general manager at the *EO* in 1993. Then, as the EOPC's operations—and the *CP* subsidiary in particular—expanded, Patterson, in 1995, found it necessary to turn over direct management of the *CP* subsidiary. In addition, as part of the restructuring in 1995, the foundering Astorian Printing Company operations were merged with the job printing arm of the *CP*. This move failed to save the Astoria job printing business, which had been in decline for a decade, so it was closed. The EOPC did salvage its profitable tidebook business by transferring it to Capital Press Printing. Eventually, though, even Capital Press Printing—a part of *CP* since 1928— had to be sold in 1998. The print shop had turned out a wide variety of printed products, such as

In the spring of 2000 the EOPC hired Laura Sellers Earl as the company's internet news editor.

brochures, company annual reports, catalogs, and election ballots. But because of the rapid and expensive changes in the printing industry, it made more sense to focus the EOPC's resources on its main business. As Mike Forrester, publisher of *CP,* noted, "we are a newspaper company, and the job printing industry is in constant techno- logical change." (*Shop Talk*, Jul. 1998)

During the last half of the 1990s, the EOPC experienced both stability and carefully orchestrated change. Financially, the corporation remained profitable and regularly contributed to the employee profit-sharing plan. The company also continued its long-standing policy of contributing to charity both through the individual papers and at the corporate level. This remained the case even when newsprint prices soared in the middle of the decade of the 1990s, putting temporary

pressure on profit margins. Overall, the EOPC's daily and weekly newspapers achieved modest circulation gains and stronger advertising growth, even though the newspaper business, in general, experienced severe economic headwinds during the 1990s. The *CP*, in particular, continued to demonstrate success. Between 1990 and 1998, circulation grew from 32,000 to 40,000 subscribers.

The EOPC also added to its newspaper portfolio. In the fall of 1999, the Don Swart family, owners of the weekly *Wallowa County Chieftain* in Enterprise, Oregon, offered to sell its paper to the EOPC. The managers and owners of the EOPC saw a great opportunity in the offer for the northeastern Oregon weekly because it fit nicely within the long-stated corporate strategy, which sought to build a portfolio of regional and strategically connected newspapers. The cluster of northeastern and coastal papers created operational and cost efficiencies, facilitated cross-selling of advertising, and supported expanded internet opportunities. Negotiations proceeded rapidly, and the purchase closed for $1.4 million in March 2000. Rick Swart remained as editor and his wife Cheryl Swart served as advertising manager. The EOPC sold the *Chieftain's* press, printing the paper on the *EO* press in Pendleton.

To meet the growth and technology demands of its newspapers and outside Goss press work, the EOPC had to expand plants and equipment during the late 1990s. The *EO* purchased property for expansion. The weeklies also bought land and invested in new buildings. The *Observer's* need to move, for example, became apparent during winter rains that flooded its rented space, forcing staff to wade through its water-logged office.

With its printing operation gone, the *CP* remodeled its building to gain new space. At the same time, the *EO* built a $200,000 metal structure to store newsprint and increase production space. The *EO* also added a four-color unit to its press, while the *DA* replaced its inserter and expanded its press capacity. In 1998, EOPC directors hired Dario Design—a Boston architectural design firm specializing in newspaper plant design, production, and material handling—to provide planning for future facilities and equipment needs.

Perhaps the biggest change in the EOPC's production of newspapers involved the adoption of computerized pagination in the early 1990s. This process allowed editors to electronically dummy and build news pages with a desktop computer instead of using the time-consuming paste-up method. This transition also eliminated mainframe computers. Once editors finished the page layout on the computer, they sent pages to the printer via an imagesetter. After plating, the pages went to the press. The *DA* began the changeover to electronic production in 1991 and the *EO* followed suit by 1994. Both papers also adopted the Baseview editorial system. By the end of the decade, the weekly papers were able to send their copy to the presses in Astoria and Pendleton electronically, ending the physical transport of pasted-up pages to the daily presses for printing. After printing, a mail truck returned the newspaper bundles to the weeklies for distribution. To keep the EOPC's papers technically up-to-date and competitive through the 1990s, the directors found the additional plant and equipment required an average yearly capital investment ranging between $250,000 and $400,000.

In the spring of 2000, the EOPC also launched an effort to make better use of the internet in disseminating the news. The company named Laura Sellers-Earl as corporate internet news editor. Sellers-Earl had been the *Daily Astorian's* first female managing editor. In her new role, she was charged with helping the weekly papers move stories from their newspapers to their web sites and to work on setting up shared electronic news archives. Sellers mostly worked from her home but traveled to each

This mock-up of *Willamette Week*'s original masthead design was used to sell stock
for the new Portland newspaper in 1973. The East Oregonian Publishing Co.
and the Forrester family were among *Willamette Week*'s original investors.
Steve Forrester became its first managing editor.

It is unusual for old, legacy media to invest in start-ups of iconoclastic media. But EOPC
did that in 1973 – buying stock in the prospective Portland newspaper *Willamette Week*. Steve
Forrester was one of the five principals who started the company. They included Ron Buel,
Ross Hall, Jack Schell and Robert Burtchaell. Forrester would be *WW*'s managing editor; Buel
was publisher.

In addition to the EOPC's and Steve's shares, Amy Aldrich Bedford would purchase
debentures that *WW* offered in the year prior to the newspaper's sale to the Eugene *Register-
Guard*. In 1983, Richard Meeker and Mark Zusman bought *WW* from the *Register-Guard*.

paper to establish relationships and train the news staffs on effective and efficient use of the web as a news gathering tool.

In addition, by the late 1990s, all the EOPC's papers had made their first attempts at creating a web presence for their advertising and news archives. Carl Earl of the *DA* staff and the corporate systems supervisor lead the effort to keep the papers and their staffs computer-literate.

Along with business expansion, the EOPC board of directors instituted several management changes. As J. W. Forrester reduced his board involvement during the 1990s, his sons Mike and Steve stepped up. Steve Forrester added publisher to his title of editor of the *DA* in January 2000, while Mike Forrester took the same steps at the *CP* in August 2000.

A major change came in February 2000 with the death of J. W. Forrester at the age of 86. His death was not anticipated but came suddenly at his Portland residence. On the following day, former U.S. Sen. Maurine Neuberger died, which had special meaning for the Forrester family. Bud had been a professional friend of Maurine's husband Dick, beginning in the 1930s. Dick had appointed Mike Forrester to be a U.S. Senate page in 1955, the first from Oregon in 40 years. Next, Maurine made Steve a Senate page in the fall of 1963.

The family's first outside director was Rob Miller, who joined the *Capital Press* board. Then Tom Brown, a New England publisher, joined the EOPC board.

Forrester's memorial service at Portland's Old Church included eulogies by former Oregon governors Victor Atiyeh and Neil Goldschmidt. Marking Forrester's longtime affinity for jazz, the cabaret pianist Dave Frishberg closed the service with "Bill Bailey, won't you please come home?" A funeral mass was held in Astoria's Grace Episcopal Church.

This passing led Eleanor Forrester and Amy Bedford, in August 2000, to retire as officers but remain on the board, leaving Mike, Steve and Jacqueline as officers. Mike continued as president, Steve as vice president and Jacqueline as secretary-treasurer.

The fourth generation became active in the late 1990s. Jacqueline's daughter, Kathryn Brown, had joined the board as a director in 1997 and subsequently was elected treasurer. Kathryn, a nurse practitioner, decided in 1999, however, to take a two-year leave-of-absence from the board to work for the Peace Corps. She would become a Peace Corps medical officer in the West African country of Togo.

Other board changes occurred during this period, as well. In line with advice from the Austin Family Business Program of Oregon State University, Steve Forrester had proposed the addition of non-family, outside directors. Amy Bedford was reluctant to make that move, saying that, "I just can't see someone else sitting here with us." An alternative was agreed to: adding a non-family director to the Capital Press Publishing Company board. Rob Miller, a Willamette Valley grower, joined the *Capital Press* board in 1999. Following that successful experiment, Tom Brown (no relation to Jacqueline), publisher of *The Monitor* of Concord, New Hampshire, became an EOPC director in 2000. With the addition of outside directors, the family directors felt it necessary to restate the corporate by-laws and alter the director fee structure.

During the turbulent final third of the twentieth century, the EOPC not only survived, it actually grew. It added weekly newspapers and achieved the growth potential of its biggest acquisition—the *CP*. The company continued its tradition of investing in technology and facilities. Most importantly, such investments enabled the EOPC to accomplish the commitment that its papers serve their individual communities by providing the best possible news gathering, advertising medium, and knowledgeable editorial voice.

The daily and weekly newspapers of the EOPC gave evidence of their quality editorial product by annually winning numerous state and regional awards from professional journalism organizations, such as the Pacific Northwest Newspaper Association and the Oregon and Washington Newspaper Publisher's Associations. Surviving as a family enterprise in the Oregon newspaper scene by the late 1980s was in itself something of a feat. As Donald J. Sterling of *The Oregonian* observed in writing about Bud Forrester's career in journalism:

> Half a century ago, every daily in Oregon was a family enterprise. Now there are only four family ownerships among the 20 dailies left in the state: his [Bud Forrester] own in Astoria and Pendleton; that of the Robert W. Chandler family in Bend, Baker and La Grande; the Alton F. Baker family in Eugene; and the John Voorhies family in Grants Pass. All the other dailies belong to out-of-state newspaper groups. (*The Oregonian*, Feb. 12, 1986)

The EOPC, in December 1998, received an award that recognized the family-

Tom Brown presents the *East Oregonian* sponsored "Let 'er Buck" trophy
to the All-Around Champion, Trevor Brazile, at the 2012 Pendleton Round-Up.

owned company's commitment to the fundamental values of solid community
newspaper publishing. It won this recognition from the OSU Austin Family Business
Program. This honor especially cited the company's ability to sustain good
journalism, its dedication to the core values of having quality newspapers, providing
community service, treating employees with respect, and prevailing as a family-owned
operation in a time of big-chain ownership of newspapers.

Speaking for the family, Mike Forrester remarked that "it felt good to be in the
company of other family-owned businesses. Like them, we have grown over the
years because serving our communities and customers has been a high priority." In
addition, Amy Bedford emphasized that the company's employees shared credit for
the award: "The key to our continued success is in hiring good people and taking
good care of them." (*Shop Talk*, Dec. 1998)

THE DAILY ASTORIAN

129th YEAR, No. 52   TUESDAY, SEPTEMBER 11, 2001   50 CENTS

Day of infamy

❑ **World Trade Center towers fall after being struck by two planes**

NEW YORK (AP) — In a horrific sequence of destruction, terrorists hijacked two airliners and crashed them into the World Trade Center in a coordinated series of attacks this morning that brought down the twin 110-story towers. A plane also slammed into the Pentagon, raising fears that the seat of government itself was under attack.

"I have a sense it's a horrendous number of lives lost," Mayor Rudolph Giuliani said. "Right now we have to focus on saving as many lives as possible."

Authorities had been trying to evacuate those who work in the twin towers, but many were thought to have been trapped. About 50,000 people work at the Trade Center. American Airlines said its two aircraft were carrying a total of 156 people.

"This is perhaps the most audacious terrorist attack that's ever taken place in the world," said Chris Yates, an aviation expert at Jane's Transport in London. "It takes a logistics operation from the terror group involved that is second to none. Only a very small handful of terror groups is on that list. ... I would name at the top of the list Osama bin Laden."

President Bush ordered a full-scale investigation to "hunt down the folks who committed this act."

Within the hour, the Pentagon took a direct, devastating hit from an aircraft. The fiery crash collapsed one side of the five-sided structure.

The White House, the Pentagon and the Capitol were evacuated along with other federal buildings in Washington and New York.

Authorities in Washington immediately began deploying troops, including an infantry regiment. The Situation Room at the White House was in full operation. And authorities went on alert from coast to coast, halting all air traffic and tightening security at strategic installations.

"This is the second Pearl Harbor. I don't think that I overstate it," said Sen. Chuck Hagel, R-Neb.

American Airlines identified the planes that crashed into the Trade Center as Flight 11, a Los Angeles-bound jet hijacked after takeoff from Boston with 92 people aboard, and Flight 77, which was seized while carrying 64 people from Washington to Los Angeles.

In Pennsylvania, United Airlines Flight 93, a Boeing 757 en route from Newark, N.J., to San Francisco, crashed about 80 miles southeast of Pittsburgh with 45 people aboard. The fate of those aboard was not immediately known and it was not clear if the crash was related to the disasters elsewhere. In a statement, United said another of its planes, Flight 175, a Boeing 767 bound from Boston to Los Angeles with 65 people on board, also crashed, but it did not say where.

Evacuations were ordered at the United Nations in New York and at the Sears Tower in Chicago. Los Angeles mobilized its anti-terrorism division, and security was intensified around the naval installations in Hampton Roads, Va. Walt Disney World in Orlando, Fla., was evacuated.

At the World Trade Center, "everyone was screaming, crying, running, cops, people, firefighters, everyone," said Mike Smith, a fire marshal. "It's like a war zone."

"I just saw the building I work in come down," said businessman Gabriel Ioan, shaking in shock outside City Hall, a cloud of smoke and ash from the World Trade Center behind him.

Nearby a crowd mobbed a man on a pay phone, screaming at him to get off the phone so that they could call relatives. Dust and dirt flew everywhere. Ash was 2 to 3 inches deep in places. People wandered dazed and terrified.

The planes blasted fiery, gaping holes in the upper floors of the twin towers. A witness said he saw bodies falling and people jumping out. About an hour later, the southern tower collapsed with a roar and a huge cloud of smoke; the other tower fell about a half-hour after that, covering lower Manhattan in heaps of gray rubble and broken glass. Firefighters trapped in the rubble radioed for help.

"Today we've had a national tragedy," Bush said in Sarasota, Fla. "Two airplanes have crashed into the World Trade Center in an apparent terrorist attack on our country." He said he would be returning immediately to Washington.

The crashes at the World Trade Center happened minutes apart beginning just before 9 a.m.

See ATTACK, Page 14

One of the towers of the World Trade Center in New York collapses in this image taken from television. Planes crashed into the upper floors of both World Trade Center towers minutes apart today.   AP/ABC

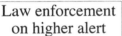

Law enforcement on higher alert

Local emergency responders were wary, but proceeding mostly according to routine in light of the attack on the World Trade Center and Pentagon today.

Clatsop County Sheriff John Raichl said that local personnel were called in at 7 a.m. to activate Astoria's Emergency Operations Center, but that otherwise all county operations were being kept as routine and normal as possible.

See LOCAL, Page 9

AP/ABC via APTN

A ball of fire explodes from one of the towers at the World Trade Center in New York after a plane crashed into it in this image taken from television.

SUZANNE PLUNKETT — Associated Press

People run from the collapse of one of teh World Trade Center towers today.

CHAPTER VI

Existential challenge arrives with the Millennium

"We know that a hallmark of healthy family-owned businesses is that they plan ahead for the retirements of key family members."
Kathryn B. Brown

Sixteen tumultuous years began the millennium at the EOPC – testing the very survival of the company. Second-generation owners dwindled while members of the fourth generation became more involved. This period would be marked by the vision of a new chief operating officer. At the close of this period, the company would hire its first female chief operating officer and its first female publisher of *The Daily Astorian.*

The owners continued to embrace the concept of having outside, non-family directors on the board. With the advance of the digital age, the family stockholders' management and investment decisions embraced a duality that included older print technology and the new publishing technology. During this new era, the owners continued to make strategic purchases of other newspaper properties that expanded the reach of the EOPC. The family owners also continued to personally participate in projects important in the cultural life of their communities.

During these first decades of the new century, the EOPC underwent major management changes, dealt with the worst economic recession since the Great Depression, absorbed new acquisitions, financed major press and building upgrades, weathered declining print circulation and advertising, tried to figure out how best to use the internet, and managed succession to the next generation. All of this happened within the context of communities along Oregon's northwest coast and eastern region that struggled to find secure footing as their natural resource-based economies contracted. The timber industry of Wallowa and Grant counties declined because of environmental and supply pressures, while the communities of northwest Oregon and southwest Washington grew evermore dependent on seasonal tourism and retirees. Agriculture provided a solid base for Umatilla County, but it was not an economic growth activity, except for food processing in the county's west end.

**The population statistics for the counties and major towns
in the EOPC territory support this regional description:**

	CLATSOP	ASTORIA	UMATILLA	PENDLETON
2000	35,630	9,813	70,548	16,354
2010	37,039	9,477	75,887	16,612

Clatsop County's inhabitants increased by only 4 percent while Umatilla's grew by 7.6 percent. Astoria actually lost population, while Pendleton only managed a small increase.

In February 2000, the EOPC lost its long-time head when J. W. Forrester died at the age of 86. In a journalism career that spanned more than a half century, Forrester left a lasting contribution to the well-being of the communities his company's newspapers served. The passing of Bud Forrester brought numerous expressions of loss across the spectrum of politics and journalism. Remembering Forrester, Doug Onyon, former copy desk chief at the *DA,* said: "I will always remember his generosity of praise, calm and steady direction and passion not only for what was right in journalism but for what was right in all of life." (*Shoptalk,* Mar. 2000) Duncan Law, retired director of the Oregon State University Seafood Laboratory in Astoria, observed that "the one thing that set Bud apart from many other newsmen was the deep belief in his own credo: that the editor of a community newspaper should not sit at his typewriter and preach. He must be active in community problems and solving them." (*Shoptalk*, Mar. 2000).

Perhaps his sons best captured his essential qualities as a journalist. Steve wrote, "As a journalist he did not take a quiet or safe course," while Mike noted, "In a time when the news media come under heavy criticism for bias, negativity and sensationalism, my dad's papers sought to be supportive and encouraging of their communities. And he believed with all his energy that a newspaper is a citizen of its community." (*Shoptalk*, Mar. 2000) Summing up Forrester's journalistic contributions, retired Congressman Wendell Wyatt said: "I've always admired his calm analysis of each day's news. He was a man on top of almost every issue." (*East Oregonian*, Feb. 23, 2000)

At the time of Bud Forrester's death, the EOPC directors had decided to buy the *Wallowa County Chieftain*, a weekly newspaper published in the northeast Oregon town of Enterprise. The effective date of the merger had been set for March 1, 2000. The purchase of the *WCC* represented a strategic addition to the EOPC fleet of community papers. The *WCC* had been a solid, respected part of Wallowa County since 1884. With a circulation of about 4,100, it had been published by the same family (Coffin-Swart) since 1941. The new plan of operation called for the existing publisher, Rick Swart, and the advertising manager, Cheryl Swart, to remain in their jobs at the *Chieftain* in Enterprise, while printing shifted from the *Chieftain* office to the presses of the *EO* in Pendleton. The move also gave the *WCC* full-color capabilities—something highly desirable but currently unavailable to the paper.

The company lost its longtime head when J.W. Forrester died in February 2000.

To oversee the EOPC's growing eastern Oregon operation, encompassing daily and weekly newspapers and free advertising publications, the company named *EO* publisher Mark Garber as its eastern regional manager. Publisher since March 1997, Garber would oversee the *EO* (daily circulation of 12,000), the *WCC* (weekly circulation, 4,100), the *BME* (weekly circulation, 3,900), the *Eastern Oregon Real Estate Guide* (a free publication with a monthly circulation of about 22,000), all of the publications' internet sites, and commercial printing. The EOPC now had the ability to sell various combinations of print and online advertising at a discount across eastern Oregon. Garber reported to corporate general manager Pat Patterson.

Taking advantage of the EOPC resources, the *Chieftain* quickly adopted complete pagination and electronic transfer to the *EO* press. It reached this milestone one year after joining the EOPC. A lot of hurdles had to be overcome as the *WCC* moved from the old "cut and paste" method to converting the PC-based Adobe Pagemaker files into PDF files so that they could be processed on the Macintosh computers in the *EO* office. Much debugging and re-transmitting occurred while the staffs at each end of the production process worked out the kinks. The key to ultimate success came with the introduction of high speed DSL connection in Wallowa County. That reduced the time necessary to send a 5-megabyte file from 30 minutes to about 2 minutes. Now, for the first time the *Chieftain* could transfer an edition faster electronically than it could by carrying hard copies of pages over the mountains by car to Pendleton. With the move to pagination, the *Chieftain* staff also carried out a redesign in modular format with a new flag. The end product was a higher-quality, more reader-friendly paper.

The company added a Sunday edition to the *East Oregonian*, beginning September 3, 2000.

At their May 2000 board meeting, the EOPC directors made a major commitment of resources to the *EO*. After seeing the results of a readers' survey, they took the plunge and voted to launch a Sunday edition of the *EO*, beginning on September 3, 2000. Existing subscribers indicated in overwhelming numbers that not only would they read a Sunday *EO*, they also were willing to pay an additional 50 cents a week for it. In addition, the survey indicated that non-subscribers would also read a Sunday paper, generating additional single-copy sales. Further surveying showed similar strong endorsement for a Sunday paper in Wallowa and Grant counties. In all, the survey takers had queried 1,100 in eastern Oregon about the need for a Sunday paper. As Board President Mike Forrester stated, "We see the opportunity for an Eastern Oregon Sunday paper that provides timely coverage of sports and news for the region. Northeastern Oregon has a distinctive character. An

Eastern Oregon Sunday paper can be in closer touch with the people and activities of the region because the news is gathered in Eastern Oregon and printed in Eastern Oregon." (*Shoptalk*, Jun. 2000)

To put out the Sunday paper, the *EO* added ten full-and part-time staffers. In the fall of 2000, the newspaper had 114 full and part-time employees. In addition, the writers at the *WCC* and *BME* also contributed to the Sunday edition. Richard Hensley, editor of the *EO*, sought a balance of coverage. Along with state, national, and international news, he stated, "Our goal will be to provide as much local news and sports as possible." (*Shoptalk*, Sept. 2000) The Sunday edition provided coverage on travel, lifestyles, business, and the stock market. The real estate section highlighted unique homes in the region, along with house plans and decorating ideas. Steve Brown (no relation to Jacqueline), the Sunday editor, also designed and implemented an expanded commentary section, presenting a variety of viewpoints. Over time, the *EO* continued to adjust the content of the Sunday edition, primarily building up regional sports coverage. Other additions included more local business news and a local "teen scene."

No sooner had the *EO* successfully launched its Sunday edition that it lost its publisher of four years. In May 2001, Mark Garber left to become vice president of the Pamplin Media Group of 18 community newspapers centered in Portland. In announcing his departure, Mike Forrester noted that Garber had done fine work during a challenging time at the *EO*:

> Mark coordinated the efforts of all company staff in Eastern Oregon to introduce a popular, well-received and regional Sunday paper. In Umatilla County, he has ensured a strong *EO* presence out of both the Pendleton and Hermiston offices. He oversaw an addition to the rear of the newspaper's plant in Pendleton, installation of press units and general expansion of *EO* business in Eastern Oregon—all the while maintaining high quality of product. (*Shoptalk*, June 2001)

In fact, at the time, EOPC papers were demonstrating their high quality of journalism by winning awards from the Oregon Newspaper Publisher Association. At its annual meeting in the summer of 2001, the Association named both the *DA* and *EO* the best daily newspapers in their size class, while presenting the *BME* with four awards in its size category. For the *DA*, the general excellence award was the third in a row.

While the *EO* introduced its Sunday edition and the EOPC absorbed the *WCC*, other company newspapers during 2000-2001 made plant upgrades and editorial changes to meet the needs of readers. The improvements included two stacked Goss Community press units and replacement of other components, which allowed more efficient use of color and faster production of papers at the *DA*. These changes to the 30-year-old press cost over $200,000. As Steve Forrester, publisher of the *DA*, noted at the time, "We're pleased to make this major investment in order to extend and improve our service to readers and to our commercial printing customers. The improvements will allow us to do these essential jobs better and faster." (*Shoptalk*, May 2001).

Over at the *CP*, the news team boosted news coverage in its four regular editions. The front five pages of the paper and some inside pages now carried news of interest directed at readers in both western and eastern Washington and Oregon editions, as well as those for California, and Idaho. Previously, only the first pages had been zoned. These changes aimed at overcoming criticism from California and Idaho readers complaining that the *CP* was an "Oregon paper." As General Manager Mike O'Brien recognized, "While ads do provide reader value, we won't capture the ad market until we have the circulation to deliver results." (*Shoptalk*, May 2001) To facilitate these adjustments at the *CP*, the EOPC directors had voted in the previous year to take out a mortgage on the *CP* building in Salem to pay for necessary remodeling and expansion.

Just as the work on the *CP* building got underway, the EOPC completed construction of an entirely new structure for the *CO* in Long Beach, Washington, in April 2000. In Pendleton, meanwhile, the company finished buying the entire block holding the *EO* building in preparation for eventually remodeling and expanding the structure built in 1956. In the short term, directors authorized spending $200,000 to construct a metal building to expand production space at the *EO*.

While the launch of the *EO* Sunday edition was generally well-received with an average circulation of 12,420 (one thousand more than the daily) in the first few months, the venture hurt the newspaper's bottom line. The launch expenses were greater than expected and revenue was lower than projected. In fact, advertising revenue was declining gradually across all company papers during that time. The board decided to stay the course and responded with staff and production cost cuts. In fact, a national economic recession and several years of declining farm prices during the early years of the decade created a challenging business environment for the various EOPC newspapers. For example, during the 2000-2001 period, EOPC profits declined 38.7 percent and circulation slid at all of the company papers except the *CP*. At the same time, an unanticipated source of pressure on circulation soon became evident: A mobile society was gaining access to new sources of information through the internet. In addition, illiteracy and English-as-a-second-language among a growing minority sector of the population made it difficult to reach new readers. Growing time demands on two-worker households and just plain apathy all took their toll on readership, as well. One study, cited in the EOPC in-house newsletter, claimed that nationwide "newspaper penetration of households has been declining every year for the past 25 years. Readership, which was 78 percent of adults 25 years ago, now is in the 50 percent range and steadily falling. Thirty years ago, 67 percent of people in the 35-and-under age group said they read a newspaper every day. Now that percentage is below 20 percent." (*Shoptalk*, May 2001).

In the fight to build circulation, EOPC's newspapers carried out a concerted campaign to capture readers' interests, calling the effort "It's the Reader." Mike Forrester, publisher of the *CP* and president of the company, led the charge, urging editors and reporters to renew their focus on their community's news and make themselves more accessible to the public by publishing their phone numbers and email addresses with their bylines. He also suggested more surveys of readers' interests, soliciting news tips from readers, enhancing customer service, and—above all— remembering the basics of effective journalism. As Forrester succinctly put it,

> It is important that all of us on the EOPC newspapers keep in touch with our communities and readers on a continuing basis. A newspaper is in most cases the prime medium of communication for a community. The extent to which a newspaper staff keeps its fingers on the pulse of the community will determine how effective it is. It is not necessary for us on these papers to love our communities—it is necessary that we understand that the newspaper is produced for thousands of people who do care about their communities. (*Shoptalk*, Sept. 2001)

The EOPC directors took other steps to keep the company abreast of media trends, such as adding outside directors to the EOPC board. Family board members also attended seminars and workshops run by Oregon State University's Austin Family Business Program to gain insights into successfully run, family-owned businesses.

The essence of the new university-based business literature held that family owners must operate in a professional, dispassionate manner, not allowing family sentiment to override businesslike judgment. That ethos became poignant for the Forresters and Amy Bedford when the family realized that Jacqueline Brown suffered from alcoholism. Following a family intervention in 1994, Brown went to a residential treatment program for women outside Seattle. In early 2006, following a second intervention, she attended another residential treatment program. When that recovery was not successful, the family took the difficult step of having Brown resign as the company's human resources director. Brown died an untimely death in 2009, at the age of 70.

After Tom Brown had served three years on the EOPC board in 2000, Lucy Mohl was elected in 2003. Mohl had extensive experience in television, print, and internet commentary and news. At the time of joining the board, she was programming director at Real Networks in Seattle, a leader in internet media delivery. Meanwhile, in 2001 Tom Beechinor, a Walla Walla, Washington, farmer joined, Rob Miller on the *CP* board.

In spite of economic headwinds, the EOPC continued to invest in posting content of its print papers to internet editions. Many community newspapers reported that big box retailers had cut back on advertising as online sites created advertising competition. EOPC papers were determined to meet this with their own enhanced internet presence and by continuing to enhance the print product through color and improved local content. Despite the financial pressure from ever-increasing employee health care expenses and declining advertising revenue, the EOPC maintained its capital expense budget at a healthy level.

In November 2002, a national survey of 100 representative newspapers from small dailies to major metropolitan papers with feedback from 37,000 readers and non-readers confirmed for the EOPC management what their own experience indicated. Paid circulation was in decline and many readers thought what they saw in their local paper only "seemed to repeat what they have already heard on other media and is not worth the time to page through and find news that may be of interest to them." (*Shoptalk*, Nov. 2002) In response to these finding, the EOPC editors sought to reenergize their papers' commitment to reporting local news and emphasizing putting the reader and customer first. It was a back to basics approach coupled with a clear sense of purpose.

Against this backdrop, the EOPC made management changes, reflecting the need to address succession at the top. During 2003, Mike Forrester first stepped down from his role as publisher and editor of the *CP* and then chose to retire as president of the EOPC. At the company's annual board meeting in August 2003, the board of directors elected Steve Forrester president and chief executive officer. Mike became chairman of the board. Also, during 2003, Kathryn Brown, the daughter of Jacqueline Brown and a board member, began to take a more active role in the company. Drawing on her background in the health care profession, she developed a health care directory for the internet site of each EOPC newspaper and began a weekly health column for the company newspapers.

EOPC management aggressively pursued opportunities and challenges presented by the internet. At a company-wide offsite meeting of key players in the summer of 2003, Pat Patterson, EOPC general manager, reminded the group that it was not cost-free to gather the news and distribute it and therefore each paper had to find a way to earn a profit on its internet product. As then *Chieftain* Editor Rick Swart noted, "The internet represents a huge opportunity for us to increase readership, grow revenue and build brand." All of this focus on the future occurred just as the EOPC marked a hundred years since Ed Aldrich arrived in Pendleton to work for the *EO*. Over time, as Aldrich became editor and part owner, he kept and strengthened the paper's commitment to community betterment. As Steve Forrester observed, "The kind of entrepreneurial community building that E. B. Aldrich practiced is

Tom Brown became the company's first non-family director. He was shortly joined by Lucy Mohl.

not what you find in most newspapers that are owned by a company that is publicly traded or one with a corporate headquarters in a faraway city." (*Shoptalk*, Dec. 2003).

In 2004, the EOPC dealt with two major decisions that had long-term consequences. First, the directors had to deal with the *EO*'s building. The structure, built in 1956, was beginning to show its age; and the original layout impaired efficient printing operations in the new age of computerized production. In addition, the directors had to decide if such a major investment was wise in a part of the state that had limited future economic growth potential. Second, Pat Patterson, the long-time company general manager, announced his decision to retire in 2005. Both decisions had to be made against the backdrop of a difficult economic environment in the newspaper business. While general economic conditions were showing gradual

Kathryn B. Brown

improvement during the 2004-2005 period, a severe recession continued in the agricultural sector, forcing consolidation of farms and agricultural firms. This situation reduced subscribers and advertisers for the *CP*, cutting into the profits of the most economically successful portion of the EOPC.

After considering various options proposed by Gail Sargent, a Hermiston-based architect, the directors decided to proceed with remodeling the existing 16,000 square feet of the *EO* building and add 7,300 square feet of new space at a cost of approximately $2 million. The plans called for unifying the new and existing portions of the structure with an attractive brick exterior. The directors assumed this major financial commitment at the same time that other company-wide capital investments in equipment, plant, and personnel had to be pursued to address normal business needs and enhance its internet presence. As President Steve Forrester stated on behalf of the board, "Our company's investment in a new building for the *East Oregonian* represents our family's commitment to the future of Pendleton and the larger region the newspaper serves." (*Shoptalk*, Mar. 2005)

Patterson in 2004 made a promotion that would assume more significance in the years ahead. He named Marissa Williams, who was an editorial assistant at the *Blue Mountain Eagle*, the paper's general manager. Eventually, she would become the *Eagle*'s publisher as well as the *Chieftain*'s publisher. And in 2016, Williams became the company's regional advertising director, with revenue responsibilities for all the eastside newspapers.

In the midst of significant management changes and an expensive building expansion at the *EO*, the EOPC community newspapers launched a major journalistic feat during 2005-06 by running a cross-paper series on global warming. The brainchild of the *DA* publisher and editor, Steve Forrester, the articles focused on how climate change would affect the Pacific Northwest readers' lives and livelihoods. Steve's plan was to use each of the company's newspapers to contribute a unique, personalized perspective to the series. Forrester saw this as an opportunity to pool the company's journalistic resources to produce a compelling, original product for both the print and internet part of the business. As he stated in July 2005, "We want to create a series of articles that will be widely read and will bring our papers new stature." (*Shoptalk*, July 2005)

Steve Forrester succeeded Mike Forrester as president in 2003, and Kathryn Brown became a more active owner.

Preparation for the series began in August 2005, when editors and other representatives from all six newspapers met to establish a focus and assign topics for coverage. This series was not to be yet another debate on whether or not global climate change was real or which industries or nations were to blame for accelerating the effects of change. Rather, the articles ambitiously looked at the impacts on agriculture, the ocean fisheries and the Columbia River Estuary, forests, recreation, tourism, public health, and population patterns throughout the region covered by the company's papers.

Kathryn Brown, EOPC health writer and company director, noted that each part of the series included cameos of local scientists, meterologists, farmers, foresters and marine biologists, who spoke about their conclusion that climate change was coming. As she wrote, "Climate change is likely to be the most important issue of the 21st century, globally as well as for the Pacific Northwest." (*Shoptalk*, Sept. 2005) Since weather impacts crops, farmers were expected to be especially interested in the stories related to climate trends. Thus, the *CP* contributed heavily to the series. The *DA* and *CO* focused on climate change effects on the ocean and mouth of the Columbia River. The *EO, BME,* and *WCC* concentrated on how climate change might affect water availability, forest management, cattle ranching, dryland agriculture, recreation, and tourism. Coverage would also include what people were doing to address greenhouse gases and prevent further damage.

Steve Forrester designated Patrick Webb, managing editor of the *DA*, to oversee the production of the series. Webb assembled the articles, profiles, photos, and graphics into a package that each paper then published, whether in part or as a whole. After almost a year of arduous work by reporters and editors, the series began running in March and April 2006 in the six EOPC papers and on the company's internet sites. At the time, Webb proudly stated, "It was great to see all of us work together on a common goal." (*Shoptalk*, May 2006)

The daily papers ran the material as a three-day series, while the weeklies selected the most relevant articles for a one-day presentation or occasional weekly examination of specific topics. Subsequent installments ran in September of that year. The second installment focused on climate change's effects on agriculture and fisheries. A logo designed by a graphic designer at the *EO*, featuring the globe in the form of a water droplet ("Earthdrop") helped tie the series' stories and photos together. In all, a total of 22 writers, 7 photographers, 7 editors, 6 page designers, and 2 logo creators from all six EOPC newspapers contributed to the series.

Steve Brown at the *CP* reflected on how difficult the series had been to produce, since it had to reach such a broad audience: "It is interesting trying to cover a fairly controversial subject for such a varied audience. Trying to balance the gloom-and-doom crowd and the passing-phase crowd is like trying to balance pumpkin pie and dark ale. Some things just don't work together!" (*Shoptalk*, Nov. 2006) In spite of the inherent difficulties in exploring such a complex and controversial subject, the climate change series received widespread praise among the environmental, scientific, and government agencies involved in the issues raised by global warming. Typical of such comments, Warren Shoemaker, of Oregon Global Warming Action Network, wrote, "This will help raise concern among the farming community, the people who stand to be most impacted by climate change. It's also excellent educational material to help others understand that the impacts are already noticeable and that we must implement some policies to speed the transition away from fossil fuels." (*Shoptalk*, Nov. 2006) Brent Searle

All EOPC newspapers contributed to a 2006 year-long series on climate change, which used this logo. The series gained national recognition.

of the Oregon Department of Agriculture stated that the articles provided "a needed introduction into the topic as most of agriculture isn't really tuned into this and there is a still a lot of questions about the politics and science." (*Shoptalk*, Nov. 2006)

Ultimate confirmation of the EOPC's climate change series' excellence came when the Metcalf Institute for Marine and Environmental Reporting at the University of Rhode Island awarded it Special Merit in the competition for the prestigious Grantham Prize for Excellence in Reporting on the Environment. According to the prize jurors, the packaging of articles "represented an extraordinary effort on the part of a group of small newspapers in the Pacific Northwest. The result is sophisticated, compelling journalism, extraordinary for publications of this size and scope. . . . These journalists gave their readers a new connection with the problem of climate change, and new motivation to act to mitigate it." (*Shoptalk*, July 2007). Juror David Boardman, who was executive editor of The *Seattle Times*, noted the difficulty of a group of such small newspapers producing a series of this scope.

While producing its part of the climate change series, the *EO* staff had to accommodate the inconvenience of the remodel and expansion of their building. Work got underway in May 2005. During the first phase, new construction at the east end of the block provided space for the news staff, a camera-plate room for pre-press operations, a locker room, lunch room, and a large-group meeting area. The second phase altered the "back shop" of the existing building to include a business office, mechanical and packaging department, and an expanded fireproof vault for the

John Perry

newspaper morgue. The third phase remodeled the front office and placed the new brick exterior around the entire structure.

John Perry's 12 years of leadership begin

As work began on the *EO* building, the EOPC concluded its search for a chief operating officer, as the position was renamed. The company directors chose John S. Perry, a 32-year veteran newspaperman, to succeed Pat Patterson on June 1, 2005. Perry's most recent job was as executive vice president of *King County Journal* (Washington) newspapers. A family-owned newspaper company like the EOPC, it published several weekly and twice-a-month papers, as well as running a sizable commercial printing business. In the course of his newspaper career, Perry started on the copy desk and worked as a reporter for the *EO* in 1976-78. As he later recounted, Perry found the EOPC job attractive because of the owners' commitment to community journalism and openness to "new ideas and innovation." He continued, "Steve (Forrester) made it very clear that he was handing me the keys to the car. That was very clear, you know, you run the day-to-day business." (Interview, Feb. 13, 2017)

While based at the *CP* in Salem, Perry planned regular visits to the EOPC's far-flung papers, providing hands-on leadership and direction. Upon taking over as COO, Perry acknowledged, "We are all aware of the challenges we face: competition from other media and for people. I get excited by challenges like that. Technology will help us. We have to be nimble enough to deliver news and advertising in whatever form people want, and deliver news that can't be gotten anywhere else." (*Shoptalk*, June 2005)

Perry took over management of the EOPC at a time of general advancement. Directors announced at the annual meeting in August 2005 that the company's financial performance had improved over the previous year, with advertising revenue up 3.5 percent, circulation at the two dailies up 2 percent, over-all newspaper profit up year-over-year, and internet sales up by 4 percent—especially at the *CP*. A decline in health-care claims and expense controls by managers had helped the bottom line, as well. As a result of the impressive financial results, the directors announced a profit-sharing contribution equaling 3.8 percent of pay, which was deposited into each employee's 401(k) plan. The general excellence of the company's journalism was reflected by its various papers winning numerous Oregon Newspaper Publishers Association awards that year. Still, Perry cautioned that many challenges lay ahead. All three weekly papers suffered declines in circulation and two of them needed new editors. In addition, the *CP* had to find ways to deal with slowing growth from the consolidation of agricultural equipment firms and farms.

Succeeding Pat Patterson, John Perry began his 12 years as chief operating officer.

Recognizing how the company had grown with six newspapers and more than 200 employees located in four states, Perry convinced the EOPC directors to hire a full-time human resources manager. As he later stated, "The person we hired was responsible for keeping the company in compliance with federal and state employment rules, a rapidly changing and litigious area of law. A human resources professional helped us recruit talent and foster a positive work environment." (Interview, Feb. 13, 2017) Taking over many tasks previously handled by members of the corporate accounting staff in Pendleton, the new human resources manager would be located in Salem, reporting to Perry. In the following year, EOPC named Ginger Anderson (now Ginger Wing) the

EO Media Group confronts the digital terrain

For a group of small newspapers, EO Media Group entered the field of digital publishing early. On July 30, 1996, *The Daily Astorian*'s website launched. Two days later, there was a blurb at the bottom of the Business page announcing that the *Astorian* was "on line" and touting the convenience of submitting letters, subscribing or giving feedback. Visitors were promised stories from the front page, meeting agendas, fair results and visitor information. The audience was probably in the teens.

The first of the East Oregonian Publishing Co.'s sites, DailyAstorian.com, was part hobby and all experiment – a way for Systems Manager Carl Earl and Managing Editor Laura Sellers-Earl to test this new medium. In 1998, the *East Oregonian* went online.

In 2002, the websites began the transition from hand-coded html pages to software hosting companies. In the years since, the hosting software has changed. The team now led by Director of Digital Services Crindalyn Lyster includes a products designer, digital support specialist and a digital ad person. Each newspaper does it's own web posting.

From one fledgling site, EOMG has grown to about 15. It also offers e-editions, mobile sites, email newsletters and, a full range of social media options.

CP office manager, as the company's assistant for human resources. At the time of her promotion, Perry noted that "Ginger has a solid grasp of employment law, and she works well with managers and employees alike." (*Shoptalk*, Oct. 2006) In time, Wing would become the company's director of human resources and a member of the corporate leadership team.

Amidst the challenges of overseeing the *DA* and EOPC, Steve Forrester also found time to help spearhead a major Astoria community improvement project. Since 1992, he had led the non-profit Astoria group, Liberty Restoration Inc., which raised funds to purchase and restore the 1925 Liberty Theater—a vaudeville-motion picture palace—to its former glory. Originally a beautifully designed and ornate theater in the heart of downtown Astoria, by the 1990s it was deteriorating and neglected. In 2000, the Astoria City Council made a $1.3 million urban renewal grant to the non-profit for the building's purchase. During the years necessary to complete the project, the newspaper absorbed the non-profit's administrative costs, while also making a monetary contribution. The successful Liberty Theater project brought new vitality to Astoria's downtown arts and culture scene.

The Daily Astorian and the Forresters became bedrock contributors to restoration of the historic Liberty Theater in downtown Astoria.

During 2006, EOPC directors and managers had to focus on challenges threatening the viability of the *East Oregonian*. While the newspaper celebrated a grand reopening of its remodeled and expanded building in July 2006, it faced a serious problem of declining circulation (dropping below 10,000 copies for the first time in many years) coupled with the high expenses of producing a seven-day paper. The board, after a year of deliberation and detailed analysis, decided to drop Monday publication beginning in August 2006.

Over the decades, the *EO* generally had been profitable following a six-day-a-week schedule. With the addition of the Sunday paper in 2000, however, the daily began to lose money. Part of the problem stemmed from the stagnant economy of eastern Oregon. As Mike Forrester wrote in a memo to fellow EOPC directors, "The *EO* [is] operating within a local economy that has restructured with fewer retail outlets, fewer locally owned outlets, more shopping trips into Washington, and larger challenges for maintaining ad linage and newspaper revenue." (Board records, May

2006) Finally, according to Perry, "The recommendation to discontinue the Monday edition ultimately came down to value. Monday newspapers, in Pendleton and across the nation, typically contain less advertising than other days of the week because fewer people do their shopping early in the week. There also is generally less news activity on Sundays to publish in Monday editions." (*Shoptalk*, Aug. 2006)

Surprisingly, the public generally had little reaction to the loss of the *EO*'s Monday edition. Few dropped their subscriptions and many simply accessed the paper's internet site for news on Monday. Managing Editor Steve Brown noted that the *EO* added new features—some in the printed paper and others on the internet site "as compensation for taking away one day of the print edition." (*Shoptalk*, Sept. 2006) Still, at the end of 2006, while circulation and advertising had once again begun to grow and financial losses decline, Perry doubted that the paper's current management team could sustain the positive trend. To better capitalize on this improvement and reinvigorate management at the *EO*, Perry replaced its publisher/editor.

Amy Aldrich Bedford's prime achievement was the Pendleton River Parkway – a 20-year quest.

Still, while the *EO* appeared to struggle during 2006, the EOPC was continuing to thrive. Year-end fiscal results announced in August 2006 showed advertising revenue gained 2 percent over the prior year, while circulation was up 1 percent. Overall company profitability increased 2 percent, while internet sales grew an impressive 14 percent.

Most notable was the journalistic success of the company's newspapers. The *EO* won the general excellence award for newspapers between 10,000 and 25,000 circulation from the Oregon Newspaper Publishers Association (it also won in 1988 and 2001), while other company papers received another 32 awards from the ONPA.

The death in July 2006 of longtime EOPC stockholder, director, and *EO* public relations manager Amy Aldrich Bedford, at the age of 94, marked another transition. For 55 years, Amy—along with her sister, Eleanor, and other family members—had served Pendleton through the *EO*'s community focus. Among her many civic activities, Amy helped found the Oregon East Symphony and the Arts Council of Pendleton. For many years, she promoted better international relations through the World Affairs Council. Perhaps her biggest community endeavor had been the twenty-year quest to construct the Pendleton River Parkway. Completed in 1997, the parkway is a paved walkway bordering the Umatilla River as it passes through Pendleton. Amy also worked to convert the former Umatilla County Library building into an arts center. As already noted above, Amy's daughter, Jacqueline Brown, retired in November from the *EO* after 18 years as human resources manager. She continued to serve on the EOPC board of directors.

No sooner had the EOPC absorbed the recent changes in family management then yet another occurred. In January 13, 2007, Eleanor Aldrich Forrester, the mother of Steve and Mike Forrester, died at the age of 90. The wife of Bud Forrester, she had worked beside her husband at both the *EO* and *DA*. Like her sister and husband, Eleanor believed deeply in the value of community journalism. She had a keen interest in politics from the local to national level and served on the Oregon Liquor Control Commission and the Oregon Council for the Humanities. In 2001, she was inducted into the Hall of Achievement of the University of Oregon's Journalism School.

Eleanor Aldrich Forrester's death followed that of her sister by one year.

As the second generation of family owners passed on, a fourth generation owner became more active in the EOPC. Kathryn Bedford Brown, Jacqueline Brown's daughter and a company director since 1997, began to assume a more direct role in day-to-day newspaper operations. In order to learn all aspects of the newspaper business, she joined the management team of the *EO* and became EOPC treasurer in the spring of 2007. In particular, she focused on human resources and the financial aspects of the *EO*'s operations and joined its editorial board. Kathryn was the oldest of six cousins in the fourth generation of owners.

With the deaths of longtime family members on the EOPC board, the remaining family shareholders made some changes in the agreement controlling stock transfers. To promote shared interests and insure continuity and stability in management of the company, the stockholders restated terms that restrict the transfer of shares. The aim was to maintain ownership by family stockholders active on the board.

Further EOPC management changes came in the fall of 2007 when Diana Porter,

"We wondered what happened to you."

In December 2007, Clatsop County and the Long Beach Peninsula were hit with a storm that became a landmark event. Called the Great Coastal Gale of 2007, winds of up to 147 mph knocked out Bonneville Power Administration trunk lines and cell towers. The region served by The Daily Astorian was without power for five days. During the height of incapacity, only ham radio operators were able to communicate with the outside world.

Using generators to power editing terminals and laptops, Managing Editor Patrick Webb led reporters to pull together five editions that were printed at The Daily News in Longview. Online Editor Crindalyn Lyster ferried discs to Laura Sellers-Earl, who was operating out of a Longview motel. Sellers fed the company's website, to inform readers outside Clatsop and Pacific counties.

The storm created an eye-popping adventure for photographer Alex Pajunas. There were washed-out railway lines, boats turned on their side, trees dropped through roofs and a dimly lit courtroom (dubbed Candelight Court).

The DA's own newsroom was illuminated by an array of candles and battery powered lights and head lamps.

When editors reached the Portland Associated Press bureau after days without phone service, the AP on the other end of the line said: "We wondered what happened to you."

the company's longtime controller, announced her retirement in March 2008. For over 25 years, Porter had responsibility for payroll, insurance, investments, expenditures, internal audits, and financial advice on company matters to stockholders. Porter had worked closely, first with general manager Pat Patterson and then with chief operating officer John Perry as the company grew and modernized. When Porter arrived in 1982, she and one other person handled personnel, payroll, and other records keeping for three newspapers largely by hand. Upon retirement, her office had grown to four and most functions were computerized.

In the Spring of 2008, Perry announced the hiring of John Shaver as chief financial officer. Shaver had a record as a newspaper financial expert, most recently for Western Communications, the Bend-based company that owned the *Bend Bulletin, La Grande Observer, Baker City Herald, Hermiston Herald*, and other publications in Oregon and California. After a brief transition in Pendleton, Shaver and the corporate accounting office moved to Salem to join other corporate functions. At the same time, the EOPC board named a new outside director to fill the vacancy left by Lucy Mohl, who retired as an outside director. Jeff Rogers, chief financial officer of a group of family-owned newspapers in Indiana, joined the board in August 2007. President Steve Forrester remarked at the time Rogers became a director why such a position existed: "Many years ago, our family made a decision to have outside directors on our board. This has paid off in good advice and deep insight into the challenges our company faces." (*Shoptalk*, Sept/Oct. 2007)

To promote continuity and stability, shareholders restated terms of the stock purchase agreement.

While management changes occurred at the EOPC, John Perry continued pushing his long-term vision for the company to become a sustainable multimedia concern. To achieve this goal, Perry moved further into the internet aspects of the news operations, continued making vital capital investments in publishing equipment and facilities, and grasped opportunities to expand business through strategic purchases of other newspapers. In each of these areas, Perry made progress during 2007.

To innovate and capture new markets, Perry focused on expanding each of the EOPC's newspapers' use of the internet, which still contributed only three percent of newspaper revenue. Perry gave Laura Sellers-Earl responsibility to drive the new media effort. Previously, she was corporate online director. Now as director of marketing and innovation, Sellers-Earl would lead the charge to reach new customers and retain current ones through print, online, and other means. Sellers-Earl said that "this a great challenge to extend our brand, reach and value with a focused effort, combining the power of all our products and engaging our customers and non-customers." (*Shoptalk*, June 2007)

One of the first products of the new internet initiative involved launching a self-service classified system (Bluefin) to allow customers to create their own ads at any time and for any of the company's newspapers and internet sites. Another example of the internet initiative was the creation—one of the first of its kind—of a community based internet site called Seaside-Sun.com.

While the internet initiative got underway, Perry also convinced the directors to move ahead with a strategic newspaper purchase. In July 2007, the EOPC bought the *North Coast Citizen*, its first newspaper purchase since taking over the *WCC* in 2000. While a detailed examination of the newspaper's financial condition and place in the community revealed no major problems, purchasing the newspaper presented risks. Absorbing a new operation and managing it to

The next pair of non-family, outside directors were Jeff Rogers and Cory Bollinger.

increase advertising and circulation without taking resources away from other properties in the company would be a challenge. The EOPC, after all, had debt related to buying *WCC* and to the construction or remodeling of its other company newspaper buildings in John Day, Salem, and Pendleton, Oregon, and Long Beach, Washington. Still, the purchase seemed a great opportunity. The *NCC*, published 26 times a year, was profitable and well-respected in the coastal community of Manzanita. There would be the ability of the *NCC* to work with the *DA* and its other niche publication, *Coast Weekend*, to better serve the businesses and residents of Oregon's north coast. Since the *DA* already printed the *NCC*, there would be no production issues. The *DA*, moreover, could take over the *NCC*'s circulation and financial functions without adding personnel. Finally, the current owners of the *NCC*

– Dave and Jan Fisher – were willing to continue running the paper for a few years, which eased the challenges associated with new management. Long term, the EOPC hoped to grow the *NCC* into a weekly that extended its market reach north to Cannon Beach and Seaside and south to other the communities along the coast.

No sooner had the EOPC consummated the deal for the *NCC* than it had the opportunity to buy another newspaper within its geographic territory. After losing money for five years, the owners of the biweekly *Hermiston Herald* put it on the market. Perry liked that the combined *EO* and *HH* would have 60 percent market penetration. In addition, the *EO* could drop its Hermiston bureau at a considerable annual savings. All but one director voted to buy the *Herald*. The EOPC completed acquisition of the *HH* – from Western Communications of Bend – during the company's third quarter of 2008. The biggest challenge would be to distinguish the *Herald* from the *EO*, grow advertising revenue, and keep circulation from dropping. Under EOPC ownership, after a brief stumble, the *Herald* forged ahead and paid off its cost of purchase in four years instead of the planned five. The *NCC*, however, took longer to become profitable.

Recession tests company's resilience

The severe economic recession lasting from 2008 to 2010 proved especially challenging. Not only had the company taken on new debt to buy the *NCC* and the *HH*, its long-time major source of company profit—the *CP*—experienced headwinds, as the agricultural economy of its four-state market area declined sharply. Perry had long believed that the company overly depended on the *CP*'s profit. Thus, four years earlier he had begun the process of improving the financial performance of the company's other newspapers, especially that of the *EO*.

The pressures of the recession were intense. The company suffered a million dollar loss in advertising, while print circulation continued a steady decline. Between 2004 and 2010—excluding the *HH* and the *NCC*—circulation dropped from 67,100 to 59,512. The *EO* experienced the largest loss of print subscribers; it went from 10,317 to 7,847 over that period.

Despite the recessionary pressures, the EOPC persevered by cost-cutting and benefitted from the decline in the price of newsprint. Other savings came through pay freezes at most EOPC papers, as well as staff cuts. Employees were furloughed as well. At the beginning of 2008, the EOPC had 211 employees; by the end of 2009, the company's roster had declined to 184. To cut its expenses, the *CP* dropped its money-losing California edition. One edition went to all four states. Perry also pushed the company's newspapers to emphasize their profitable niche publications, such as real estate and visitor guides. Remarkably, through all the tough times, the company managed to eke out a small profit, contribute to its employee profit sharing, and continue the 401k match.

Late in 2009—during an otherwise gloomy year for the EOPC—*The Daily Astorian* caught a lucky break. The project to replace the press that dated to 1970 had proved too expensive to undertake during the depths of the recession. Attempts to outsource printing to the Longview, Washington, *Daily News* also went nowhere. In December 2009, however, Perry learned that a press owned by the Pioneer Press of Northfield, Illinois, was available. The Chicago Sun Times Co., owner of the Pioneer Press, had declared bankruptcy and had put the smaller company's printing press on the market for $400,000. The *DA*'s systems manager, Carl Earl, and press foreman, Jim Stanovich, inspected the printing equipment and found it to be in good shape. In addition, this opportunity occurred at the moment the EOPC had paid off two long-term debts, so bank financing was available. The new press consisted of two, four-high Tensor towers, an upgraded folder, five newer Goss Community units, and new roll splicers.

Pressures of the recession were intense – including a $1 million loss in advertising.

The EOPC's major investment in the press quickly produced notable results. The modern press offered 50 percent more color capacity, greater page capacity, and improved reproduction quality. The readers of the *DA* noticed an improvement in the print quality of the daily paper and its commercial products. The new press also helped the bottom line by reducing newsprint waste. Speaking for the EOPC board, Steve Forrester observed, "Our investment [in the press] represents our belief in the economy and culture of the Columbia-Pacific region and the future of our own enterprise." (*Shoptalk*, Jan. 2010)

In his efforts to strengthen the *EO*'s management team, Perry asked the Board to name Tom Brown as editor and publisher of the paper in early 2010. A native

Oregonian, Brown had served ten years on the EOPC Board, while president and CEO of a family-owned newspaper group in New England. Brown had recently retired from his newspaper position. Perry said: "We are fortunate that Tom has agreed to postpone his retirement and accept our invitation to help guide the *East Oregonian* during these turbulent economic times. He brings to the *EO* an enormous track record of successful newspapering and award-winning journalism." (*Shoptalk*, Mar. 2010)

Brown responded to the challenge presented by the *EO* by noting that "My understanding of the *EO* and appreciation of the family and managers has grown over the years that I have served on the company board. The EOPC . . . is easily one of the best community newspaper companies in our industry. My goal will be to take the *EO* and its online edition to an even higher level of service to its readers and advertisers." (*Shoptalk*, Mar. 2010) Specifically, the Board charged Brown with preparing the *EO* for its future in print, internet, and mobile formats. They were counting on his 40 years of newspaper experience to lead the *EO* into publishing in the age of new media.

Brown was also charged with mentoring Kathryn Brown to take over as publisher after his eventual retirement. As associate publisher of the *EO* and Board director, Kathryn Brown observed, "Over the last decade, I have learned much from Tom at our company's quarterly board meetings. I am looking forward to working with Tom on a daily basis at the *EO*, and continuing to learn about all aspects of the newspaper business from him. He'll be a mentor to me as well as a great addition to our management team." (*Shoptalk*, Mar. 2010)

The flip side of the recession was a printing press purchased out of the bankruptcy of the Chicago Sun-Times Co.

Another special project led by Steve Forrester that was several years in the making came to fruition during 2009-2010. Forrester, with the Board's backing, put together three book projects. For the most significant publication, he assembled a team of talented and knowledgeable writers and historians to produce a comprehensive history of the Pendleton Round-Up to commemorate the rodeo's one hundredth anniversary in 2010. The lavishly illustrated volume came out in July 2009 and by the time of the actual anniversary of the Round-Up, the widely acclaimed book had gone through three printings.

Aryan Nation threatens to enter John Day

Scotta Callister

Wearing combat boots and a brown-shirt style uniform, Paul Mullet strode into the Eagle office to announce his plan for an Aryan Nations world headquarters in John Day.

I suggested an interview, and he agreed readily. I started with some softball questions about his plans and the white supremacist philosophy. He grew expansive, obviously enjoying the prospect of publicity. I began to question his assumptions, and his eyes seemed to blaze as he laid out his vision – insisting the townspeople would welcome him and minority residents would feel so much safer with his troops patrolling the streets. My heart sank as the implications of this crazed vision sank in. Even if he turned out to be a lone lunatic, it was clear jackboot patrols and swastika flags would seriously harm the community's image, and worse, spread fear among the minorities and religious groups he clearly disdained.

I asked to take a picture. Posing with a couple of "lieutenants," Mullet carefully arranged his shirt sleeve so the swastika patch would be visible. After he left, I went online and sought background information – and advice – from the Northern Idaho experts who had defeated a neo-Nazi stronghold there. Attorney Norm Gissel urged us not to be silent, not to dismiss the threat, but to tackle it head-on and vocally. Publisher Marissa Williams and I decided to immediately post a story online – not the norm for a traditional print weekly in those days. As word spread and the community grew alarmed, we realized people needed help understanding this threat and how to respond safely. We began planning two town hall sessions to educate the community about the white supremacist movement and what might happen here.

Gissel and fellow activist Tony Stewart agreed to come to John Day to speak at the town halls. The turnout was so large the state fire marshal warned us to limit the standing-room-only crowd.

— *Scotta Callister*

Detracting from this otherwise highly successful project was the unexpected bankruptcy of Graphic Arts Center Publishing Co. of Portland, which left unpaid royalties in excess of $30,000 due the EOPC. Fortunately, the University of Oklahoma Press was impressed with the Round-Up book and became its distributor.

In recognition of Astoria's bicentennial, Forrester assembled another team of historians to create two books—"Eminent Astorians" and "Eccentric and Extraordinary Astorians." The Clatsop County Historical Society partnered with the EOPC for the Astoria books. Oregon State University Press was the books' distributor. The EOPC's books have made a lasting contribution by accurately recording and preserving the histories of the communities served by the company.

For an example of the fearless journalism practiced by the EOPC newspapers, one need only turn to the *BME*'s coverage of the Aryan Nation's attempt to establish a white homeland and headquarters in Grant County. A Neo-Nazi leader and three confederates walked into the *BME*'s office in February 17, 2010 and announced that they were going to create a white homeland in the county. After the paper put out this astounding news, local officials did not immediately respond to the challenge, so the *Eagle* stepped into this leadership vacuum. As *BME*'s editor, Scotta Callister, later recalled, the paper went

> beyond the traditional role of arm's length observer, we became the clearing house for rumors, the distiller of ideas and the facilitator of community solutions. We blended traditional strengths—through reporting and reasoned editorials—with digital innovations including web-streaming, video and social media. And we quickly organized two town hall meetings, bringing in human rights experts to talk about hate groups. (Pulitzer Prize Nomination, Jan. 15, 2011)

In addition to convening public meetings led by civil rights experts to aid the community in responding to the hate group's attempt to take over the county, the paper encouraged the formation of a county human rights coalition. Callister also investigated and reported on the Aryan Nation leader's criminal past, giving the community vital information and empowering citizens to unite and resist hate. By the end of the year, the Aryan Nation leader had given up his project and left the county.

In recognition of its journalistic leadership, the newspaper's work received special honors from the Rural Organizing Project and Ecumenical Ministries of Oregon. As

Callister put it, the *BME* demonstrated that "community newspapers—no matter how small—can harness the power of print and emerging advantages of multimedia to connect with their readers and serve the public good." (Pulitzer Prize Nomination, Jan. 15, 2011) This would not be the last time the *BME* had to cover the activities of extreme right-wing, anti-government groups in eastern Oregon.

In January 2016, a cadre of armed, out-of-state, anti-government agitators took over the Malheur National Wildlife Refuge in neighboring Harney County. This action started a standoff with federal authorities that lasted 41 days, drawing national attention. The occupation was ostensibly a protest over the re-imprisonment of two Harney County ranchers, Dwight and Steven Hammond, who had been convicted of arson on public range land. The Hammond "Cause" and subsequent refuge occupation exacerbated existing community tensions, arising out of disagreements over federal land management practices. These issues had been brewing since the early 1990s, when environmental concerns began reducing timber harvests and restricting grazing access on public lands in eastern Oregon.

Before the occupation, controversial Grant County Sheriff Glenn Palmer had shown sympathy with the anti-government cause. The standoff between the occupiers and the federal authorities climaxed when the FBI arrested the main leaders, while they were in route to a meeting with Sheriff Palmer in John Day.

The Grant County community expressed deep division over the refuge occupation, some believing it a positive step in a fight against federal overreach, while others saw it as a criminal act. In this heated environment, the *BME* responded as it had to the previous outburst of anti-government sentiment in Grant County. As the *Eagle* editor, Sean Hart, later noted, the paper provided coverage that sought "to explain the sentiments of each side, to dispel myths and misconceptions, to provide context and to hold public officials accountable—ultimately to be a trusted, neutral voice to bring a fractured community together." He felt that despite insults and negativity on both sides of the issue, "the *Eagle* succeeded by remaining objective and reporting the local angle of this national story." (personal communication, May 2018)

While the first half of the 2010-11 fiscal year contained positive financial results for the EOPC, the last half was dismal. The lingering effects of a weak economy continued to take a toll. As Perry put it, "this recession seems interminable, oppressive, and exhausting." (Shop Talk, Jan. 2011) For the year, annual revenue, net operating costs, and profit all hit a ten-year low. The declines struck every part of the company.

The fact that the entire newspaper industry was suffering seemed cold comfort to EOPC directors. Besides holding a tight rein on expenses, EOPC top management took several steps to improve overall revenue and profit.

In the spring of 2011, Perry engineered the sale of the money-losing *NCC* to the Country Media group of newspapers along the Oregon coast. In exchange for the *NCC*, Country Media entered into a long-term commercial printing contract with the EOPC for all of its newspapers. This agreement had an immediate, positive impact on the EOPC's revenue line. Nevertheless, as Steve Forrester said, "Choices like this are never easy." (*Shoptalk*, June 2011) The decision, the directors believed, would help pay for the substantial investment the EOPC owners had made in new press equipment in Astoria the year before.

Next, the EOPC directors invested in technological changes that would produce long-term benefits for its legacy newspapers. Both the *DA* and *EO* adopted a digital computer-to-plate production process. The technology removed a step in the process by creating a page image directly on a metal plate, eliminating a photo negative. This improved the quality of print reproduction, reduced waste, and saved on labor. The new process was also environmentally friendly, since it eliminated chemicals that were used in the photographic process. The two

The Rural Organizing Project and Ecumenical Ministries of Oregon recognized the Eagle's leadership on responding to the arrival of the Aryan Nation in John Day.

newspapers could now take on more commercial jobs, as well. To further increase the efficiency of the Astoria press, the directors also agreed to buy a new inserter.

At the *EO*, the EOPC directors made another strategic technological investment. On the roof of the *EO* building they installed a solar array consisting of 132 panels that would meet 16 percent of the newspaper's total energy needs and pay for itself in five years. At the time of its installation, this was the largest privately owned solar project in eastern Oregon and one of just two newspapers in the nation to use solar power. The project took advantage of a number of energy incentives and tax credits, as well as a zero-interest loan from the city of Pendleton. Kathryn Brown, *EO*'s associate publisher, vowed that the company would continue "efforts to reduce our energy usage and . . . our carbon footprint." (*Shoptalk*, Nov. 2011)

Steve Forrester

A key part of Perry's strategy to grow the company involved expanding its digital efforts with a greater sense of urgency. While the newspapers of the EOPC had a strong record of innovation in the online world, he felt this initiative had gotten bogged down in the mechanics of uploading news and advertising content and dealing with software issues. To reenergize the digital focus, the EOPC hired a digital project developer and reoriented the six-person digital team toward growing revenue and creating new products and services. In the past, most digital efforts by the team simply took the reportage and advertising produced by the company's newspapers and posted that material to each paper's internet site. Now, Perry wanted the individual newspaper staffs to post their own content—news, features, photographs, and advertisements.

Two results of this new digital emphasis that showed great promise were the *CP*'s OnlyAg.com internet site and the *DA*'s DiscoverOurCoast.com internet-and-mobile magazine. The former was an internet site devoted to buying and selling agricultural equipment and supplies. It was a search engine and database that served agriculture business across the country, creating revenue potential beyond the newspaper's primary market.

The joint *DA-CO* project—DiscoverOurCoast.com—resulted in a glossy magazine produced by the staffs of the two papers that replaced visitor guides. The older guides had grown stale and were losing profitability. The new magazine – *Our Coast* – circulated regionally. *Daily Astorian* Advertising Manager Betty Smith conceived the new magazine's distribution as well as its ad sales strategy.

During 2011, the EOPC continued to excel at traditional journalism. Steve Forrester spearheaded a project drawing on the news and editorial staffs of the EOPC newspapers to produce an important regional environmental investigation. The series, "The Fate of Our Forests," focused on the changing patterns of forest ownership. Patrick Webb, managing editor of the *DA*, coordinated the writers from the companies' newspapers in this award-winning effort. The EOPC won the Northwest's top environmental journalism award for the series, given by the Pacific Northwest Newspaper Association. Judges described the series as "Local journalism at its best. This series not only explained the changes and odd-bedfellows arrangements sweeping forest management in Oregon, it also explained in clear, lively prose the politics and economics of the issue as well." (*Shoptalk*, Oct. 2011)

Recessionary cost saving measures included pay freezes, staff cuts and furloughs.

The *EO*'s decade of unprofitability became the biggest problem for the owners and managers of the EOPC. As a first step, the *EO* and corporate management teams recommended that the newspaper move from afternoon to morning publication. In doing so, they were following a national trend of afternoon papers switching to a morning audience. The managers found that advertisers generally liked a morning publication, that it improved the timeliness of the news product, and enabled the paper to compete better against radio and internet with breaking news. Also, since *The Oregonian* had retreated to its metropolitan territory and abandoned statewide-news coverage and print sales, the *EO* had one less competitor. The changeover would be cost neutral as well. At their annual meeting in August 2011, the EOPC directors voted to convert the newspaper to mornings in March 2012. This would not be the last big change for the *EO*.

Halfway through the 2011-12 fiscal year, it became clear that the EOPC might end the fiscal year with a loss. To prevent that, the company directors voted January

2012 to reduce the shareholders' yearly dividend. Individual company newspapers took other cost-saving steps, such as furloughs and increasing subscription and single copy prices. Fortunately, the EOPC was on schedule to dramatically reduce its long-term debt over the next two years. The most consequential step the directors took, though, was to reduce the frequency of the *EO* to five days by combining the Saturday and Sunday editions. They set this dramatic move to occur by October 2012. Despite earlier concerns, the EOPC managed to end the 2011-12 fiscal year with a gain in total sales for the first time in four years. Much of the increase came in commercial printing, while the newspapers continued to lag, with paid circulation and ad count continuing to decline.

Despite the wrenching changes at the *EO* during 2012, the paper continued to produce quality journalism, winning another first-place ONPA general excellence award.

Another good opportunity for the company appeared when EOPC directors bought *Oregon Coast Today*, a free distribution publication located in Lincoln City, Oregon. In the short term, Mike O'Brien, publisher of the *CP*, would serve as publisher of the new acquisition. The entertainment-focused weekly served Lincoln City, Tillamook, and Newport. As John Perry noted, "The acquisition is part of a strategy to strengthen our portfolio of free-distribution products, which includes shoppers, a real estate guide, a parenting magazine and an Idaho farming publication." (*Shoptalk*, Nov. 2012) He strategized that free publications would provide revenue and profits to supplement the other company print and digital products. Free publications, moreover, reach a different audience than paid newspapers. Finally, free newspapers had the advantage of discouraging competitors from entering the market with their own free publications. With the addition of *OCT*, the EOPC publications now had a market reach stretching from southwestern Washington to the central Oregon coast.

> ***Oregon Coast Today* was the company's first free-circulation newspaper purchase.**

At their annual meeting in August 2012, the EOPC directors voted to change the name of the company to EO Media Group. John Perry said: "EO Media Group is a better brand to market to regional and national advertisers. Our former name referenced our geographic origin in Eastern Oregon. Our company now does business on the Oregon and Washington coasts, in Idaho and—as with OnlyAg.com—on a national scale." (*Shoptalk*, Dec. 2012)

To carry out the upgrading of the EOMG's technical capability, Perry announced in November 2012 that the company was investing in a new generation of software for use across all operations. He stated, "For the first time, all of our newsrooms will use a common editing system, allowing our reporters and editors to easily share information, articles and photos for print, our internet sites, social media and mobile communication devices such as the iPhone or iPad." (*Shoptalk*, Nov. 2012) The new system also improved internet site navigation and display.

While pushing digital upgrades, Perry did not neglect the print side of operations. Management and board had to consider upgrading the *EO* press. This stemmed from the *Capital Press* losing its long-time printer. The Salem *Statesman-Journal*, which had printed the *CP* for many years, had outsourced its printing to *The Oregonian*. As a result of this change, the printing costs of the *CP* had increased over 8.5 percent and would likely go up even more. There was also the danger that *The Oregonian* would stop printing and that any alternative printing venues would be even more expensive.

While there would be considerable savings to print at the *EO*—something the EOMG directors had studied before—the move would require a large up-front cost. The EOMG would need to invest approximately $1.2 million in press modifications and additional equipment to print 36 pages of color for each edition of the *CP*. The Board decided to do the press modernization, with the installation taking place in the summer of 2013 and eventually costing $1.5 million. The press project was led by Tom Brown, who stayed on to lead the effort after he retired as publisher in early 2013.

If the *EO* press upgrade project and the company-wide conversion to new software and central pagination were not challenging enough, the EOMG management had to integrate new acquisitions into their operations. Country Media, a newspaper company, wanted to sell the *Cannon Beach Gazette*, *Seaside Signal*, and *Coast River Business Journal*, and the EOMG directors decided to make the purchase. Perry explained to EOMG employees, "the purchase price and strategic fit seemed reasonable," and he felt confident the "we can operate the new publications profitably and with quality content." (*Shoptalk*, Mar. 2013)

By the end of 2014, Perry had carried out four major projects. The new press at the *EO* had been installed and was beginning to realize savings in production costs, especially in printing the *CP*. The company had also installed new editing/publishing software to integrate all the newsrooms and support the implementation of central desk pagination initiative. The final project, almost completed by the end of the year involved creating metered internet sites, in which readers were charged for access after reading a threshold number of articles.

Over the preceding ten years, the newspaper business had faced enormous change. At the EOMG annual meeting in August 2014, Perry presented a comparison of certain benchmarks, showing how the company had fared during those years. Newspapers under ownership increased from six to eleven, while full-time employees declined from 198 to 188. Print circulation declined 21 percent, while the digital audience grew 461 percent. Over the ten-year period, the EOMG's paid circulation dropped 21 percent, but this beat the industry average, which was down 47 percent. Company revenue decreased 1.2 percent, but expenses dropped 1.6 percent. Pre-tax profit rose 13.3 percent. In addition, long-term debt, despite acquisitions and major capital expenditures, declined significantly. Finally, Perry noted that the company beat the industry average in fighting the loss of classified advertising revenue. The company was down 35 percent, while the industry average dropped 74 percent.

Perry noted that industry classified advertising dropped 74 percent while EOMG's papers dropped 35 percent.

Looking ahead, Perry became particularly concerned about the steady decline in the EOMG newspapers' net paid circulation. As he told the stockholders, "the company spends more on circulation than newsrooms and costs are above the industry average." He went on to note that "sales and promotion efforts are inconsistent and the papers aren't sharing [information] between themselves." (EOMG Board minutes, Oct. 2014) It frustrated him that circulation practices were inconsistent across the company and that staff had to be constantly retrained. In short, the current system was expensive, not getting results, nor preparing for the future.

To remedy what he saw as a flawed circulation system, Perry proposed a reorganization that emphasized improved sales, retention, and customer service. Each newspaper would focus on all aspects of customer service, while a central circulation office at *CP* in Salem would do sales, retention, and operations. Specifically, the local circulation mangers would handle issues related to delivery, single copy placement, data entry, carrier oversight, and payment processing. The central office circulation staff—led by long-time circulation manager Samantha McLaren—would deal with budgeting, pricing, reporting of analytics and metrics, postal interactions, subscriber lists, and overseeing local mangers.

Perry hired a veteran newspaper executive with broad experience in marketing and advertising, Michael Keith, to oversee all circulation marketing efforts, including research, strategy, and promotion. After a full year of operation, the new approach appeared to have staunched the decline in net-paid circulation. To continue this positive trend, the EOMG directors approved yet another round of expensive advertising and circulation software upgrades at their annual meeting in August 2016.

While keeping a sharp watch on expenses and looking for ways to improve operations, the EOMG directors searched for opportunities to expand their market reach. Watching *The Oregonian* retreat from state-wide political news coverage, the directors sought to fill the gap with an innovative news product. At Steve Forrester's instigation, EOMG struck an agreement with Pamplin Media to establish a news bureau in Salem to cover state government news and produce copy for both companies' newspapers and a newsletter called the *Oregon Capital Insider*. The newsletter initially went to subscribers of the company's newspapers as well as Pamplin's. After more than a year of negotiation, EOMG and Pamplin reached an agreement with the City Club of Portland, by which club members receive the newsletter and the newsletter publishes the City Club's heavily researched reports to a wider audience. By building circulation numbers, the newsletter became attractive to advertisers. The capital bureau, after much planning, began operation in February 2015 out of the *CP*'s office

While concerned about the continuing long-term slide in advertising revenue, the EOMG directors and top managers had to engage in succession planning during 2015-2016. Both Steve Forrester and John Perry indicated that they wished to retire in August 2016 and August 2017, respectively. While Forrester would be stepping down as publisher and editor of the *DA*, he planned to remain as president and CEO of EOMG. To replace Forrester, the EOMG named David Pero to the post. Pero had most recently been chief operating officer of the Eugene *Register-Guard*.

Other initiatives taken to ensure a smooth transition in the family management of the EOMG included bringing in a new outside director, Cory Bollinger, to replace Tom Brown when he stepped down after 15 years of service on the Board. Bollinger served as vice president of publishing for Schurz Communication and publisher of the *Aberdeen News* in Aberdeen, South Dakota. In 2016, Bollinger was named regional publisher for Schurz Communications and moved to Bloomington, Indiana. Schurz Communications, like EOMG, is a family-owned publisher of 11 daily and weekly newspapers and operator of TV, radio stations, and cable businesses across the United States. The board also added Susan Forrester Rana as a company director. Rana is the daughter of Steve Forrester and a stockholder in the EOMG. She subsequently became the company's treasurer. Steve's son Harrison was elected to the board in August 2017.

In December 2017, Kari Borgen was hired to replace Pero as regional publisher of the coast papers. She became the first woman to be *The Daily Astorian* publisher. Borgen had been regional publisher in eastern Oregon for Western Communications, heading newspapers in Baker City and La Grande. She was also chief revenue officer of Western Communications.

The steps pursued in 2015-16 to carry out the EOMG leadership transition manifested planning that had been going on for some time at the company. As Kathryn Brown noted at the time the company announced Steve Forrester's retirement, "Our family began actively planning for succession more than 20 years ago, and has managed smooth transitions as Steve's parents, my grandmother and my mother retired over the years. I'm confident that we will manage well through this transition." (*Shoptalk*, Apr. 2016)

Throughout the transition planning process and the continuing need to run a profitable enterprise, the owners have always kept a larger view of the meaning of family. Their sense of family extended beyond just the relationship of the owners in a closely held company. The EOMG has attempted to provide decent and fair working conditions for its employees. Pay and benefits met and often exceeded industry standards. Whenever financial conditions allowed, the company maintained a policy of profit sharing with employees—the money being paid into retirement accounts. The company also promoted from within and provided training and growth opportunities to make that option possible. Recognizing that each newspaper has a somewhat

Kari Borgen

unique environment, the EOMG upper management has given local managers considerable autonomy to serve the needs of their readers and communities.

The EOMG of the twenty-first century is an example of a once common but now endangered enterprise: the family-owned and run newspaper. The company traces its roots to the Bull and Jackson families of the nineteenth century and continues with the Aldrich, Forrester, Bedford, and Brown and Chessman families of the twentieth and twenty-first centuries. Across time, the connecting link always has been a commitment to providing objective reporting and honoring the diverse opinions and values of the communities served by their newspapers.

This devotion to community journalism has faced many political, economic, and technical challenges. Sharp-eyed business people as well as committed journalists, the family owner-managers of the EOMG have never let the drive for profit be their sole concern. Rather, they have sought sufficient returns on investment necessary to support excellence in independent, community journalism. Whether it was Edwin Aldrich and Merle Chessman standing up to the KKK or the *BME* doing frontline reporting on the white nationalists trying to move into Grant County, Oregon, the EOMG newspapers stoutly resisted the threats and economic pressure brought by those being exposed for their questionable views.

EO Media Group Board of Directors 2017 (from left): Jeff Rogers, Heidi Wright, Cory Bollinger, Kathryn Brown, Susan Forrester Rana, John Perry, Harrison Forrester and Steve Forrester

EPILOGUE

The Way Ahead

"Local journalism in our country is in dire shape.
Pick your metric—numbers of reporters, newspapers,
readers—nearly all the trendlines veer downhill."
[Kyle Pope, editor in chief and publisher,
Columbia Journalism Review (Spring, 2017), 12]

The newspaper business faces a constant struggle to secure and then expand its two main revenue components: circulation and advertising. The explosion of digital media in the twenty-first century has called into question the traditional approaches to attracting subscribers and advertisers. The potential audience for printed newspapers now has multiple media options for finding news, opinion, or product information. Clearly, meeting the financial and management challenges of running a successful newspaper business has only gotten more demanding over time. Regardless of the ever-changing nature of the media competition, the newspaper publisher/editor still must put out a paper in both print and digital form that can keep the necessary subscriber and advertiser base to remain financially viable.

Recent findings by the Pew Research Center indicate how tenuous the traditional newspaper business formula for chasing circulation and advertising has become. Between 2000 and 2016, for example, weekday readership of America's newspaper fell from 55.7 million to 34.6 million, while advertising revenue dropped from $48.6 billion to $18.2 billion. All three streams of advertising—run-of-paper, classified, and preprint—contributed to the financial slump of the newspaper business. In response to this industry-wide economic decline, the number of papers and employment levels also dropped. The number of daily newspapers across the country slid by 126 between 2004 and 2014, falling from 1,457 to 1,331. In the same timeframe, newsroom employment levels deteriorated from approximately 65,000 in 2004 to 41,000 in 2015. The one bright spot was the percentage of newspaper advertising revenue coming from digital sources. Digital advertising represented 29 percent of newspaper advertising in 2016, up from 17 percent in 2011. (www.pewresearch.org/fact-sheet/newspapers)

The number of daily newspapers across the country slid by 126 between 2004 and 2014 – from 1,457 to 1,331.

The assault of digital media on traditional print media also had a physical aspect as well. As the internet became more graphic and access speeds increased, print media also tried to transform. Newspapers changed from gray, picture-less broadsheets compiling mostly national news to vibrant, colorful, slimmed-down sheets delivering more local than national or international news. The search for relevance in an ever-changing media environment also led to a renewed focus on the reader. As Liz Spayed, the public editor for *The New York Times*, noted "now that the monopolistic era of print is giving way to an accelerating stampede of digital, the relationship between newsrooms and their audiences is in a period of manifest change." (July 10, 2016) Newspaper management, she continued, "is aiming to produce a product that consumers have a greater say in creating." (July 10, 2016) Still, in this new environment, the publisher/editor's goal remained the same: capture and retain more subscribers in order to grow circulation revenue.

Of course, the EOMG was not immune to the newspaper industry turmoil of the past fifteen years. In 2000, the company owned two dailies and four weeklies with a combined print circulation of 70,109. By 2015, the circulation numbers for those same papers had declined to 48,596. The number of EOMG employees also fell from an average high of 201 in 2008 to 174 in 2016. These drops in circulation and employment levels, however, occurred while the company was expanding its portfolio of print publications. In 2008, it bought the *Hermiston Herald*, picked up another publication in 2012, and then three more in 2013. While one, the *HH*, was in eastern Oregon, the other papers were located along the Oregon coast and all published either weekly, bi-weekly, or monthly. The EOMG's largest publications experienced especially heavy losses in advertising revenue between FY 2005-06 and FY 2015-16. At the *EO*, *DA*, and *CP*, combined revenue from advertising decreased 30 percent. Employment at these three papers also declined 23 percent during that timeframe.

Over the ten-year period from 2005 to 2015, the EOMG's main goal was to be the leading media company in the communities it served, while maintaining the company's ability to remain an independent, sustainable, family-owned business. To accomplish this goal, the EOMG Board and management team pursued several strategic objectives:

- Serve as the principal source of news, information and advertising in its markets
- Adopt a "digital-first" publishing model with paywall
- Remain in the printing business by printing its own papers and offering commercial printing
- Solidify market share in Clatsop and Umatilla counties
- Reduce reliance on the *Capital Press* for profitability
- Modernize and standardize infrastructure and management tools
- Strengthen financial resources

While focusing on these objectives, the Board had to manage a succession process for both family ownership and key management personnel.

Beginning in 2000, second and third generation family stockholders and directors either passed on or retired from day-to-day involvement over the subsequent decade-and-a-half. Fortunately, members of the fourth generation of the family chose to follow them into active involvement in the company. Other transitions on the non-family side of business operations also had to be dealt with. By 2017, long-serving, non-family members of the EOMG management team, John Perry and John Shaver, were in the

Heidi Wright

process of retiring. Despite the danger of the company losing its sense of direction or risk becoming a take-over target for another media concern, the EOMG has managed to stay true to its commitment to community journalism and remain a financially viable family-owned business. Undoubtedly, this success stemmed from its focus on and consistent execution of the strategic objectives listed above.

Within its geographic territories in coastal Oregon and northeastern Oregon, the EOMG, through its paid daily and weekly newspapers and free publications, has established and retained its news and advertising dominance in print. It has aggressively pushed a digital-first strategy for over ten years. Management invested in creating a digital team devoted to adopting and training the company's staff on the best available software tools for exploiting social media and internet-based opportunities. One exciting outcome of the digital team's efforts was the creation of a powerful internet platform, called the Marketplace, which houses classified advertising, job listings, farm implement dealers and individual sellers. A successful launch of the *CP* Marketplace led to the development of Coast and Eastern Oregon Marketplaces. The EOMG has also partnered with the Pamplin Media Group to publish a successful online weekly newsletter devoted to news and opinion covering the political scene of Oregon's state government. Monetizing digital media, however, remains a work in progress.

The EOMG achieved its commitment to traditional print by large investments in maintaining and continually upgrading its presses in both Astoria and Pendleton. These printing plants not only enabled the company to print its own daily and weekly papers but also to produce other's newspapers and to take on outside commercial printing and other types of profitable publications—all of which added to the EOMG's financial bottom line. Remaining in the print business, moreover, allowed the company to control the cost and quality of print products, especially in the use of color. In addition, since 2000, the EOMG has expended substantial sums to remodel and expand its Salem and Pendleton office buildings, as well as building new ones in John Day and Enterprise, Oregon. The company has not ignored investing in its employees, either. It paid industry-competitive wages, maintained a strong benefits package, and provided an employee profit-sharing arrangement when finances allowed it.

Over the ten-year period from 2005 to 2015, the EOMG board and management team focused with laser-like intensity upon one key strategic objective as they carried out community journalism. The company strived to be the leading media operation in the communities it served, while maintaining its ability to remain an independent, sustainable, family-owned business. This goal assumed the high importance of informing and connecting its papers' readers with the ever-evolving interests and values of their

Within its geographical territories, the EOMG has retained news and advertising dominance.

communities through accurate reportage and thoughtful editorial commentary. In sustaining this commitment to quality community journalism, EOMG has kept a close watch on the bottom line and followed prudent business practices.

To keep this focus on sustainable community journalism going forward, the EOMG hired a new COO, Heidi Wright, in early 2017. Wright came to the company with a strong business and newspaper background gained at both publicly and family-owned news organizations in Montana and Oregon. She was attracted to the EOMG position because of the family owners' long-term, continuing commitment to community journalism in both print and digital formats. Since arriving at the company, she has focused on better monetizing the digital portion of the company's media mix, while strengthening the print side of the operation with new products.

Wright believes strongly that the EOMG must grow profitability in both the print and digital products. This can be done by centralizing certain production functions and reducing operating or shared costs across the company's various news and advertising platforms, while improving top line growth through diversifying revenue streams. She emphasizes that the latter effort requires intensive training of the sales force so that they can better match the advertising message to the medium, whether print or digital, with the goal of enabling the advertiser to reach the right audience. This approach requires a major focus on collecting demographic and marketing data and aggregating it so that the sales representative can propose tailored ad campaigns that will provide measurable results to the advertisers.

Wright is also concerned with finding new ways to deliver the news to readers in an age seemingly saturated with information from all types of media. The goal, as Wright sees it, is to produce content that readers see as relevant, credible and reflective of the community they live in. That process entails developing direct, two-way communications with readers that builds on the trust and credibility that the EOMG's newspapers have in their respective communities. Wright also is overseeing the development of new digital platforms to assist advertisers in its market areas to use the broad spectrum of available data and analytics to reach potential customers. Finally,

Heidi Wright has focused on monetizing the digital side while strengthening print with new products.

EOMG is not ignoring the print side of its business. New publishing ventures will include both magazine and other formats to serve unmet needs for news, features, and opinions throughout Oregon.

In support of the EOMG family-owners' faith in community journalism, a recent study has shown that there is a strong relationship between civically engaged citizens—those activity engaged in community life—and interest in local news. The study found that citizens who regularly vote, volunteer, and connect with local organizations also display a keen interest in local news sources, such as newspapers. The study, while not claiming a causal relationship between civic involvement and news habits, suggests that the consumption of local news may trigger a greater civic engagement and that the more active one becomes in a local community, the more that person is likely to consume news. Community newspapers like those published by the EOMG are uniquely positioned to benefit from and contribute to sustaining healthy communities. (Pew Research Center, "Civic Engagement Strongly Tied to Local News Habits," www.journalism.org/2016/11/03/)

How should today's community newspapers such as those operated by the EOMG respond to the complications they face? In a recent survey of the problems besetting local journalism, the *Columbia Journalism Review (CJR)* identified two promising models to keep community journalism alive. One approach is the online, nonprofit news startups. These are not comprehensive news sites, but endeavors concentrating on a few areas of community interest such as local politics, criminal justice, the environment, or health care. They rely on small staffs and contributions from individual donors and local and national foundations for support. While not needing to sell advertising to exist, the nonprofit does need grant writers, membership services employees, and fundraisers to manage the year-to-year funding cycle to stay alive. Still, the approach has gained traction, with about 200 sites currently in operation. The *CJR* noted that between 2009 and 2016, ten national foundations gave $500 million to journalism nonprofits. ("The Future of Local News," *CJR*, Spring, 2017)

New publishing ventures will include magazine and book formats.

The other model for saving local journalism detailed by the *CJR* is the strategy employed by the Gannett Corporation. This approach involves buying local papers around the nation and fitting them into an existing business structure and news gathering process to create a network that manages content by moving some local news to a broader audience through cross-publishing stories, while sending national news gathered by the *USA TODAY* team out to all properties in the chain. The concern, though, is that since the Gannett business model depends upon each media property reducing the number of reporters, while centralizing production and consolidating business operations, the local newspapers will have very shallow roots in their respective communities. For its markets, an independent EOMG may offer a better approach to keeping alive hometown journalism.

A recent study by the University of Oregon School of Journalism and

Communication looked at the experience of ten local media outlets in the Pacific Northwest as they responded to the disruptive impact of digital technologies on local journalism. As Damian Radcliffe, the study's author explained, "Combining desk analysis with new qualitative work, this report aims to support this goal [of learning from others] by sharing experiences from the Pacific Northwest related to business models, the evolving practices of local journalism, use of digital tools and platforms, as well as real life engagement with audiences and communities." (Radcliffe, "Local Journalism in the Pacific Northwest," Sept. 2017)

While acknowledging the challenges the profession faced, the report presented an upbeat view of local journalism in Oregon and Washington. It found a consensus among the media outlets surveyed that local journalism remained important for its civic value, but an equally intense belief that survival in the new digital media environment required newsrooms to continue embracing changes: editors and publishers needed to experiment with new formats; create smaller, more visually driven newsrooms; explore multiple ways to increase revenue; and find new approaches to engaging with audiences—whether in print, digitally, or at events.

In an interview, Penelope Abernathy, author of Saving Community Journalism, has succinctly summed up the value of community newspapers, asserting that "Newspapers, when they're at their best, they interpret life for you. And they connect you. And . . . it's coming out of that [tradition of providing local information] with a real strong passion, too, for making sure that the good newspapers that want to change, that don't want to die, can actually have the tools to do it." (www.niemanlab.org/2014/06/) Echoing such sentiments, noted journalist Christiane Amanpour recently observed, "One of the big issues is that because of money, so much journalism is being cut back . . . in local markets, where it really counts. . . . You don't have as much of that great indigenous local reporting that you used to have. That's what harms the country, because that's where you get the real story." (*New York Times Magazine*, Jan. 21, 2018, p. 54) The EOMG was founded on and has maintained a determination to not let such journalism disappear in its territory.

Based on its past and present commitment to and keen understanding of community journalism's value, the family-owned EOMG gives every evidence of having the tools and skills to successfully play a vital role in continuing to cover and provide context to the news and opinion of the communities its newspapers serve in both print and digital form.

General and Specific Rules Governing the East Oregonian News Office

E. B. Aldrich

The newspaper business is a high calling. It offers great opportunities for service and involves responsibilities. If you do not find the work congenial, if you are not enthused by its possibilities or do not wish to observe the ethical requirements of good journalism, you should go into some other line of work.

Accuracy and fairness are the main requisites of a good news story. Get both sides of a story. Be just in handling the facts. Don't do anything as a newspaper worker that you would not do as a man or woman. Keep confidences.

Remember that all the people hereabouts are our friends and neighbors. We wish to help people, not hurt them. We desire to be as kind and generous as possible. Yet we must publish the news fearlessly and impartially when the public interest demands and must not be deterred by friendships. Be extremely careful when a story reflects on a man's good name and doubly so and then some when the good name of a woman is involved. Write nothing in malice or for revenge. Publish no jokes on women or girls.

Even if a man is an opponent of the paper, give him a fair deal with the news. The integrity of our news columns is above all quarrels. The paper will not tolerate an employee who 'hands it' to the people he or she may dislike.

In getting news, get all the facts. If it is a good story all details are needed. If it is a little story or item the details make it a better story. Don't let a man get away until he has given you all the dope. Otherwise you may waste a lot of time trying to phone him.

Be very careful about names. Have people spell out a name, taking no chances on mistakes. Be especially careful when news comes over the phone. Talk courteously over the phone or elsewhere and thank people for news.

Don't merely look for big stories. Little items are the standby of a small daily. Don't merely ask people if they know any news. Most of them will say no. Ask leading questions.

Mere scandal is not newspaper material. If it is a domestic or business quarrel the rule is to wait; until the matter goes into court, until an arrest is made or a suit filed. Then it is a public matter.

The *East Oregonian* invariably publishes all suits, civil or criminal, filed in the circuit court. If a suit is withdrawn or settled immediately or before press time it may be considered as not having been filed. Sometimes action is taken through mistake and this plan avoids doing an injustice. While all circuit court cases must be published, it is permissible to hold a story down when the facts justify. We do not scandalize divorce suits.

In the police or justice's courts it is not necessary to publish every trivial case. All cases are to be published that involve traffic offenses, bootlegging, gambling, white slavery or serious attacks. A safe rule is to publish cases that may become state court cases, but more leniency may be shown mild offenders if the public good permits. Aim to treat all people alike in such cases, however. As to news justice, a washerwoman or anyone else without much influence should have the same courtesy and consideration as the richest man in the community.

It is an unpardonable sin on the East Oregonian for anyone to take money or other payment for publishing or suppressing news. If anyone wants to advertise let him do so openly through the business office.

— E.B. Aldrich
East Oregonian editor 1908-1950

Abernathy, Penelope Muse. *Saving Community Journalism*. Chapel Hill, NC: University of North Carolina Press, 2014.

Bell, Emily, et al. "The Future of Local News: Lasting problems and new models for hometown journalism." *Columbia Journalism Review*, Vol. LVI, No. 1 (Spring 2017): 36-112.

Brown, Kate, complier. *Oregon Blue Book, 2011-2012*. Salem, OR: Office of the Secretary of State, 2011.

Byrd, Joann Green. *Calamity: The Heppner Flood of 1903*. Seattle: University of Washington Press, 2009.

Cassino, Kip. The Future of Legacy Media. Williamsburg, VA: Borrell Associates, January 2014.

Cloud, Barbara. *The Business of Newspapers on the Western Frontier*. Reno, NV: University of Nevada Press, 1992.

Cornish, Audie. "Christine Amanpour Wants More Local News." *The New York Times Magazine* (Jan. 28, 2018): 54.

Daily Astorian, 1919-2017.

East Oregonian, 1875-2017.

EO Media Group. Board Minutes, 2012-2017.

East Oregonian Publishing Company, Archives and Board Minutes, 1875-2012.

East Oregonian Publishing Company, ShopTalk, 1990-2013.

Gordon, Linda. *The Second Coming of the KKK*. New York: Liveright Publishing Co., 2017.

Haarsager, Sandra. "Molding Astoria—The Role of Two Editors." In *Eminent Astorians*, edited by Karen Kirtley, 215-250. Salem, OR: East Oregonian Publishing Company, 2010.

Hedberg, John. "The Pacific Coast's First Linotype," *The Portland Craftsman* (June 1926): 13-14.

Johnston, Robert D. *The Radical Middle Class: Populist Democracy and the Question of Capitalism in Progressive Era Portland, Oregon*. Princeton, NJ: Princeton University Press, 2003.

Kirchmeier, Mark. "The Stewards." *Northwest Magazine* (Dec. 1, 1985): 12-13, 16, 20.

Lockley, Fred. "Charles Samuel Jackson." In *History of the Columbia River Valley from The Dalles to the Sea*, 986-87. Chicago: S. J. Clarke Publishing Co., 1928.

Lockley, Fred. "Lee Drake." In *History of the Columbia River Valley from The Dalles to the Sea*, 785-87. Chicago: S. J. Clarke Publishing Co., 1928.

Lomax, Alfred. *Later Woolen Mills in Oregon.* Portland, OR: Binfords & Mort, Publishers, 1974.

Lucas, Peggy Chessman. "Merle Chessman, Editor Statesman." *Cumtux*, Vol. 6, No. 4 (Fall, 1986): 3-15.

Meinig, D. W. *The Great Columbia Plain: A Historical Geography, 1805-1910.* Seattle: University of Washington Press, 1968.

MacColl, Kimbark. *Growth of a City: Power and Politics in Portland, Oregon, 1915-1950.* Portland, OR: The Georgian Press, 1979.

MacColl, Kimbark. *Merchants, Money, and Power: The Portland Establishment, 1843-1913.* Portland, OR: The Georgian Press, 1988.

Macnab, Gordon. *A Century of News and People in the East Oregonian, 1875-1975.* Pendleton, OR: East Oregonian Publishing Co., 1975.

McLain, Annie. *Unmasking the Oregon Klansman: The Ku Klux Klan in Astoria, 1922-1925.* Master's thesis, 2003 www.pacificu.edu/sites/default/files/documents/Anne%20Mclain.pdf (accessed December 1, 2017).

Pendleton Tribune, 1878-1923.

Oregon. *House and Senate Journals*, 4th Session. Salem, Oregon, 1866.

Oregon. *Biennial Report of the Secretary of State*, 1876, 1886, 1897, and 1907. Salem, Oregon.

The Oregonian. Portland.

Pew Research Center. Newspaper Fact Sheets. June 15, 2016, June 1, 2017. www.pewresearch.org. (accessed December 14, 2017).

Pew Research Center. State of the News Media 2016. June 15, 2016. www.pewresearch.org. (accessed December 14, 2017).

Pew Research Center. "Civic Engagement Strongly Tied to Local News Habits." www.journalism.org/2016/11/03/... (accessed December 14, 2017)

Radcliffe, Damian. *Local Journalism in the Pacific Northwest: Why it Matters, How its Evolving and Who Pays for It.* Eugene, OR: University of Oregon, 2017.

Robbins, William G. "The Malheur Occupation and the Problem with History." *Oregon Historical Quarterly.* Vol. 117, No. 4 (Winter, 2016): 574-603.

Russo, David J. *American Towns: An Interpretive History.* Chicago, Ivan R. Dee, 2001.

Schwantes, Carlos Arnaldo. *The Pacific Northwest: An Interpretive History.* 2nd ed. Lincoln, NE: University of Nebraska Press, 1996.

Spayd, Liz. "Want to Attract Readers? Listen to Them." *The New York Times* (July 10, 2016): Opinion Section, 10.

Stein, Harry H. "Printers and Press Operators: *The Oregonian* Remembered." *Oregon Historical Quarterly,* Vol. 115, No. 2 (Summer 2014):208-223.

Stein, Harry H. "*The Oregonian* Navigates the Great Depression." *Oregon Historical Quarterly,* Vol. 114, No. 2 (Summer, 2013): 174-203.

Sullivan, Margaret. "Public Editor No. 5 Is Yesterday's News." *The New York Times* (April 17, 2016): Opinion Section, 9.

Toy, Eckard V. "The Ku Klux Klan." In *Experiences in a Promised Land: Essays in Pacific Northwest History,* edited by G. Thomas Edwards and Carlos A. Schwantes, 269-86. Seattle: University of Washington Press, 1986.

Turnbull, George S. *History of Oregon Newspapers.* Portland, OR: Binfords & Mort, 1939.

United States Census Bureau. *Ninth Census of the United States, Statistics of Population.* Washington, D. C.: U. S. Government Printing Office, 1872.

United States Census Bureau. *Compendium of the Tenth Census.* Washington, D. C.: U. S. Government Printing Office, 1883.

United States Census Bureau. *Compendium of the Eleventh Census.* Washington, D. C.: U. S. Government Printing Office, 1892.

United States Census Bureau. *Twelfth Census of the United States Taken in the Year 1900.* Washington, D. C.: U. S. Government Printing Office, 1902.

United States Census Bureau. *Thirteenth Census of the United States Taken in the Year 1910.* Washington, D. C.: U. S. Government Printing Office, 1916.

United States Census Bureau. *Fourteenth Census of the Untied States, State Compendium, Oregon.* Washington, D. C.: U. S. Government Printing Office, 1924.

Willingham, William. "The First 100 Years of the Pendleton Round-Up." In *Pendleton Round-Up at 100: Oregon's Legendary Rodeo*, by Michael Bales and Ann Terry Hill, with Karen Kirtley, editor, 10-43. Pendleton, OR: East Oregonian Publishing Company, 2009.

Willingham, William. Interview with John Perry and John Shaver. Feb. 13, 2017.

Willingham, William. Interview with Mike Forrester. Nov. 9, 2015.

Willingham, William. Interview with Heidi Wright. May 31. 2018.

Willingham, William. Personal communication from Sean Hart. May 25, 2018.

Willingham, William. *Starting Over: Community Building on the Eastern Oregon Frontier.* Portland, OR: Oregon Historical Society Press, 2006.

Zucker, Jeff, Kay Hummel and Bob Hogfoss. *Oregon Indians: Culture, History and Current Affairs.* Portland, OR: Oregon Historical Society Press, 1983.

About the Author

William F. Willingham is a native of Pendleton, Oregon and a consulting historian working in the fields of American history, historic preservation, architectural history, and water resources development. He is the author of numerous scholarly articles, consultant reports, and books, including The Classic Houses of Portland, Oregon, 1850-1950, Starting Over: Community Building on the Eastern Oregon Frontier, Waterpower in the Wilderness: A History of the Bonneville Lock and Dam, and Two Centuries of Experience in Water Resources Management: A Dutch US-Retrospective. He received his Ph. D. in Early American History from Northwestern University and his BA from Willamette University.

R. Gregory Nokes is author of Massacred for Gold: The Chinese in Hells Canyon, Breaking Chains: Slavery on Trial in the Oregon Territory, and The Troubled Life of Peter Burnett: Oregon Pioneer and First Governor of California.